UML
FOR JAVA™
PROGRAMMERS

Robert C. Martin Series

This series is directed at software developers, team-leaders, business analysts, and managers who want to increase their skills and proficiency to the level of a Master Craftsman.

The series contains books that guide software professionals in the principles, patterns, and practices of programming, software project management, requirements gathering, design, analysis, testing, and others.

UML FOR JAVA™ PROGRAMMERS

Robert Cecil Martin

Object Mentor Inc.

www.objectmentor.com

PRENTICE
HALL
PTR

Prentice Hall Professional Technical Reference
Upper Saddle River, NJ 07458
www.phptr.com

Library of Congress Cataloging-in-Publication available

Editorial/production supervision: *Kathleen M. Caren*
Executive Editor: *Paul Petralia*
Editorial Assistant: *Michelle Vincenti*
Marketing Manager: *Chris Guzikowski*
Manufacturing Manager: *Alexis Heydt-Long*
Cover Design Director: *Jerry Votta*
Interior Illustrations: *Angela Brooks*

© 2003 Pearson Education Inc.
Publishing as Prentice Hall PTR
Upper Saddle River, NJ 07458

10 9 8 7 6 5 4 3 2 1

ISBN 0-13-142848-9

Pearson Education LTD.
Pearson Education Australia PTY, Limited
Pearson Education Singapore, Pte. Ltd.
Pearson Education North Asia Ltd.
Pearson Education Canada, Ltd.
Pearson Educación de Mexico, S.A. de C.V.
Pearson Education—Japan
Pearson Education Malaysia, Pte. Ltd.

This book is dedicated to my grandchildren:

Alexis Josephine Brooks, *the daughter of Angela and Matt,*
and
Luka Jean Martin, *the son of Micah and Angelique.*

It is my privilege, and my joy,
to watch these new families grow and flourish.

Source Code and Contact Information:

Much of the source code presented in this book can be obtained from the Object Mentor Inc. Web site: *www.objectmentor.com/UMLFJP*

Robert C. Martin: *unclebob@objectmentor.com*

Object Mentor Inc.:   *info@objectmentor.com*
                      www.objectmentor.com

Contents

Figures xiii

Listings xvii

Foreword xxi

Preface xxiii

   Acknowledgements xxiv

Chapter 1: Overview of UML for Java™ Programmers 1

  Diagram Types 3

    Class diagrams 4

    Object diagrams 5

    Sequence diagrams 6

    Collaboration diagrams 7

    State diagrams 7

  Conclusion 8

  Notes 8

Chapter 2: Working with Diagrams 9

  Why Model? 9

    Why build models of software? 10

    Why should we build comprehensive designs before coding? 10

  Making Effective use of UML 11

    Communicating with others 11

    Road maps 13

    Back-end documentation 13

    What to keep and what to throw away 14

  Iterative Refinement 15

    Behavior first 16

    Check the structure 17

    Envisioning the code 20

    Evolution of diagrams 20

  Minimalism 21

  When and How to Draw Diagrams 21

    When to draw diagrams and when to stop. 22

CASE tools 22
But what about documentation? 23
And Javadocs™? 24
Conclusion 24

Chapter 3: Class Diagrams 27
  The Basics 28
    Classes 28
    Association 29
    Inheritance 30
  An Example Class Diagram 31
  The Details 33
    Class stereotypes 33
    Abstract classes 34
    Properties 35
    Aggregation 36
    Composition 36
    Multiplicity 38
    Association stereotypes 39
    Inner classes 40
    Anonymous inner classes 40
    Association classes 41
    Association qualifiers 42
  Conclusion 42
  Notes 43

Chapter 4: Sequence Diagrams 45
  The Basics 45
    Objects, lifelines, messages, and other odds and ends 46
    Creation and destruction 47
    Simple loops 48
    Cases and scenarios 49
  Advanced Concepts 51
    Loops and conditions 51
    Messages that take time 53
    Asynchronous messages 55

Multiple threads..59
Active objects...59
Sending messages to interfaces 60
Conclusion 61

Chapter 5: Use Cases 63
  Writing Use Cases 64
    What is a use case? 64
    The primary course...64
    Alternate courses..65
    What else? 65
  Use Case Diagrams 66
    System boundary diagram..66
    Use case relationships..67
  Conclusion 67

Chapter 6: Principles of OOD 69
  Design Quality 69
    Design smells 70
    Dependency management 70
  The Single Responsibility Principle (SRP)...........................71
  The Open–Closed Principle (OCP) 73
  The Liskov Substitution Principle (LSP)..............................84
  The Dependency Inversion Principle (DIP) 86
  The Interface Segregation Principle (ISP)...........................87
  Conclusion 88
  Notes 89

Chapter 7: The Practices: dX 91
  Iterative Development 91
    The initial exploration 92
    Estimating the features...92
    Spikes 93
  Planning...93
    Planning releases..93
    Planning iterations 93

The midpoint 94
Velocity feedback 95
Organizing the Iterations into Management Phases 95
What's in an Iteration? 96
Developing in pairs 96
Acceptance tests 96
Unit tests 97
Refactoring 98
Open office 98
Continual integration 98
Conclusion 99
Notes 99

Chapter 8: Packages 101
Java Packages 101
Packages 102
Dependencies 103
Binary Components — .jar Files 103
Principles of Package Design 104
The Release/Reuse Equivalency Principle (REP) 104
The Common Closure Principle (CCP) 104
The Common Reuse Principle (CRP) 105
The Acyclic Dependencies Principle (ADP) 105
The Stable Dependencies Principle (SDP) 105
The Stable Abstractions Principle (SAP) 106
Conclusion 107
Notes 107

Chapter 9: Object Diagrams 109
A Snapshot in Time 109
Active Objects 111
Conclusion 114

Chapter 10: State Diagrams 115
The Basics 115
Special events 117

Superstates 118

Initial and final pseudostates 119

Using FSM Diagrams 120

SMC 121

ICE: A case study 123

Conclusion 125

Chapter 11: Heuristics and Coffee 129

The Mark IV Special Coffee Maker 130

A challenge 132

A common, but hideous, coffee maker solution 132

Missing methods 133

Vapor classes 134

Imaginary abstraction 134

God classes 135

A Coffee Maker Solution 136

Crossed wires 136

The coffee maker user interface 137

Use Case 1: User pushes brew button 137

Use Case 2: Containment vessel not ready 139

Use Case 3: Brewing complete 139

Use Case 4: Coffee all gone 140

Implementing the abstract model 140

Use Case 1: User pushes Brew button 141

Implementing the isReady() functions 143

Implementing the start() functions 144

How does M4UserInterface.checkButton get called? 145

Completing the Coffee Maker 147

The benefits of this design 147

How did I really come up with this design? 148

OOverkill 158

Notes 159

Chapter 12: SMC Remote Service: Case Study 161

Caveat Emptor 161

Unit Tests 162

The SMCRemote System 162
SMCRemoteClient 162
   SMCRemoteClient Command Line 162
   SMCRemote Communication Protocols............................... 163
   SMCRemoteClient 165
   The Loggers 171
   The Remote Sessions... 172
   RemoteSessionBase 173
   RemoteRegistrar.. 176
   RemoteCompiler 178
   FileCarrier 183
   SMCRemoteClient Conclusion 184
SMCRemoteServer 185
   SocketService... 185
   SMCRemoteService.. 189
   SMCRemoteServer... 193
   ServerSession 196
   Three-Level FSM... 196
   UserRepository 205
   OReillyEmailSender 207
   PasswordGenerator.. 208
Conclusion... 208
Tests for SMCRemoteClient 209
Tests for SocketService 216
Tests for SMCRemoteServer 219
Other Tests.. 229
ServerController (SMC Generated) 232
Notes 240

Index... 241

Figures

Figure 1–1 : Conceptual UML Diagram: A dog is an animal. 2

Figure 1–2 : Class diagram of `TreeMap`. 5

Figure 1–4 : `TreeMap.add`. 6

Figure 1–3 : `TreeMap` Object diagram. 6

Figure 1–5 : Collaboration diagram of one case of `TreeMap.add`. 7

Figure 1–6 : State machine of a subway turnstile. 8

Figure 2–1 : `LoginServlet`. 11

Figure 2–2 : `BubbleSorter`. 12

Figure 2–3 : `BubbleSorter` sequence diagram. 13

Figure 2–4 : Road map diagram. 14

Figure 2–5 : A bad (but all too common) example. 15

Figure 2–6 : Cell phone collaboration diagram. 17

Figure 2–7 : Cell phone class diagram. 18

Figure 2–9 : Adapting `Buttons` to `Dialers`. 19

Figure 2–8 : Isolating `Button` from `Dialer`. 19

Figure 2–10 : Adding adapters to the dynamic model. 21

Figure 3–1 : Class icon. 28

Figure 3–2 : Class icon compartments with corresponding code. 28

Figure 3–3 : Association. 29

Figure 3–5 : Inheritance. 30

Figure 3–6 : Realizes relationship. 31

Figure 3–7 : Lollipop interface Indicator. 31

Figure 3–8 : ATM class diagram. 32

Figure 3–9 : «interface» class stereotype. 33

Figure 3–10 : «utility» class stereotype. 34

Figure 3–11 : Abstract classes. 34

Figure 3–12 : Unofficial denotation of abstract classes. 35

Figure 3–13 : Properties. 35

Figure 3–14 : Aggregation. 36

Figure 3–15 : Illegal cycles of aggregation between instances. 36

Figure 3–16 : Composition. 37

Figure 3–17 : Illegal composition. 37

Figure 3–19 : Simple multiplicity. 38

Figure 3–18 : Deep copy is implied by composition. 38

Figure 3–20 : Association stereotypes. 39

Figure 3–21 : Inner class. 40

Figure 3–23 : Association class. 41

Figure 3–24 : Association class denoting a weak reference. 41

Figure 3–22 : Anonymous inner class. 41

Figure 3–26 : Association qualifier. 42

Figure 3–25 : Stereotype denoting a weak reference. 42

Figure 4–1 : Typical sequence diagram. 46

Figure 4–2 : Creating an object. 47

Figure 4–4 : A simple loop. 48

Figure 4–3 : Releasing an object to the garbage collector. 48

Figure 4–5 : This sequence diagram is too complex. 50

Figure 4–6 : One small scenario. 51

Figure 4–7 : A high-level view. 52

Figure 4–8 : Sequence diagram with loops and conditions. 52

Figure 4–9 : Normal phone call. 53

Figure 4–10 : Failed phone call. 54

Figure 4–11 : Asynchronous message. 55

Figure 4–12 : Older and better way to depict asynchronous messages. 55

Figure 4–13 : Multiple threads of control. 59

Figure 4–15 : Simple logger design. 60

Figure 4–14 : Active object. 60

Figure 4–17 : Sending to a derived type through an interface. 61

Figure 4–16 : Sending to an interface. 61

Figure 5–1 : System boundary diagram. 66

Figure 6–1 : Class knows too many things. 71

Figure 6–3 : Two ways to use `Persistable`. 72

Figure 6–2 : Separation of concerns. 72

Figure 6–4 : Violation of OCP. 73

Figure 6–6 : Isolating GUI from data manipulation. 74

Figure 6–5 : Conforming to the OCP. 74

Figure 6–7 : Interaction between the `model` and `dialog`. 78

Figure 6–8 : Simple payroll example. 85

Figure 6–9 : Unsegregated enrollment system. 87

Figure 6–10 : Segregated enrollment system. 88

Figure 8–1 : Simple UML package. 102

Figure 8–2 : UML package showing contents. 102

Figure 8–3 : UML package nesting. 102

Figure 8–4 : Package dependency. 103

Figure 8–5 : A component — possibly a .jar file. 103

Figure 8–6 : A violation of the SDP. 106

Figure 9–1 : Floor plan. 110

Figure 9–2 : Lunch room and kitchen. 110

Figure 9–3 : `SocketService` class diagram. 113

Figure 9–4 : `SocketService` object diagram. 114

Figure 10–1 : Simple login state machine. 116

Figure 10–2 : States and special events in UML. 117

Figure 10–3 : Reflexive transition. 117

Figure 10–4 : Transition: Multiple states and superstate. 118

Figure 10–5 : Overriding superstate transitions. 119

Figure 10–6 : Hierarchical invocation of `entry` and `exit` actions. 119

Figure 10–8 : Subway turnstile STD. 120

Figure 10–7 : Initial and final pseudo states. 120

Figure 10–9 : Subway turnstile STT. 121

Figure 10–10 : ICE FSM. 124

Figure 11–1 : Hyper-concrete coffee maker. 133

Figure 11–2 : Crossed wires. 136

Figure 11–3 : Starting the flow of hot water. 137

Figure 11–4 : Brew button pressed, checking for ready. 138

Figure 11–5 : Brew button pressed, complete. 138

Figure 11–6 : Pausing and resuming the flow of hot water. 139

Figure 11–7 : Detecting when brewing is complete. 140

Figure 11–8 : Coffee all gone. 141

Figure 11–9 : Class diagram. 141

Figure 11–10 : Detecting the Brew button. 142

Figure 11–11 : Implementing the `isReady` methods. 143

Figure 11–12 : Pollable coffee maker. 146

Figure 11–13 : Coffee maker components. 148

Figure 12–1 : Deployment. 162

Figure 12–2 : Registration protocol. 164

Figure 12–3 : Compile protocol. 164

Figure 12–4 : SMCRemoteClient static structure. 165

Figure 12–5 : `SMCRemoteClient.main()` 166

Figure 12–6 : Registration. 167

Figure 12–7 : Compilation. 167

Figure 12–8 : Remote sessions. 172

Figure 12–9 : Compile process. 179

Figure 12–10 : SocketService. 185

Figure 12–11 : SocketService object diagram. 186

Figure 12–12 : High-level structure of SMCRemoteService. 189

Figure 12–13 : SMCRemoteServer structure: The transaction Visitor pattern. 194

Figure 12–14 : SMCRemoteServer transaction decoding. 194

Figure 12–15 : ServerSession finite state machine. 197

Figure 12–16 : Three-Level FSM. 198

Listings

Listing 1–1 :   `TreeMap.java` 3

Listing 2–1 :   `BubbleSorter.java` 12

Listing 2–2 :   `ButtonDialerAdapter.java` 20

Listing 3–1 :   `UI.java` 33

Listing 4–1 :   `EmployeeDB.java` 47

Listing 4–2 :   `ShapeFactory.java` 47

Listing 4–3 :   `TreeMap.java` 48

Listing 4–4 :   `Payroll.Java` 50

Listing 4–5 :   `TestLog.java` 56

Listing 4–6 :   `AsynchronousLogger.java` 57

Listing 6–1 :   `EmployeeTerminatorView.java` 75

Listing 6–2 :   `EmployeeTerminatorController.java` 75

Listing 6–3 :   `EmployeeTerminatorModel.java` 75

Listing 6–4 :   `EmployeeTerminatorDialog.java` 76

Listing 6–5 :   `TestEmployeeTerminatorModel.java` 79

Listing 6–6 :   `TestEmployeeTerminatorDialog.java` 80

Listing 6–7 :   `ShowEmployeeTerminator.java` 83

Listing 9–1 :   `SocketService.java` 111

Listing 10–1 :   `Turnstile.sm` 121

Listing 10–2 :   `TurnStile.java (Generated)` 122

Listing 10–3 :   `ice.sm` 125

Listing 11–1 :   `CofeeMakerAPI.java` 131

Listing 11–2 :   `Light.java` 134

Listing 11–3 :   `Heater.java` 135

Listing 11–4 :   `Sensor.java` 135

Listing 11–5 :   `M4UserInterface.java` 142

Listing 11–6 :   `UserInterface.java` 142

Listing 11–7 :   `M4HotWaterSource.java` 143

Listing 11–9 :   `M4HotWaterSource.java` 144

Listing 11–10 : `M4ContainmentVessel.java` 144

Listing 11–8 :   `M4ContainmentVessel.java` 144

Listing 11–11 : `Pollable.java` 145

Listing 11–12 : `CoffeeMaker.java` 146

Listing 11–13 : `M4UserInterface.java` 147

Listing 11–14 : `UserInterface.java` 149

Listing 11–15 : `M4UserInterface.java` 149

Listing 11–16 : `HotWaterSource.java` 150

Listing 11–17 : `M4HotWaterSource.java` 150

Listing 11–18 : `ContainmentVessel.java` 151

Listing 11–19 : `M4ContainmentVessel.java` 152

Listing 11–20 : `Pollable.java` 153

Listing 11–21 : `CoffeeMaker.java` 153

Listing 11–22 : `TestCoffeeMaker.java` 153

Listing 12–1 : `SMCRemoteClient.java` 167

Listing 12–2 : `ClientCommandLine.java` 169

Listing 12–4 : `MessageLogger.java` 171

Listing 12–5 : `NullMessageLogger.java` 171

Listing 12–6 : `ConsoleMessageLogger.java` 171

Listing 12–3 : `ClientCommandLineProcessor.java` 171

Listing 12–7 : `RemoteSessionBase.java` 173

Listing 12–8 : `LoginTransaction.java` 175

Listing 12–9 : `LoginResponseTransaction.java` 175

Listing 12–10 : `SocketTransaction.java` 176

Listing 12–11 : `RemoteRegistrar.java` 176

Listing 12–12 : `RegistrationTransaction.java` 177

Listing 12–13 : `RegistrationResponseTransaction.java` 177

Listing 12–14 : `RemoteCompiler.java` 179

Listing 12–15 : `CompileFileTransaction.java` 181

Listing 12–16 : `CompilerResultsTransaction.java` 182

Listing 12–17 : `FileCarrier.java` 183

Listing 12–18 : Socket Service That Says "Hello". 185

Listing 12–19 : A client that tests HelloService. 186

Listing 12–20 : `SocketServer.java` 187

Listing 12–21 : `SocketService.java` 187

Listing 12–22 : `SMCRemoteService.java` 190

Listing 12–23 : `UserDirectory.java` 193

Listing 12–24 : `EmailSender.java` 193

Listing 12–25 : `SMCRemoteServer.java` 195

Listing 12–26 : `SocketTransactionProcessor.java` 196

Listing 12–27 : `server.sm` 197

Listing 12–28 : `ServerControllerContext.java` 199

Listing 12–29 : `ServerSession.java` 200

Listing 12–30 : `UserRepository.java` 205

Listing 12–31 : `OReillyEmailSender.java` 207

Listing 12–32 : `PasswordGenerator.java` 208

Listing 12–33 : `TestClientBase.java` 209

Listing 12–34 : `TestClientCommandLine.java` 210

Listing 12–35 : `TestRemoteCompiler.java` 211

Listing 12–36 : `TestRemoteRegistration.java` 214

Listing 12–37 : `TestSocketService.java` 216

Listing 12–38 : `TestBase.java` 219

Listing 12–39 : `TestCommandLine.java` 220

Listing 12–40 : `TestCompilation.java` 221

Listing 12–41 : `TestOReillyEmail.java` 224
Listing 12–42 : `TestRegistration.java` 225
Listing 12–43 : `TestServerLogin.java` 226
Listing 12–44 : `TestUserRepository.java` 227
Listing 12–45 : `TestFileCarrier.java` 229
Listing 12–46 : `ServerController.java` 232

Foreword

Ho-hum, just what we need, another book about the UML. Doesn't *UML Distilled* cover everything a developer really needs to know about the UML? *UML Distilled* covers all of the UML diagram types; this book doesn't even cover all of the different diagrams.

Hang on a minute, this book covers all of the diagrams I use on real projects. It omits all of the diagrams I have to remind teams not to use. Maybe Robert Martin has written something that will surpass *UML Distilled...*

Uh-oh, first glances can be deceptive. This is a great book that deserves to become a classic. *UML for Java Programmers* is the first book I have ever read that treats the UML as a tool for programmers to help them make their day job easier. A welcome change from all of the UML books that assume you want to become a language lawyer.

I really like the way that this book focuses on the specification and implementation level use of the UML, to communicate precise, unambiguous descriptions of a proposed design and existing code. Uncle Bob promotes the idea that an occasional UML diagram can save time by prescreening ideas before going to the expense of writing the code and that sometimes a UML diagram can be a great way of explaining how a part of an existing application works.

This is a book that explains how to use the UML on real projects, one that focuses on getting practical value out of using the UML. Simple things that make a big difference, like using UML diagrams to choose between alternatives, explaining design ideas on a white board using the UML, and the need to erase diagrams once they have achieved their purpose.

Having seen all too many shelfware CASE tools, I appreciate Robert's warnings about CASE tools. Personally I'd rather see organizations invest in decent meeting rooms with photocopying white boards rather than waste money on CASE tools. Yes, CASE tools can be kind of cool, but there are many other investment opportunities that will give much better payback in terms of developer productivity.

This book challenges developers to understand the value that can derive from drawing UML diagrams, and encourages developers to push back against the language lawyers and the UML police who encourage the inappropriate use of precision in UML diagrams.

Uncle Bob has done a great job in not only showing how to use the UML effectively, but in also explaining how to recognize when the UML diagrams are depicting bad design ideas. After all you can have a beautiful diagram that would make a language lawyer happy, but if the design stinks, you need to fix it.

The design guidelines and heuristics in this book transform it from a simple guide to the UML to a great book on how to do OO design. This book demonstrates that there is much more to OO design than simply drawing UML diagrams. The diagrams do not really make much of a difference; what matters is the critical thinking about the consequences of each of the design decisions. Yes, the diagrams can make it easier to see these consequences, but what really matters is that people know how to look for and deal with these consequences.

This book deserves to become a classic because it exposes the dirty little secret of software development: good design evolves out of many iterations of hard work on a problem.

This also explains why this book uses Java. Java has been through enough iterations that it is now useful. We have been through the hype and come out the other side. Uncle Bob does a great job of showing lots of straightforward Java code that is a massive step beyond the normal, toy code samples that many books show.

The combination of Java and the UML works well to show what good OO design looks like. Uncle Bob, many thanks for a great book.

Pete McBreen
author, *Software Craftsmanship*
April 2003

Preface

It was 1991 when I got my first copy of Booch's classic *Object Oriented Design with Applications* (first edition). I had learned several OO languages by then, including C++ and Smalltalk. I was absolutely thrilled by the concept of Booch's notation. Those clouds! Those relationships! Those message passing diagrams! As a software designer it was *just* what I needed!

I also needed a tool to draw the diagrams. So I started writing a CASE tool in Think-C for the Macintosh. I remember spending a *lot* of time getting the cloud icon to look *just right*. Though I never finished that CASE tool, one artifact of it remains. The cloud icon I created has followed me from computer to computer, from Macintosh to Windows, and has been the source of all the cloud icons I have ever drawn in any book or article.

I remember the incredible day that my office partner, Billy Vogel, was talking on the phone to a head-hunter. He looked over at me and said: "Uncle Bob, I think you should take this call." The recruiter was looking for consultants to work at Rational, with Grady Booch, on a CASE tool to draw Booch Diagrams! How could such luck drop right into my lap?

A dozen years have passed. I still have my original copy of Booch's book. It's a bit frayed and dog-eared, but the book still has the power to evoke echoes of the same old thrills.

Today, of course, we use UML — the one-third offspring of Booch's notation. UML is a powerful and comprehensive notation, far grander in its sweep and scope than Booch's was. Whereas Booch's notation was good for drawing pictures of software, UML is apparently good for creating models of just about anything you can imagine — or so say some of its pundits. As grand and all-encompassing as UML may be, I find that a reasonable subset is all I need for drawing pictures of software. The same kind of pictures I used to create with Booch's notation.

This book is about that subset, and about those pictures, and about reasserting that old thrill. This book takes the vast richness of UML 2.0 and boils it down into a simple notation that programmers can easily use to draw pictures of software designs. This book reduces the panoply of UML widgets, icons, diagrams, relationships, arrowheads, and semantics, into a simple suite of tools that Java programmers can use to record their design decisions.

Make no mistake about it. This book will *not* teach you everything about UML. But if you are a Java programmer, it will teach you what you *need* to know; and perhaps it'll help you experience an echo of that old thrill.

Acknowledgements

I would like to extend my special thanks to each of the following people:

Ann Marie Martin	Micah Daniel Martin
Angela Dawn Martin Brooks	Gina Leanne Martin
Justin Michael Martin	Angelique Thouvenin Martin
Mathew Brooks	Alexis Josephine Brooks
Luka Jean Martin	Lowell Lindstrom
Lance Welter	Bob Koss
Michael Feathers	Brian Button
Talisha Jefferson	Chris Biegay
Martin Fowler	Kent Beck
Grady Booch	Kathleen Caren
Patrick Lindner	Alan Apt
Paul Petralia	A. G. McDowell
Phil Pidgeon	David Laurance
Mike Clark	Robert Wenner
Adriano Comai	Nicholas Robinson
William H. Mitchell	Erik Meade
Jeff Langr	Alan Francis
David Farber	Alexandra Weber Morales
Ron Jeffries	Ward Cunningham
Michael Hill	James Grenning
Billy Vogel	Dave Lasker
Mike Higgs	Bob Weissman
Pete McBreen	Ken Auer

My sincerest apologies to the many people I have undoubtedly forgotten to mention.

1

Overview of UML for Java™ Programmers

Angela Brooks

The Unified Modeling Language (UML) is a graphical notation for drawing diagrams of software concepts. One can use it for drawing diagrams of a problem domain, a proposed software design, or an already completed software implementation. Fowler[1] describes these three different levels as *Conceptual*, *Specification*, and *Implementation*. This book deals with the last two.

Specification- and *Implementation*-level diagrams have a strong connection to source code. Indeed, it is the intent for a *Specification*-level diagram to be turned into source code. Likewise, it is the intent for an *Implementation*-level diagram to describe existing source code. As such there are rules and semantics that diagrams at these levels must follow. Such diagrams have very little ambiguity, and a great deal of formality.

On the other hand, diagrams at the *Conceptual* level are not strongly related to source code. Rather, they are related to *human* language. They are a shorthand used to describe concepts and abstractions that exist in the human problem domain. They don't follow

implementation diagrams — trying to understand code written by somebody else

---

1. [Fowler1999a]

strong semantic rules and therefore their meaning can be ambiguous and subject to inter-
pretation.

Consider, for example, the following sentence: *A dog is an animal*. We can create a
Conceptual UML diagram that represents this sentence. (See Figure 1–1.)

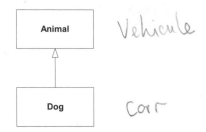

Figure 1–1
Conceptual UML Diagram: A dog is an animal.

This diagram depicts two entities named *Animal* and *Dog* connected by *generalization* relationship. An *Animal* is a generalization of a *Dog*. A *Dog* is a special case of an
Animal. That's all the diagram means. Nothing more can be inferred from it. We might be
asserting that our pet dog, Sparky, is an animal; or we might be asserting that dogs, as a
biological species, belong to the animal kingdom. Thus, the diagram is subject to interpre-
tation.

However, the same diagram at the *Specification* or *Implementation* level has a much
more precise meaning:

```
public class Animal {}
public class Dog extends Animal {}
```

This source code defines `Animal` and `Dog` as classes connected by an *inheritance*
relationship. Whereas the *Conceptual* model says nothing at all about computers, data processing, or programs, the *Specification* model *describes part of a program*.

It is unfortunate that the diagrams themselves don't communicate what level they are
drawn at. Failure to recognize the level of a diagram is the source of significant miscom-
munication between programmers and analysts. A *Conceptual* level diagram *does not*
define source code, nor should it. A *Specification* level diagram that describes the solution
to a problem does not have to look anything like the *Conceptual* level diagram that
describes that problem.

All the rest of the diagrams in this book will be at the *Specification/Implementation*
level, and will be accompanied by corresponding source code where feasible. We have
seen our last *Conceptual*-level diagram.

Diagram Types

[handwritten note: You have to tell them what abstract classes are!]

Below is a very quick tour of the primary diagrams used in UML. Once you read through it, you will be able to read and write most of the UML diagrams you will usually need. What remains, and what subsequent chapters address, are the details and formalisms that you will need to become proficient in UML.

UML has three main kinds of diagrams. *Static diagrams* describe the unchanging logical structure of software elements by depicting classes, objects, and data structures, and the relationships that exist between them. *Dynamic diagrams* show how software entities change during execution by depicting the flow of execution, or the way entities change state. *Physical diagrams* show the unchanging physical structure of software entities by depicting physical entities such as source files, libraries, binary files, data files, and the like, and the relationships that exist between them.

Consider the code in Listing 1–1. This program implements a map based upon a simple binary tree algorithm. Familiarize yourself with the code before you consider the diagrams that follow.

Listing 1–1 TreeMap.java

```java
public class TreeMap {
  TreeMapNode topNode = null;

  public void add(Comparable key, Object value) {
    if (topNode == null)
      topNode = new TreeMapNode(key, value);
    else
      topNode.add(key, value);
  }

  public Object get(Comparable key) {
    return topNode == null ? null : topNode.find(key);
  }
}

class TreeMapNode {
  private final static int LESS = 0;
  private final static int GREATER = 1;
  private Comparable itsKey;
  private Object itsValue;
  private TreeMapNode nodes[] = new TreeMapNode[2];

  public TreeMapNode(Comparable key, Object value) {
    itsKey = key;
    itsValue = value;
  }

  public Object find(Comparable key) {
    if (key.compareTo(itsKey) == 0) return itsValue;
    return findSubNodeForKey(selectSubNode(key), key);
  }
```

Listing 1–1 (Continued) TreeMap.java

```java
  private int selectSubNode(Comparable key) {
    return (key.compareTo(itsKey) < 0) ? LESS : GREATER;
  }

  private Object findSubNodeForKey(int node, Comparable key) {
    return nodes[node] == null ? null : nodes[node].find(key);
  }

  public void add(Comparable key, Object value) {
    if (key.compareTo(itsKey) == 0)
      itsValue = value;
    else
      addSubNode(selectSubNode(key), key, value);
  }

  private void addSubNode(int node, Comparable key,
                          Object value) {
    if (nodes[node] == null)
      nodes[node] = new TreeMapNode(key, value);
    else
      nodes[node].add(key, value);
  }
}
```

Class diagrams

The *class diagram* in Figure 1–2 shows the major classes and relationships in the program. It shows that there is a TreeMap class that has public methods named add and get. It shows that TreeMap holds a reference to a TreeMapNode in a variable named topNode. It shows that each TreeMapNode holds a reference to two other TreeMapNode instances in some kind of container named nodes. And it shows that each TreeMapNode instance holds references to two other instances in variables named itsKey and itsValue. The itsKey variable holds a reference to some instance that implements the Comparable interface. The itsValue variable simply holds a reference to some object.

We'll go over the nuances of class diagrams in a subsequent chapter. For now, there are only a few things you need to know.

- Rectangles represent classes, and arrows represent relationships.

- In this diagram all the relationships are *associations*. Associations are simple data relationships in which one object holds a reference to, and invokes methods upon, the other.

- The name on an association maps to the name of the variable that holds the reference.

- A number next to an arrowhead typically shows the number of instances held by the relationship. If that number is greater than one then some kind of container, usually an array, is implied.

[handwritten annotations: "why these methods only in TreeMapNode?", "object name", "2 references to TreeMapNode instances (e.g. objects)"]

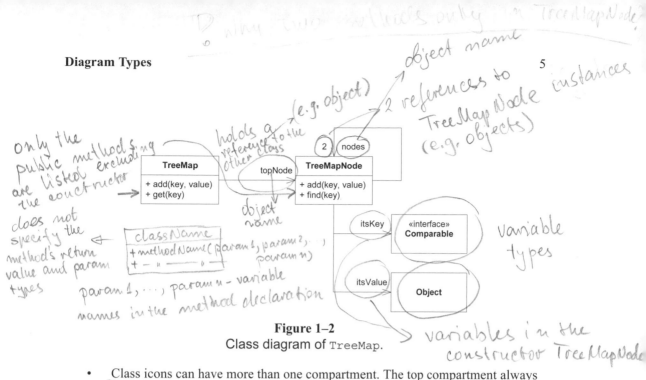

[handwritten annotations surrounding figure: "only the public methods are listed excluding the constructor", "does not specify the method's return value and param types", "holds a reference to the other class (e.g. object)", "className", "+methodName(param1, param2, ... param n)", "+ - " ", "param1, ..., param n - variable names in the method declaration", "object name", "itsKey", "itsValue", "variable types", "variables in the constructor TreeMapNode"]

Figure 1–2
Class diagram of `TreeMap`.

- Class icons can have more than one compartment. The top compartment always holds the name of the class. The other compartments describe functions and variables.

- The «interface» notation means that `Comparable` is an interface.

- Most of the notations shown are optional.

Look carefully at this diagram and relate it to the code in Listing 1–1. Notice how the association relationships correspond to instance variables. For example, the association from `TreeMap` to `TreeMapNode` is named `topNode` and corresponds to the `topNode` variable within `TreeMap`.

Object diagrams

Figure 1–3 is an *object diagram*. It shows a set of objects and relationships at a particular moment in the execution of the system. You can view it as a snapshot of memory.

In this diagram the rectangle icons represent objects. You can tell that they are objects because their names are underlined. The name after the colon is the name of the class that the object belongs to. Note that the lower compartment of each object shows the value of that object's `itsKey` variable.

The relationships between the objects are called *links*, and are derived from the associations in Figure 1–2. Note that the links are named for the two array cells in the `nodes` array.

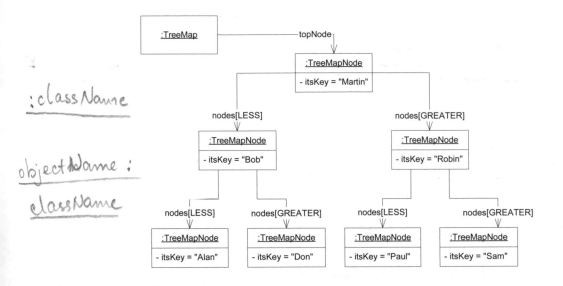

Figure 1–3
`TreeMap` Object diagram.

Sequence diagrams

Figure 1–4 is a *sequence diagram*. It describes how the `TreeMap.add` method is implemented.

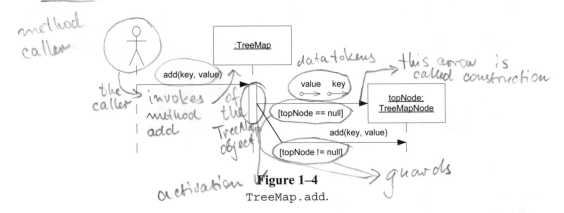

Figure 1–4
`TreeMap.add`.

The stick figure represents an unknown caller. This caller invokes the `add` method on a `TreeMap` object. If the `topNode` variable is `null`, then `TreeMap` responds by creating a new `TreeMapNode` and assigning it to `topNode`. Otherwise the `TreeMap` sends the `add` message to `topNode`.

The boolean expressions inside square brackets are called *guards*. They show which path is taken. The message arrow that terminates on the `TreeMapNode` icon represents *construction*. The little arrows with circles are called *data tokens*. In this case they depict the construction arguments. The skinny rectangle below `TreeMap` is called an *activation*. It depicts how much time the `add` method executes.

Collaboration diagrams

Figure 1–5 is a *collaboration diagram* depicting the case of `TreeMap.add` where `treeNode` is not null. Collaboration diagrams contain the same information that sequence diagrams contain. However, whereas sequence diagrams make the order of the messages clear, collaboration diagrams make the relationships between the objects clear.

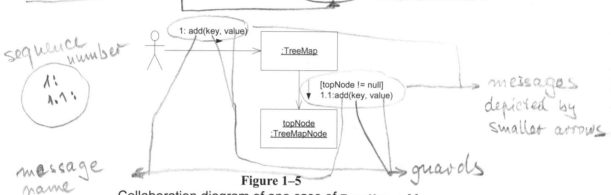

Figure 1–5
Collaboration diagram of one case of `TreeMap.add`.

The objects are connected by relationships called links. A link exists wherever one object can send a message to another. Traveling over those links are the messages themselves. They are depicted as the smaller arrows. The messages are labeled with the name of the message, its sequence number, and any guards that apply.

The dot structure of the sequence number shows the calling hierarchy. The `TreeMap.add` function (message 1) invokes the `TreeMapNode.add` function (message 1.1). Thus, message 1.1 is the first message sent by the function invoked by message 1.

State diagrams

UML has a very comprehensive notation for finite state machines. Figure 1–6 shows just the barest subset of that notation.

Figure 1–6 shows the state machine for a subway turnstile. There are two *states* named `Locked` and `Unlocked`. Two *events* may be sent to the machine. The `coin` event means that the user has dropped a coin into the turnstile. The `pass` event means that the user has passed through the turnstile.

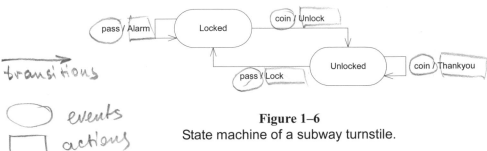

transitions

events
actions

Figure 1–6
State machine of a subway turnstile.

The arrows are called *transitions*. They are labeled with the *event* that triggers the transition and the *action* that the transition performs. When a transition is triggered it causes the state of the system to change.

We can translate Figure 1–6 to English as follows:

- If we are in the Locked state and we get a coin event, then we transition to the Unlocked state and we invoke the Unlock function.

- If we are in the Unlocked state and we get a pass event, then we transition to the Locked state and we invoke the Lock function.

- If we are in the Unlocked state and we get a coin event, then we stay in the Unlocked state and we call the Thankyou function.

- If we are in the Locked state and we get a pass event, then we stay in the Locked state and we call the Alarm function.

Diagrams like this are extremely useful for figuring out the way a system behaves. They give us the opportunity to explore what the system should do in unexpected cases, such as when a user deposits a coin, and then deposits *another* coin for no good reason.

Conclusion

The diagrams shown in this chapter are enough for most purposes. Most programmers could live without any more knowledge of UML that what is shown here.

Notes

[Fowler1999a]: : Martin Fowler and Kendall Scott, *UML Distilled: A Brief Guide to the Standard Object Modeling Language*, 2nd ed. Reading, Mass.: Addison-Wesley, 1999.

2

Working with Diagrams

Angela Brooks

Before we explore the details of UML, it would be wise to talk about when and why we use it. Much harm has been done to software projects through the misuse and overuse of UML.

Why Model?

Why do engineers build models? Why do aerospace engineers build models of aircraft? Why do structural engineers build models of bridges? What purposes do these models serve?

These engineers build models to find out if their designs will work. Aerospace engineers build models of aircraft and then put them into wind tunnels to see if they will fly. Structural engineers build models of bridges to see if they will stand. Architects build models of buildings to see if their clients will like the way they look. *Models are built to find out if something will work.*

This implies that models must be testable. It does no good to build a model if there are no criteria you can apply to that model in order to test it. If you can't evaluate the model, the model has no value.

Why don't aerospace engineers just build the plane and try to fly it? Why don't structural engineers just build the bridge and then see if it stands? Because airplanes and bridges are a *lot* more expensive than the models. *We investigate designs with models when the models are much cheaper than the real thing we are building.*

Why build models of software?

Can a UML diagram be tested? Is it much cheaper to create and test than the software it represents? In both cases the answer is nowhere near as clear as it is for aerospace engineers and structural engineers. There are no firm criteria for testing a UML diagram. We can look at it, evaluate it, and apply principles and patterns to it, but in the end the evaluation is still very subjective. UML diagrams are less expensive to draw than software is to write, but not by a huge factor. Indeed, there are times when it's easier to change source code than it is to change a diagram. So when does it make sense to use UML?

I wouldn't be writing this book if UML didn't make sense to use. However, the above illustrates just how easy UML is to misuse. *We make use of UML when we have something definitive we need to test, and when using UML to test it is cheaper than using code to test it.* For example, let's say I have an idea for a certain design. I need to test whether the other developers on my team think it is a good idea. So I write a UML diagram on the white board and ask my teammates for their feedback.

Why should we build comprehensive designs before coding?

Architects, aerospace engineers, and structural engineers all draw blueprints. Why? Because one person can draw the blueprints for a home that will require five or more people to build. A few dozen aerospace engineers can draw blueprints for an airplane that will require thousands of people to build. Blueprints can be drawn without digging foundations, pouring concrete, or hanging windows. In short, it is *much* cheaper to plan a building up front than it is to try to build it without a plan. It doesn't cost much to throw away a faulty blueprint, but it costs a *lot* to tear down a faulty building.

Once again things are not so clear-cut in software. It is not at all clear that drawing UML diagrams is much cheaper than writing code. Indeed, many project teams have spent *more* on their diagrams than they have on the code itself. It is also not clear that throwing away a diagram is much cheaper than throwing away code. Therefore, it is not at all clear that creating a comprehensive UML design before writing code is a cost-effective option.

Making Effective use of UML

Apparently neither architecture, nor aerospace engineering, nor structural engineering provide a clear metaphor for software development. We cannot blithely use UML the way those other disciplines use blueprints and models. So, when and why *should* we use UML?

Communicating with others

UML is enormously convenient for communicating design concepts among software developers. A lot can be done with a small group of developers at a white board. If you have some ideas that you need to communicate to others, UML can be a big benefit.

Angela Brooks

UML is very good for communicating focused design ideas. For example, the diagram in Figure 2–1 is very clear. We see LoginServlet implementing the Servlet interface and using the UserDatabase. Apparently the classes HTTPRequest and HTTPResponse are needed by LoginServlet. One could easily imagine a group of developers standing around a white board debating a diagram like this. Indeed, the diagram makes it very clear what the code structure would look like.

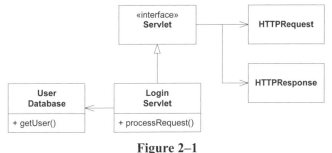

Figure 2–1
LoginServlet.

On the other hand, UML is not particularly good for communicating algorithmic detail. Consider the simple bubble sort code in Listing 2–1. Expressing this simple module in UML is not very satisfying.

Listing 2–1 `BubbleSorter.java`

```
public class BubbleSorter
{
  static int operations = 0;
  public static int sort(int [] array)
  {
    operations = 0;
    if (array.length <= 1)
      return operations;

    for (int nextToLast = array.length-2;
         nextToLast >= 0; nextToLast--)
      for (int index = 0; index <= nextToLast; index++)
        compareAndSwap(array, index);

    return operations;
  }

  private static void swap(int[] array, int index)
  {
    int temp = array[index];
    array[index] = array[index+1];
    array[index+1] = temp;
  }

  private static void compareAndSwap(int[] array, int index)
  {
    if (array[index] > array[index+1])
      swap(array, index);
    operations++;
  }
}
```

The diagram in Figure 2–2 gives us a rough structure, but is cumbersome and reflects none of the interesting details. The diagram in Figure 2–3 is no easier to read than the code and is substantially more difficult to create. UML for these purposes leaves much to be desired.

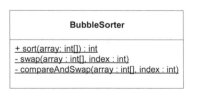

Figure 2–2
`BubbleSorter.`

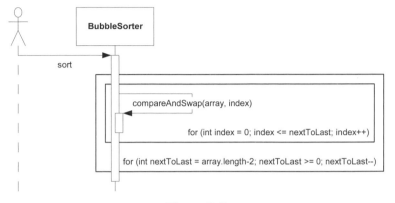

Figure 2–3
`BubbleSorter` sequence diagram.

② *Road maps*

UML can be useful for creating road maps of large software structures. Such road maps give developers a quick way to find out which classes depend upon which others and provide a reference to the structure of the whole system.

For example, in Figure 2–4 it is easy to see that `Space` objects have a `PolyLine` constructed of many `Lines` that are derived from `LinearObject` that contains two `Points`. Finding this structure in code would be tedious. Finding it in a road map diagram is trivial.

Such road maps can be useful teaching tools. However, any team member ought to be able to throw such a diagram up on the white board at a moment's notice. Indeed, I drew the one above from my memory of a system I was working on five years ago. Such diagrams capture the knowledge that all the developers must keep in their heads in order to work effectively in the system. So, for the most part, there is not much point in going to a lot of trouble to create and archive such documents. Their best use is, once again, at the white board.

③ *Back-end documentation*

When is the best time to create a design document? At the end of the project as the last act of the team. Such a document will accurately reflect the state of the design as the team left it, and could certainly be useful to an incoming team.

However, there are some pitfalls. UML diagrams need to be carefully considered. We don't want a thousand pages of sequence diagrams! Rather, we want a few very salient diagrams that describe the major issues in the system. No UML diagram is worse than one that is cluttered with so many lines and boxes that you get lost in the tangle (See Figure 2–5). **Don't do this**.

4) *most of all UML diagrams help you to understand the problem better*

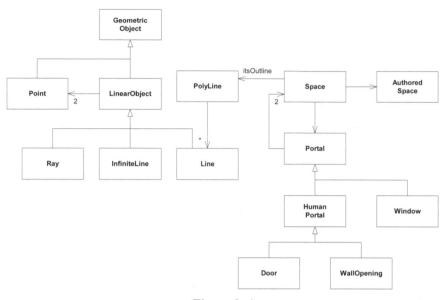

Figure 2–4
Road map diagram.

What to keep and what to throw away

Get into the habit of throwing UML diagrams away. Better yet, get into the habit of not creating them on a persistent medium. Write them on a white board, or on scraps of paper. Erase the white board frequently, and throw the scraps of paper away. Don't use a case tool or a drawing program as a rule. There is a time and place for such tools, but most of your UML should be short-lived.

Some diagrams, however, are useful to save: These are the diagrams that express a common design solution in your system. These are the diagrams that record complex protocols that are hard to see in the code. These are the diagrams that provide road maps for areas of the system that aren't touched very often. These are the diagrams that record designer intent in a way that is better than code can express it.

There is no point in hunting for these diagrams; you'll know them when you see them. There's no point in trying to create these diagrams up front. You'll be guessing, and you'll guess wrong. The real useful diagrams will keep showing up over and over again. They'll show up on white boards or scraps of paper in design session after design session. Eventually someone will make a persistent copy of the diagram just so it doesn't have to be drawn again. That is the time to place the diagram in some common area that everyone has access to.

It is important to keep common areas convenient and uncluttered. Putting useful diagrams on a Web server or a networked knowledge base is a good idea. However, don't

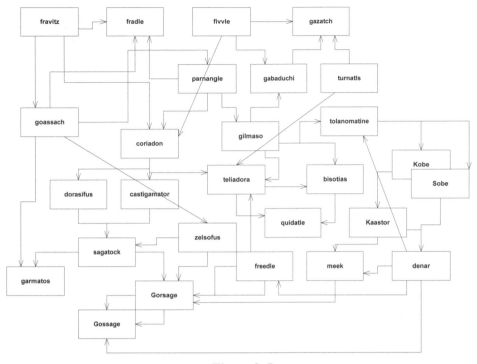

Figure 2–5
A bad (but all too common) example.

allow hundreds or thousands of diagrams to accumulate there. Be judicious about which diagrams are truly useful, and which could be recreated by anybody on the team at a moment's notice. Keep only those whose long-term survival has lots of value.

Iterative Refinement = Wirth
Stepwise

How do we create UML diagrams? Do we draw them in one brilliant flash of insight? Do we draw the class diagrams first and then the sequence diagrams? Should we scaffold the whole structure of the system before we flesh in any of the details?

The answer to all these questions is a resounding NO. Anything humans do well they do by taking tiny little steps

and then evaluating what they have done. The things that humans do not do well are things that they do in great leaps. We desire to create useful UML diagrams. Therefore we will create them in tiny little steps.

Steps in creating UML Diagrams

1)
Behavior first

I like to start with behavior. For those problems where I think UML will help me think the problem through, I'll start by drawing a simple sequence diagram of the problem. Consider, for example, the software that controls a cellular phone. How does this software make the phone call?

We might imagine that the software detects each button press and sends a message to some object that controls dialing. So we'll draw a Button object and a Dialer object and show the Button sending many digit messages to the Dialer. The star means *many*.

1* many

What will the Dialer do when it receives a digit message? Well, it needs to get the digit displayed on the screen. So perhaps it'll send displayDigit to the Screen object.

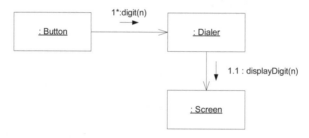

Next the Dialer had better cause a tone to be emitted from the speaker. So we'll have it send the tone message to the Speaker object.

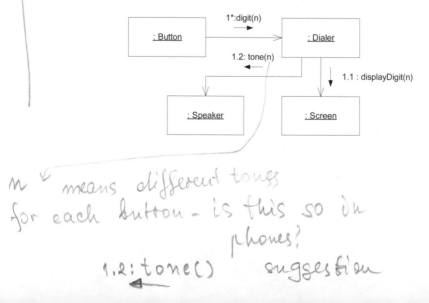

n * means different tones
for each button - is this so in
phones?
1.2: tone()   suggestion

?What is a cellular phone?

At some point the user will press the Send button, indicating that he wants the call to go through. At that point we'll have to tell the cellular radio to connect to the cellular network and pass along the phone number that was dialed.

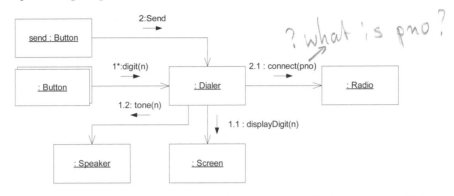

? what is pno?

Once the connection has been established, the Radio can tell the Screen to light up the "in use" indicator. This message will almost certainly be sent in a different thread of control (which is denoted by the letter in front of the sequence number). The final collaboration diagram is shown in Figure 2–6.

I do not understand that!

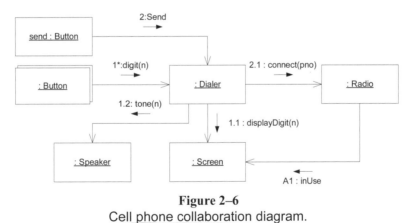

Figure 2–6
Cell phone collaboration diagram.

Check the structure

This little exercise has shown how we build a collaboration from nothing. Notice how we invented objects along the way. We didn't know these objects were going to be there ahead of time, we just knew we needed certain things to happen, so we invented objects to do them.

But now, before we go much further, we need to examine what this collaboration means to the structure of the code. So we'll create a class diagram that supports the collaboration. This class diagram will have a class for each object in the collaboration, and an association for each link in the collaboration.

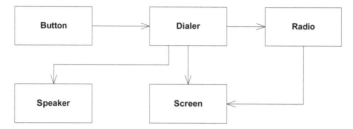

Figure 2–7
Cell phone class diagram.

Those of you who are familiar with UML will note that I have ignored aggregation and composition. That's intentional. There'll be plenty of time to consider whether any of those relationships apply.

What's important to me right now is an analysis of the dependencies. Why should Button depend upon Dialer? If you think about this, it's pretty hideous. Consider the implied code:

```
public class Button
{
   private Dialer itsDialer;
   public Button(Dialer dialer)
   {itsDialer = dialer;}
   ...
}
```

I don't want the source code of Button mentioning the source code of Dialer. Button is a class that I can use in many different contexts. For example, I'd like to use the Button class to control the on/off switch, or the menu button, or the other control buttons on the phone. If I bind the Button to the Dialer, then I won't be able to reuse the Button code for other purposes.

I can fix this by inserting an interface between Button and Dialer, as shown in Figure 2–8. Here we see that each Button is given a token that identifies it. When the Button class detects that the button has been pressed, it invokes the buttonPressed method of the ButtonListener interface, passing the token. This breaks the dependence of Button upon Dialer and allows Button to be used virtually anywhere that needs to receive button presses.

Notice that this change has had no effect upon the dynamic diagram in Figure 2–6. The objects are all the same, it's just the classes that have changed.

its tricky i do not? .

i do not understand! .

? .

how did we ended up with this diagram?

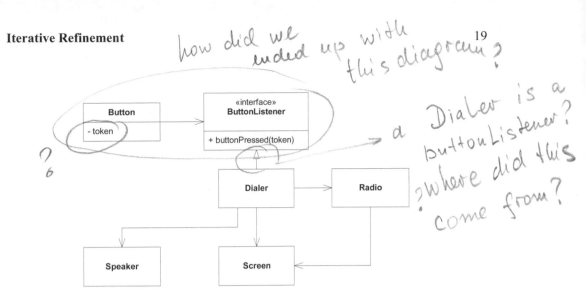

a Dialer is a buttonListener? where did this come from?

? b

Figure 2–8
Isolating Button from Dialer.

Unfortunately, now we've made Dialer know something about Button. Why should Dialer expect to get its input from ButtonListener? Why should it have a method within it named buttonPressed? What has the Dialer got to do with Button?

We can solve this problem, and get rid of all the token nonsense, by using a batch of little adapters. The ButtonDialerAdapter implements the ButtonListener interface. It receives the buttonPressed method and sends a digit(n) message to the Dialer. The digit passed to the Dialer is held in the adapter.

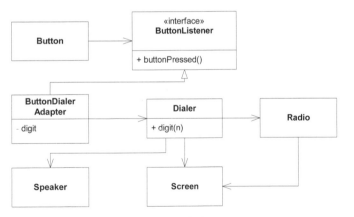

Figure 2–9
Adapting Buttons to Dialers.

Envisioning the code

We can easily envision the code for the `ButtonDialerAdapter`. It appears in Listing 2–2. Being able to envision the code is *critically* important when working with diagrams. We use the diagrams as a shortcut for code, not a replacement for it. If you are drawing diagrams and cannot envision the code that they represent, then you are building castles in the air. *Stop what you are doing and figure out how to translate it to code.* Never let the diagrams become an end unto themselves. You must always be sure you know what code you are representing.

```
Listing 2–2   ButtonDialerAdapter.java
public class ButtonDialerAdapter implements ButtonListener
{
  private int digit;
  private Dialer dialer;
  public ButtonDialerAdapter(int digit, Dialer dialer)
  {
    this.digit = digit;
    this.dialer = dialer;
  }

  public void buttonPressed()
  {
    dialer.digit(digit);
  }
}
```

Evolution of diagrams

Note that the last change we made in Figure 2–9 has invalidated the dynamic model back in Figure 2–6. The dynamic model knows nothing of the adapters. We'll change that now. See Figure 2–10.

This shows how the diagrams evolve together in an iterative fashion. You start with a little bit of dynamics. Then you explore what those dynamics imply to the static relationships. You alter the static relationships according to the principles of good design. Then you go back and improve the dynamic diagrams.

Each of these steps is *tiny*. We don't want to invest any more than *five minutes* into a dynamic diagram before exploring the static structure implied. We don't want to spend any more than five minutes refining that static structure before we consider the impact on the dynamic behavior. Rather, we want to evolve the two diagrams together using very short cycles.

Remember, we're probably doing this at a white board, and we are probably not recording what we are doing for posterity. We aren't trying to be very formal or very precise. Indeed, the diagrams I have included in the preceding figures are a bit more precise and formal than you would normally have to be. The goal at the white board is not to get all the dots right on your sequence numbers. The goal is to get everybody standing at the

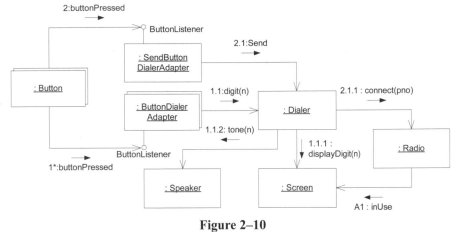

Figure 2–10
Adding adapters to the dynamic model.

board to understand the discussion. The goal is to stop working at the board and start writing code.

Minimalism

This book will show you all the various widgets and icons you can adorn a UML diagram with. Using these adornments you can make your diagrams very complex. It is possible to represent an amazing amount of detail in a UML diagram. However, I advise against this.

As we'll discuss below, diagrams are most useful for communicating with others, and for helping you work out design problems. It is important that you only use the amount of detail necessary to accomplish your goal. Loading a diagram with lots of adornments is possible, but counter-productive. Keep your diagrams simple and clean. UML diagrams are not source code and should not be treated as the place to declare every method, variable, and relationship.

When and How to Draw Diagrams

Drawing UML diagrams can be a very useful activity. It can also be a horrible waste of time. A decision to use UML can be a very good thing, or it can be a very bad thing. It depends upon how, and how much, you choose to use it.

When to draw diagrams and when to stop.

Don't make a rule that everything must be diagrammed. Such rules are worse than useless. Enormous amounts of project time and energy can be wasted in pursuit of diagrams that no one will ever read.

When to draw diagrams:

- Draw diagrams when several people need to understand the structure of a particular part of the design because they are all going to be working on it simultaneously. Stop when everyone agrees that they understand.

- Draw diagrams when two or more people disagree on how a particular element should be designed, and you want team consensus. Put the discussion into a time box, then choose a means for deciding, such as a vote or an impartial judge. Stop at the end of the time box, or when the decision can be made. Then erase the diagram.

- Draw diagrams when you just want to play with a design idea, and the diagrams can help you think it through. Stop when you've gotten to the point that you can finish your thinking in code. Discard the diagrams.

- Draw diagrams when you need to explain the structure of some part of the code to someone else, or to yourself. Stop when the explanation would be better done by looking at code.

- Draw diagrams when it's close to the end of the project and your customer has requested them as part of a documentation stream for others.

*When **not** to draw diagrams:*

- Don't draw diagrams because the process tells you to.

- Don't draw diagrams because you feel guilty not drawing them or because you think that's what good designers do. Good designers write code and draw diagrams only when necessary.

- Don't draw diagrams to create comprehensive documentation of the design phase prior to coding. Such documents are almost never worth anything and consume immense amounts of time.

- Don't draw diagrams for other people to code. True software architects participate in the coding of their designs, so that they can be seen to lie in the bed they have made.

CASE tools

UML CASE tools can be beneficial, but they can also be expensive dust collectors. Be *very* careful about making a decision to purchase and deploy a UML CASE tool.

- ***Don't UML CASE tools make it easier to draw diagrams?***
  No, they make it significantly harder. There is a long learning curve to get proficient, and even then the tools are more cumbersome than white boards. White

boards are very easy to use. Developers are usually already familiar with them. If not, there is virtually no learning curve.

- ***Don't UML CASE tools make it easier for large teams to collaborate on diagrams?***
  In some cases. However, the vast majority of developer and development projects do not need to be producing diagrams in such quantities and complexities that they require an automated collaborative system to coordinate their activities. In any case, the best time to purchase a system to coordinate the preparation of UML diagrams is when a manual system has first been put in place, is starting to show the strain, and there is no other choice but to automate.

- ***Don't UML CASE tools make it easier to generate code?***
  The sum total effort involved in creating the diagrams, generating the code, and then using the generated code is not likely to be less than the cost of just writing the code in the first place. If there is a gain, it is not an order of magnitude, or even a factor of two. Developers know how to edit text files and use IDEs. Generating code from diagrams may sound like a good idea, but I strongly urge you to measure the productivity increase before you spend a lot of money.

- ***What about these CASE tools that are also IDEs and show the code and diagrams together?***
  These tools are definitely cool. However, I don't think the constant presence of UML is important. The fact that the diagram changes as I modify the code, or that the code changes as I modify the diagram, does not really help me much. Frankly, I'd rather buy an IDE that has put its effort into figuring out how to help me manipulate my programs rather than my diagrams. Again, measure productivity improvement before making a huge monetary commitment.

In short, look before you leap, and look very hard. There *may* be a benefit to outfitting your team with an expensive CASE tool, but verify that benefit with your own experiments before buying something that could very well turn into shelf ware.

But what about documentation?

Angela Brooks

Good documentation is essential to any project. Without it the team will get lost in a sea of code. On the other hand, too much documentation of the wrong kind is worse because then you have all this distracting and misleading paper, and you still have the sea of code.

Documentation must be created, but it

must be created prudently. Often the choice *not* to document is just as important as the choice to document. A complex communication protocol needs to be documented. A complex relational schema needs to be documented. A complex reusable framework needs to be documented.

However, none of these things need a hundred pages of UML. Software documentation should be *short and to the point*. The value of a software document is inversely proportional to its size.

For a project team of 12 people working on a project of a million lines of Java, I would have a total of 25 to 200 pages of persistent documentation, with my preference being for the smaller. These documents would include UML diagrams of the high-level structure of the important modules, ER diagrams of the relational schema, a page or two about how to build the system, testing instructions, source code control instructions, and so forth.

I would put this documentation into a wiki[1] or some collaborative authoring tool so that anyone on the team can have access to it on their screens and search it, and anyone can change it as need be.

It takes a lot of work to make a document small, but that work is worth it. People will read small documents. They won't read 1,000-page tomes.

And Javadocs™?

Javadocs are excellent tools. Create them. But keep them small and focused. Those that describe functions that others will use should be written with care, and should contain enough information to help the user understand. Javadocs that describe private utility functions or methods that aren't for wide distribution can be much smaller.

Conclusion

A few folks at a white board can use UML to help them think through a design problem. Such diagrams should be created iteratively, in very short cycles. It is best to explore dynamic scenarios first, and then determine their implications on static structure. It is important to evolve the dynamic and static diagrams together using very short iterative cycles on the order of five minutes or less.

UML CASE tools can be beneficial in certain cases, but for the normal development team they are likely to be more of a hindrance than a help. If you think you need a UML CASE tool, even one integrated with an IDE, run some productivity experiments first. Look before you leap.

---

1. A web based collaborative document authoring tool. See: http://c2.com and http://fitnesse.org

UML is a tool, not an end in itself. As a tool, it can help you think through your designs and communicate them to others. Use it sparingly and it will give you great benefit. Overuse it and it will waste a lot of your time. When using UML, *think small*.

3

Class Diagrams

Angela Brooks

UML class diagrams allow us to denote the static contents of — and the relationships between — classes. In a class diagram we can show the member variables, and member functions of a class. We can also show whether one class inherits from another, or whether it holds a reference to another. In short, we can depict all the *source code dependencies* between classes.

This can be valuable. It can be much easier to evaluate the dependency structure of a system from a diagram than from source code. Diagrams make certain dependency structures visible. We can *see* dependency cycles, and determine how best to break them. We can see when abstract classes depend upon concrete classes, and determine a strategy for rerouting such dependencies.

The Basics

Classes

Figure 3–1 shows the simplest form of class diagram. The class named `Dialer` is represented as a simple rectangle. This diagram represents nothing more than the code shown to its right.

```
public class Dialer
{
}
```

Figure 3–1
Class icon.

This is the most common way you will represent a class. The classes on most diagrams don't need any more than their name to make clear what is going on. *providing the name is meaningful*

A class icon can be subdivided into compartments. The top compartment is for the name of the class, the second is for the variables of the class, and the third is for the methods of the class. Figure 3–2 shows these compartments and how they translate into code.

class name
class variables
class method

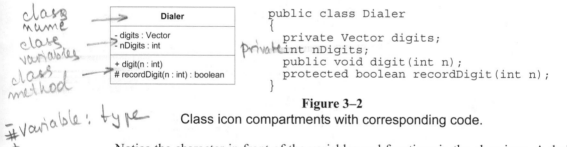

```
public class Dialer
{
    private Vector digits;
    private int nDigits;
    public void digit(int n);
    protected boolean recordDigit(int n);
}
```

Figure 3–2
Class icon compartments with corresponding code.

#Variable : type
+

Notice the character in front of the variables and functions in the class icon. A dash (−) denotes `private`, a hash (#) denotes `protected`, and a plus (+) denotes `public`.

The type of a variable, or a function argument is shown after the colon following the variable or argument name. Similarly, the return value of a function is shown after the colon following the function.

This kind of detail is sometimes useful, but should not be used very often. UML diagrams are not the place to declare variables and functions. Such declarations are better done in source code. Use these adornments only when they are essential to the purpose of the diagram.

+method : (variable : type) : method type
#

Association

Associations between classes most often represent instance variables that hold references to other objects. For example, in Figure 3–3 we see an association between `Phone` and `Button`. The direction of the arrow tells us that `Phone` holds a reference to `Button`. The name near the arrowhead is the name of the instance variable. The number near the arrowhead tells us how many references are held.

how many references of the variable

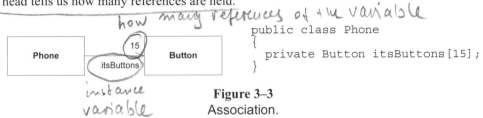

```
public class Phone
{
    private Button itsButtons[15];
}
```

instance variable

Figure 3–3
Association.

In Figure 3–3 we saw that 15 `Button` objects were connected to the `Phone` object. In Figure 3–4, we see what happens when there is no limit. A `Phonebook` is connected to *many* `PhoneNumber` objects. The star means *many*. In Java this is most commonly implemented with a `Vector`, a `List`, or some other container type.

many

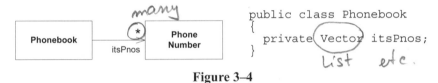

```
public class Phonebook
{
    private Vector itsPnos;
}
```

List   etc.

Figure 3–4

You may have noticed that I avoided using the word "has". I could have said: "A `Phonebook` *has* many `PhoneNumbers`." This was intentional. The common OO verbs HASA and ISA have lead to a number of unfortunate misunderstandings. We'll explore some of them later in Chapter 6. For now, don't expect me to use the common terms. Rather, I'll use terms that are descriptive of what actually happens in software, such as: "is connected to."

is connected to = has

is a
has   *find out more? → ch. 6*

generalization

define generalization

Inheritance

You have to be very careful with your arrow-heads in UML. Figure 3–5 shows why. The little arrowhead pointing at `Employee` denotes *inheritance*[1]. If you draw your arrowheads carelessly, it may be hard to tell whether you mean inheritance or association. To make it clearer, I often make inheritance relationships vertical and associations horizontal.

In UML all arrowheads point in the direction of *source code dependency*. Since it is the `SalariedEmployee` class that mentions the name of `Employee`, the arrowhead points at `Employee`. So, in UML, inheritance arrows point at the base class.

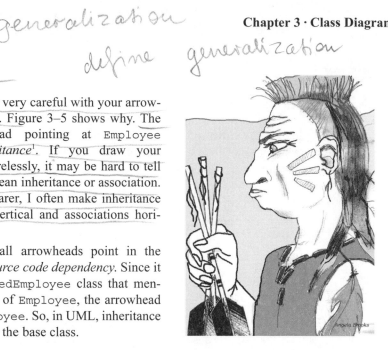

base class

derived class

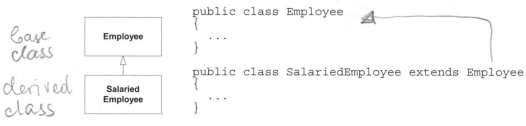

```
public class Employee
{
    ...
}

public class SalariedEmployee extends Employee
{
    ...
}
```

Figure 3–5
Inheritance.

UML has a special notation for the kind of inheritance used between a Java class and a Java interface. It is shown, in Figure 3–6, as a dashed inheritance arrow[2]. In the diagrams to come, you'll probably catch me forgetting to dash the arrows that point to interfaces. I suggest you forget to dash the arrows that you draw on white boards too. Life's too short to be dashing arrows.

Figure 3–7 shows another way to convey the same information. Interfaces can be drawn as little lollipops on the classes that implement them. We often see this kind of notation in COM designs.

---

1. Actually, it denotes *generalization*, but as far as a Java programmer is concerned, the difference is moot.
2. This is called a *realizes* relationship. There's more to it than just inheritance of interface, but the difference is beyond the scope of this book.

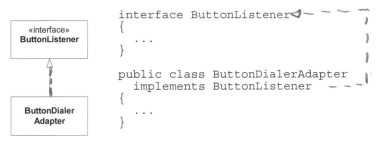

```
interface ButtonListener
{
    ...
}

public class ButtonDialerAdapter
    implements ButtonListener
{
    ...
}
```

Figure 3–6
Realizes relationship.

Figure 3–7
Lollipop interface Indicator.

An Example Class Diagram

Figure 3–8 shows a simple class diagram of part of an ATM system. This diagram is interesting both for what it shows, and for what it does not show. Note that I have taken pains to mark all the interfaces. I consider it crucial to make sure my readers know what classes I intend to be interfaces and which I intend to be implemented. For example, the diagram immediately tells you that `WithdrawalTransaction` talks to a `CashDispenser` interface. Clearly some class in the system will have to implement the `CashDispenser`, but in this diagram we don't care which class it is.

Note that I have not been particularly thorough in documenting the methods of the various UI interfaces. Certainly `WithdrawalUI` will need more than just the two methods shown there. What about `promptForAccount` or `informCashDispenserEmpty`? Putting those methods in the diagram would just clutter it. By providing a representative batch of methods, I've given the reader the idea. That's all that's really necessary.

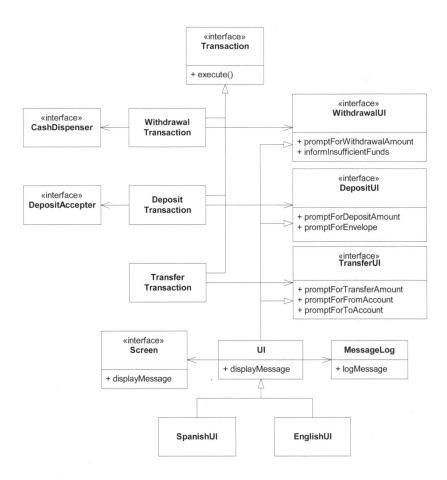

Figure 3–8
ATM class diagram.

Again note the convention of horizontal association and vertical inheritance. This really helps to differentiate these vastly different kinds of relationships. Without a convention like this it can be hard to tease the meaning out of the tangle.

Notice how I've separated the diagram into three distinct zones. The transactions and their actions are on the left, the various UI interfaces are all on the right, and the UI implementation is on the bottom. Note also that the connections between the grouping are minimal and regular. In one case it is three associations, all pointing the same way. In the other case it is three inheritance relationships all merged into a single line. The grouping, and the way they are connected, help the reader to see the diagram in coherent pieces.

You should be able to *see* the code as you look at the diagram. Is Listing 3–1 close to what you expected for the implementation of UI?

```
Listing 3–1  UI.java
public class UI implements
   WithdrawalUI, DepositUI, TransferUI
{
  private Screen itsScreen;
  private MessageLog itsMessageLog;

  public void displayMessage(String message)
  {
    itsMessageLog.logMessage(message);
    itsScreen.displayMessage(message);
  }
}
```

The Details

There are a vast number of details and adornments that can be added to UML class diagrams. Most of the time these details and adornments should not be added. But there are times when they can be helpful.

Class stereotypes

Class stereotypes appear between guillemet[3] characters, usually above the name of the class. We have seen them before. The «**interface**» denotation in Figure 3–8 is a class stereotype. «interface» is one of two standard stereotypes that can be used by Java programmers. The other is «utility».

«**interface**». All the methods of classes marked with this stereotype are abstract. None of the methods can be implemented. Moreover, «interface» classes can have no instance variables. The only variables they can have are static variables. This corresponds exactly to Java interfaces. See Figure 3–9.

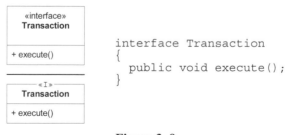

```
interface Transaction
{
    public void execute();
}
```

Figure 3–9
«interface» class stereotype.

---

3. The quotation marks that look like double angle brackets « ». These are *not* two less-than, and two greater-than signs. If you use doubled inequality operators instead of the appropriate and proper guillemet characters, the UML police *will* find you.

I draw interfaces so often that spelling the whole stereotype out at the white board can be pretty inconvenient. So I often use the shorthand in the lower part of Figure 3–9 to make the drawing easier. It's not standard UML, but it's much more convenient.

«utility». All the methods and variables of a «utility» class are static. Booch[4] used to call these *class utilities*. See Figure 3–10.

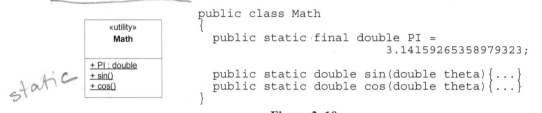

```
public class Math
{
    public static final double PI =
                          3.14159265358979323;

    public static double sin(double theta){...}
    public static double cos(double theta){...}
}
```

static

Figure 3–10
«utility» class stereotype.

You can make your own stereotypes if you like. I often use stereotypes like «persistent», «C-API», «struct», or «function». You just have to make sure that the people who are reading your diagrams know what your stereotype means.

Abstract classes

In UML there are two ways to denote that a class or a method is abstract. You can write the name in italics, or you can use the {abstract} property. Both options are shown in Figure 3–11.

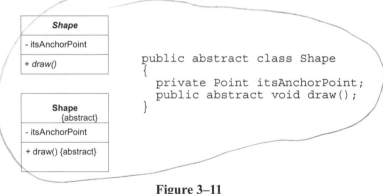

```
public abstract class Shape
{
    private Point itsAnchorPoint;
    public abstract void draw();
}
```

Figure 3–11
Abstract classes.

It's a little difficult to write italics at a white board, and the {abstract} property is wordy. So at the white board, if I need to denote a class or method as abstract, I use the

---

4. [Booch1994], p. 186.

convention shown in Figure 3–12. Again, this isn't standard UML, but at the white board it is a lot more convenient.[5]

Figure 3–12
Unofficial denotation of abstract classes.

Properties *should I include this one or skip it?*

Properties, like {abstract} can be added to any class. They represent extra information that's not usually part of a class. You can create your own properties at any time.

Properties are written in a comma separated list of name–value pairs, like this:

```
{author=Martin, date=20020429, file=shape.java, private}
```

The properties in the preceding example are not part of UML. The {abstract} property is the only defined property of UML that Java programmers would find useful.

If a property does not have a value, it is assumed to take the boolean value `true`. Thus, {abstract} and {abstract = true} are synonyms.

Properties are written below and to the right of the name of the class, as shown in Figure 3–13.

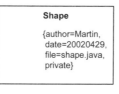

Figure 3–13
Properties.

Other than the {abstract} property, I don't know when you'd this useful. Personally, in the many years that I've been writing UML diagrams, I've never had occasion to use class properties for anything.

---

5. Some of you may remember the Booch notation. One of the nice things about that notation was its convenience. It was truly a white board notation.

Aggregation

Aggregation is a special form of association that connotes a "whole/part" relationship. Figure 3–14 shows how it is drawn and implemented. Notice that the implementation shown in Figure 3–14 is indistinguishable from association. That's a hint.

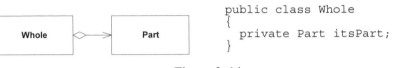

```
public class Whole
{
    private Part itsPart;
}
```

Figure 3–14
Aggregation.

Unfortunately, UML does not provide a strong definition for this relationship. This leads to confusion because various programmers and analysts adopt their own pet definitions for the relationship. For that reason I don't use the relationship at all, and I recommend that you avoid it as well. In fact, this relationship has been dropped from UML 2.0.

The one hard rule that UML gives us regarding aggregations is simply this: A whole cannot be its own part. Therefore *instances* cannot form cycles of aggregations. A single object cannot be an aggregate of itself, two objects cannot be aggregates of each other, three objects cannot form a ring of aggregation, and so on. See Figure 3–15.

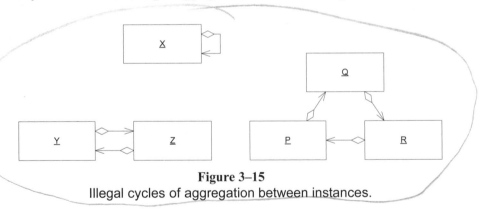

Figure 3–15
Illegal cycles of aggregation between instances.

I don't find this to be a particularly useful definition. How often am I concerned about making sure that instances form a directed acyclic graph? Not very often. Therefore I find this relationship useless in the kinds of diagrams I draw.

Composition

Composition is a special form of aggregation, as shown in Figure 3–16. Again, notice that the implementation is indistinguishable from association. However, this time the reason is not due to a lack of definition; this time it's because the relationship does not have a lot of use in a Java program. C++ programmers, on the other hand, find a *lot* of use for it.

```
public class Owner
{
    private Ward itsWard;
}
```

Figure 3–16
Composition.

The same rule applies to composition that applied to aggregation. There can be no cycles of instances. An owner cannot be its own ward. However, UML provides quite a bit more definition.

- An instance of a ward cannot be owned simultaneously by two owners. The object diagram in Figure 3–17 is illegal. Note, however, that the corresponding class diagram is not illegal. An owner can transfer ownership of a ward to another owner.

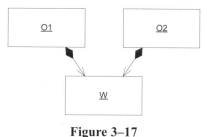

Figure 3–17
Illegal composition.

- The owner is responsible for the lifetime of the ward. If the owner is destroyed, the ward must be destroyed with it. If the owner is copied, the ward must be copied with it.

In Java destruction happens behind the scenes by the garbage collector, so there is seldom a need to manage the lifetime of an object. Deep copies are not unheard of, but the need to show deep copy semantics on a diagram is rare. So, though I have used composition relationships to describe some Java programs, such use is infrequent.

Figure 3–18 shows how composition is used to denote deep copy. We have a class named Address that holds many Strings. Each string holds one line of the address. Clearly, when you make a copy of the Address, you want the copy to change independently of the original. Thus, we need to make a deep copy. The composition relationship between the Address and the Strings indicates that copies need to be deep.[6]

---

6. Exercise: Why was it enough to clone the itsLines vector? Why didn't I have to clone the actual String instances?

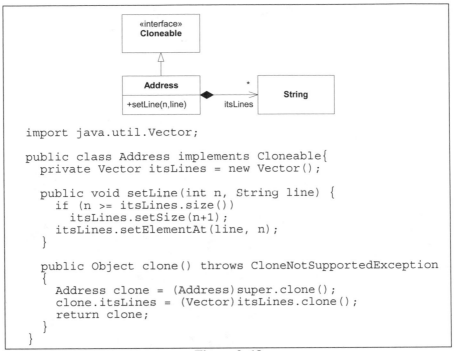

```
import java.util.Vector;

public class Address implements Cloneable{
   private Vector itsLines = new Vector();

   public void setLine(int n, String line) {
      if (n >= itsLines.size())
         itsLines.setSize(n+1);
      itsLines.setElementAt(line, n);
   }

   public Object clone() throws CloneNotSupportedException
   {
      Address clone = (Address)super.clone();
      clone.itsLines = (Vector)itsLines.clone();
      return clone;
   }
}
```

Figure 3–18
Deep copy is implied by composition.

Multiplicity

Objects can hold arrays or vectors of other objects, or they can hold many of the same kind of objects in separate instance variables. In UML this can be shown by placing a *multiplicity* expression on the far end of the association. Multiplicity expressions can be simple numbers, ranges, or a combination of both. For example, Figure 3–19 shows a BinaryTreeNode, using a multiplicity of 2.

```
public class BinaryTreeNode
{
   private BinaryTreeNode leftNode;
   private BinaryTreeNode rightNode;
}
```

Figure 3–19
Simple multiplicity.

Here are the allowable forms:

- Digit.   The exact number of elements.

- * or 0..*   Zero to many.

- 0..1   Zero or one. In Java this is often implemented with a reference that can be `null`.

- 1..*   One to many.

- 3..5   Three to five.

- 0, 2..5, 9..* Silly, but legal.

Association stereotypes

Associations can be labeled with stereotypes that change their meaning. Figure 3–20 shows the ones that I use most often.

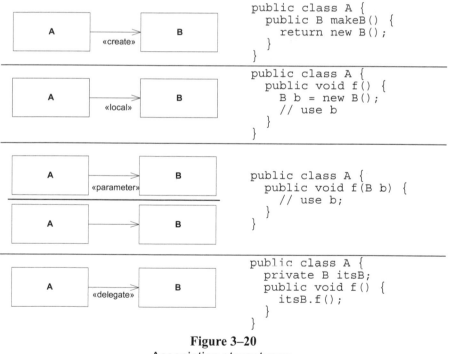

Figure 3–20
Association stereotypes.

The **«create»** stereotype indicates that the target of the association is created by the source. The implication is that the source creates the target and then passes it around to other parts of the system. In the example I've shown a typical factory.

The **«local»** stereotype is used when the source class creates an instance of the target and holds it in a local variable. The implication is that the created instance does not survive the member function that creates it. Thus, it is not held by any instance variable nor passed around the system in any way.

The **«parameter»** stereotype shows that the source class gains access to the target instance though the parameter of one of its member functions. Again, the implication is that the source forgets all about this object once the member function returns. The target is not saved in an instance variable.

Using dashed dependency arrows, as the diagram shows, is a common and convenient idiom for denoting parameters. I usually prefer it to using the **«parameter»** stereotype.

The **«delegate»** stereotype is used when the source class forwards a member function invocation to the target. There are a number of design patterns where this technique is applied, such as PROXY, DECORATOR, and COMPOSITE[7]. Since I use these patterns a lot, I find the notation helpful.

Inner classes

Inner (nested) classes are represented in UML with an association adorned with a crossed circle, as shown in Figure 3–21.

Figure 3–21
Inner class.

Anonymous inner classes

One of Java's more interesting features is anonymous inner classes. While UML does not have an official stance on these, I find the notation in Figure 3–22 works well for me. It is concise and descriptive. The anonymous inner class is shown as a nested class that is given the «anonymous» stereotype, and is also given the name of the interface it implements.

---

7. [Gamma1995] pp. 207, 175, 163.

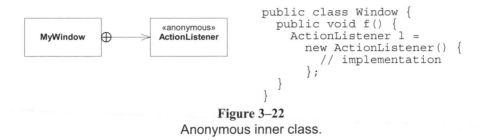

Figure 3–22
Anonymous inner class.

Association classes   ~~skip this!~~

Associations with multiplicity tell us that the source is connected to many instances of the target, but the diagram doesn't tell us what kind of container class is used. This can be depicted by using an association class, as shown in Figure 3–23.

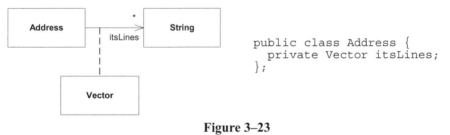

Figure 3–23
Association class.

Association classes show how a particular association is implemented. On the diagram they appear as a normal class connected to the association with a dashed line. As Java programmers we interpret this to mean that the source class really contains a reference to the association class, which in turn contains references to the target.

Association classes can also be used to indicate special forms of references, such as weak, soft, or phantom references. See Figure 3–24. On the other hand, this notation is a bit cumbersome and is probably better done with stereotypes as in Figure 3–25.

Figure 3–24
Association class denoting a weak reference.

Figure 3–25
Stereotype denoting a weak reference.

Association qualifiers   ~~skip this~~

Association qualifiers are used when the association is implemented through some kind of key or token, instead of with a normal Java reference. The example in Figure 3–26 shows a `LoginServlet` associated with an `Employee`. The association is mediated by a member variable named `empid`, which contains the database key for the `Employee`.

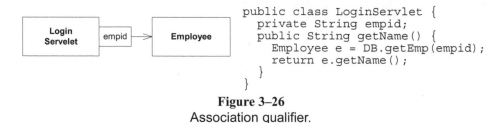

Figure 3–26
Association qualifier.

I find this notation useful in rare situations. Sometimes it's convenient to show that an object is associated to another through a database or dictionary key. It is important, however, that all the parties reading the diagram know how the qualifier is used to access the actual object. This is not something that's immediately evident from the notation.

Conclusion

There are lots of widgets, adornments, and whatchamajiggers in UML. There are so many that you can spend a long time becoming an UML language lawyer, enabling you to do what all lawyers can — write documents nobody else can understand.

In this chapter I have avoided most of the arcana and byzantine features of UML. Rather I have showed you the parts of UML that *I* use. I hope that along with that knowledge I have instilled within you the values of minimalism. Using too little of UML is almost always better than using too much.

Notes

[Booch1994]: Grady Booch, *Object Oriented Analysis and Design with Applications.* Redwood City, CA.: Benjamin Cummings, 1994.

[Gamma1995]: Erich Gamma, Richard Helm, Ralph Johnson, and John Vlissides. *Design Patterns.* Reading, Mass.: Addison-Wesley, 1995.

4

Sequence Diagrams

Sequence diagrams are the most common of the dynamic models drawn by UML users. As you might expect, UML provides lots and lots of goodies to help you draw truly incomprehensible diagrams. In this chapter we'll study those goodies, and try to convince you to use them with great restraint.

I once consulted for a team that had decided to create sequence diagrams for every method of every class. Please don't do this, it's a terrible waste of time. Use sequence diagrams when you have an immediate need to describe to someone how a group of objects collaborate, or when you want to visualize that collaboration for yourself. Use them as a tool that you use occasionally to hone your analytical skills, rather than as necessary documentation.

The Basics

I first learned to draw sequence diagrams in 1978. James Grenning, a longtime friend and associate, showed them to me while we were working on a project that involved complex communication protocols between computers connected by modems. What I am going to show you here is very close to the simple notation he taught me then, and should suffice for the vast majority of sequence diagrams that you will need to draw.

Objects, lifelines, messages, and other odds and ends

Figure 4–1 shows a typical sequence diagram. The objects and classes involved in the collaboration are shown at the top. We can distinguish objects from classes because objects have underlined names. The stick figure (actor) at left represents an anonymous object. It is the source and sink of all the messages entering and leaving the collaboration. Not all sequence diagrams have such an anonymous actor, but many do.

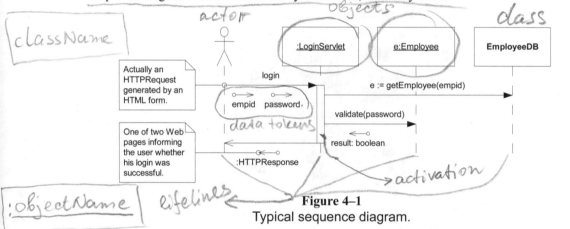

Figure 4–1
Typical sequence diagram.

The dashed lines hanging down from the objects and the actor are called *lifelines*. A message being sent from one object to another is shown as an arrow between the two lifelines. Each message is labeled with its name. Arguments appear either in the parentheses that follow the name, or next to *data tokens* (the little arrows with the circles on the end). Time is in the vertical dimension, so the lower a message appears the later it is sent.

The skinny little rectangle on the lifeline of the LoginServlet object is called an *activation*. Activations are optional; most diagrams don't need them. They represent the time that a function executes. In this case it shows how long the login function runs. The two messages leaving the activation to the right were sent by the login method. The unlabeled dashed arrow shows the login function returning to the actor, and passing back a return value.

Note the use of the e variable in the getEmployee message. This signifies the value returned by getEmployee. Notice also that the Employee object is named e. You guessed it, they're one and the same. The value that getEmployee returns is a reference to the Employee object.

Finally, notice that `EmployeeDB` is a class, not an object (its name is not underlined). This can only mean that `getEmployee` is a static method. Thus, we'd expect `EmployeeDB` to be coded as in Listing 4–1.

```java
Listing 4–1  EmployeeDB.java
public class EmployeeDB
{
  public static Employee getEmployee(String empid)
  {
    . . .
  }
  . . .
}
```

Creation and destruction

We can show the creation of an object on a sequence diagram using the convention shown in Figure 4–2. An unlabeled message terminates on the object to be created, not on its lifeline. We would expect `ShapeFactory` to be implemented as shown in Listing 4–2.

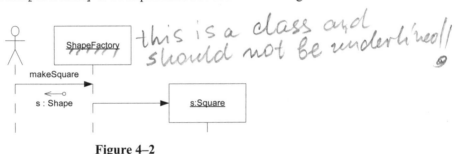

this is a class and should not be underlined!!

Figure 4–2
Creating an object.

```java
Listing 4–2  ShapeFactory.java
public class ShapeFactory
{
  public Shape makeSquare()
  {
    return new Square();
  }
}
```

In Java we don't explicitly destroy objects. The garbage collector does all the explicit destruction for us. However, there are times when we want to make it clear that we are done with an object and that, as far as we are concerned, the garbage collector can have it.

Figure 4–3 shows how we denote this in UML. The lifeline of the object to be released comes to a premature end at a large X. The message arrow terminating on the X represents the act of releasing the object to the garbage collector.

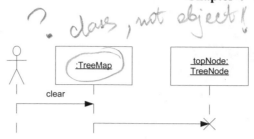

Figure 4–3
Releasing an object to the garbage collector.

Listing 4–3 shows the implementation we might expect from this diagram. Notice that the `clear` method sets the `topNode` variable to `nil`. Since the `TreeMap` is the only object that holds a reference to that `TreeNode` instance, it will be released to the garbage collector.

```
Listing 4–3  TreeMap.java
public class TreeMap
{
  private TreeNode topNode;
  public void clear()
  {
    topNode = nil;
  }
}
```

Simple loops

You can draw a simple loop in a UML diagram by drawing a box around the messages that repeat. The loop condition is enclosed in square brackets and is placed somewhere in the box, usually at the lower right. See Figure 4–4.

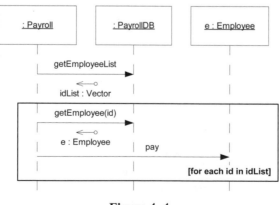

Figure 4–4
A simple loop.

This is a useful notational convention. However, it is not wise to try to capture algorithms in sequence diagrams. Sequence diagrams should be used to expose the connections between objects, not the nitty gritty details of an algorithm.

Cases and scenarios

Rule: Don't draw sequence diagrams like Figure 4–5, with lots of objects and scores of messages. Nobody can read them. Nobody *will* read them. They're a huge waste of time. Rather, learn how to draw a few smaller sequence diagrams that capture the essence of what you are trying to do. Each sequence diagram should fit on a single page, with plenty of room left for explanatory text. You should not have to shrink the icons down to tiny sizes to get them to fit on the page.

Also, don't draw dozens or hundreds of sequence diagrams. If you have too many, they won't be read. Find out what's common about all the scenarios and focus on that. *In the world of UML diagrams, commonalities are much more important than differences.* Use your diagrams to show common themes and common practices. Don't use them to document every little detail. If you really need to draw a sequence diagram to describe the way messages flow, then do them succinctly, and sparingly. Draw as few of them as possible.

First of all, ask yourself if the sequence diagram is necessary at all. Code is often more communicative and economical. Listing 4–4, for example, shows what the code for the `Payroll` class might look like. This code is very expressive, and stands on its own. We don't need the sequence diagram to understand it, so there's no need to draw the sequence diagram. When code can stand on its own, then diagrams are redundant and wasteful.

Can code really be used to describe part of a system? In fact, *this should be a goal* of the developers and designers. The team should strive to create code that is expressive and readable. The more the code can describe itself, the fewer diagrams you will need and the better off the whole project will be.

Secondly, if you feel a sequence diagram is necessary, ask yourself if there is a way to split it up into a small group of scenarios. For example, we could break the large sequence diagram in Figure 4–5 into several much smaller sequence diagrams that would be much easier to read. Consider how much easier the small scenario in Figure 4–6 is to understand.

Thirdly, think about what you are trying to depict. Are you trying to show the details of a low-level operation like Figure 4–6, which shows how to calculate hourly pay? Or are you trying to show a high-level view of the overall flow of the system as in Figure 4–7? In general, high-level diagrams are more useful than low-level ones. They help the reader tie the system together in his mind. They expose commonalities more than differences.

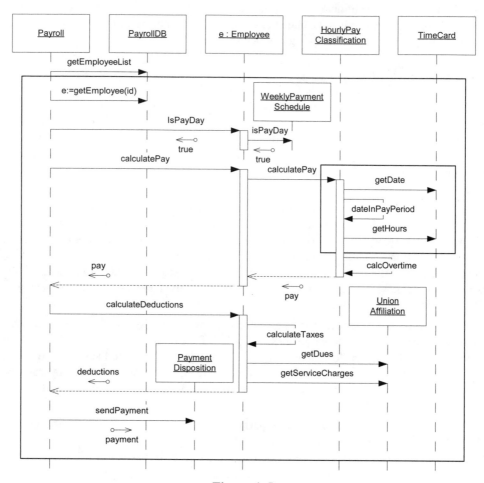

Figure 4–5
This sequence diagram is too complex.

```
Listing 4–4   Payroll.Java
public class Payroll
{
  private PayrollDB itsPayrollDB;
  private PayrollDisposition itsDisposition;
  public void doPayroll()
  {
    List employeeList = itsPayrollDB.getEmployeeList();
    for (Iterator iterator = employeeList.iterator();
         iterator.hasNext();)
    {
      String id = (String) iterator.next();
      Employee e = itsPayrollDB.getEmployee(id);
      if (e.isPayDay())
```

Listing 4–4 (Continued) `Payroll.Java`
```
    {
      double pay = e.calculatePay();
      double deductions = e.calculateDeductions();
      itsDisposition.sendPayment(pay - deductions);
    }
  }
}
}
```

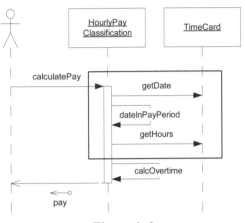

Figure 4–6
One small scenario.

Advanced Concepts

Loops and conditions

It is possible to draw a sequence diagram that completely specifies an algorithm. In Figure 4–8 you can see the payroll algorithm, complete with well-specified loops and `if` statements.

The `payEmployee` message is prefixed with a *recurrence* expression that looks like this:

```
    *[while id = idList.next()]
```

The star tells us that this is an iteration; the message will be sent repeatedly until the *guard* expression in the square brackets is false. Though UML has a specific syntax for guard expressions, I find it more useful to use a Java-like pseudo code that suggests the use of an iterator.

The `payEmployee` message terminates on an activation rectangle that is touching, but offset from, the first. This denotes that there are now two functions executing in the

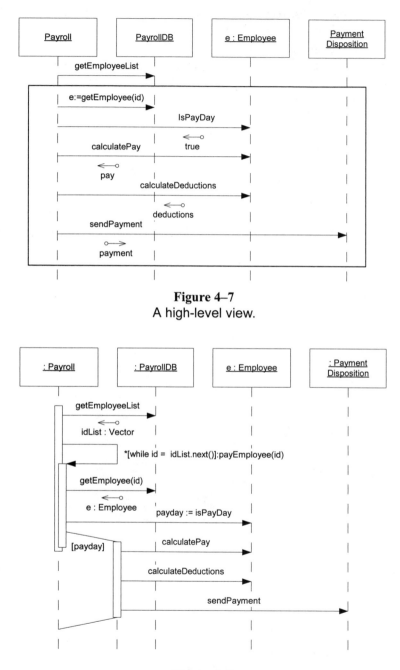

Figure 4–7
A high-level view.

Figure 4–8
Sequence diagram with loops and conditions.

same object. Since the `payEmployee` message is recurrent, the second activation will also be recurrent, and so all the messages depending from it will be part of the loop.

Note the activation that is near the `[payday]` guard. This denotes an `if` statement. The second activation only gets control if the guard condition is true. Thus, if `isPayDay` returns `true`, then `calculatePay`, `calculateDeductions`, and `sendPayment` will be executed. Otherwise they won't.

The fact that it is *possible* to capture all the details of an algorithm in a sequence diagram should not be construed as a license to capture all your algorithms in this manner. The depiction of algorithms in UML is clunky at best. Code such as shown in Listing 4–4 is a *much* better way of expressing an algorithm.

Messages that take time

Usually we don't consider the time it takes to send a message from one object to another. In most OO languages that time is virtually instantaneous. That's why we draw the message lines horizontally — they don't take any time. However, in some cases messages *do* take time to send. We could be trying to send a message across a network boundary, or in a system where the thread of control can break between the sending and reception of a message. When this is possible, we can denote it by using angled lines as shown in Figure 4–9.

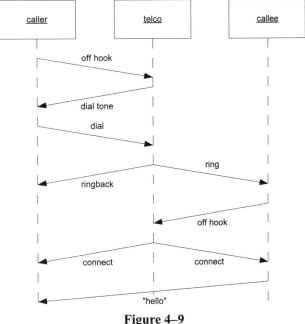

Figure 4–9
Normal phone call.

This figure shows a phone call being made. There are three objects in this sequence diagram. The `caller` is the person making the call. The `callee` is the person being called. The `telco` is the telephone company.

When the caller lifts the phone from the receiver it sends the off hook message to the telco. The telco responds with dial tone. Having received dial tone the caller dials the phone number of the callee. The telco responds by ringing the callee and playing ringback tone to the caller. The callee picks up the phone in response to the ring. The telco makes the connection. The callee says "Hello," and the phone call has succeeded.

However, there is another possibility that demonstrates the usefulness of these kinds of diagrams. Look carefully at the diagram in Figure 4–10. Note that it starts exactly the same. However, just before the callee's phone rings, he picks it up to make a call himself. The caller is now connected to the callee, but neither parties know it. The caller is waiting for a "Hello" and the callee is waiting for dial tone. The callee eventually hangs up in frustration, and the caller hears dial tone.

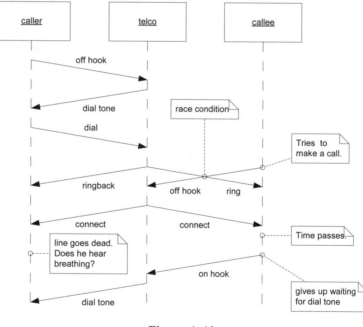

Figure 4–10
Failed phone call.

The crossing of the two arrows in Figure 4–10 is called a *race condition*. Race conditions occur when two asynchronous entities can simultaneously invoke incompatible operations. In our case the telco invoked the *ring* operation, and the callee went off hook. At this point the parties all had a different notion of the state of the system. The caller thought he was waiting for "Hello," the telco thought its job was done, and the callee thought he was waiting for dial tone.

Race conditions in software systems can be remarkably difficult to discover and debug. These diagrams can be helpful in finding and diagnosing them. Mostly they are useful in explaining them to others, once discovered.

Asynchronous messages

Usually, when you send a message to an object you don't expect to get control back until the receiving object has finished executing. Messages that behave this way are called *synchronous messages*. However, in distributed or multithreaded systems it is possible for the sending object to get control back immediately, and for the receiving object to execute in another thread of control. Such messages are called *asynchronous messages*.

Figure 4–11 shows an asynchronous message. Note that the arrowhead is open instead of filled. Look back at all the other sequence diagrams in this chapter. They were all drawn with synchronous (filled arrowhead) messages. It is the elegance (or perversity, take your pick) of UML that such a subtle difference in the arrowhead can have such a profound difference in the represented behavior.

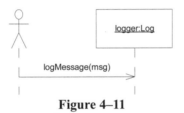

Figure 4–11
Asynchronous message.

Previous versions of UML used half-arrowheads to denote asynchronous messages as shown in Figure 4–12. This is much more visually distinctive. The reader's eye is immediately drawn to the asymmetry of the arrowhead. Therefore I continue to use this convention even though it has been superseded in UML 2.0.

Figure 4–12
Older and better way to depict asynchronous messages.

Listing 4–5 and Listing 4–6 show code that could correspond to Figure 4–11. Listing 4–5 shows a unit test for the `AsynchronousLogger` class in Listing 4–6. Note that the `logMessage` function returns immediately after queueing the message. Note also that the message is actually processed in a completely different thread that is started by the constructor. The `TestLog` class makes sure that the `logMessage` method behaves asynchronously by first checking to see if the message was queued but not processed, then yielding the processor to other threads, and finally by verifying that the message was processed and removed from the queue.

This is just one possible implementation of an asynchronous message. Other implementations are possible. In general, we denote a message to be asynchronous if the caller can expect it to return before the desired operations are performed.

Listing 4–5 `TestLog.java`

```java
import junit.framework.TestCase;
import junit.swingui.TestRunner;

public class TestLog extends TestCase {
  private AsynchronousLogger logger;
  private int messagesLogged;
  public static void main(String[] args) {
    TestRunner.main(new String[]{"TestLog"});
  }

  public TestLog(String name) {
    super(name);
  }

  protected void setUp() throws Exception {
    logger = new AsynchronousLogger(System.out);
    pause();
  }

  protected void tearDown() throws Exception {
    logger.stop();
  }

  public void testOneMessage() throws Exception {
    logger.logMessage("the message");
    checkMessagesFlowToLog(1);
  }

  public void testTwoConsecutiveMessages() throws Exception {
    logger.logMessage("another");
    logger.logMessage("and another");
    checkMessagesFlowToLog(2);
  }

  public void testManyMessages() throws Exception {
    for (int i = 0; i < 10; i++) {
      logger.logMessage("message:" + i);
      checkMessagesFlowToLog(1);
    }
  }
```

Listing 4–5 (Continued) `TestLog.java`

```java
  private void
  checkMessagesFlowToLog(int queued) throws Exception {
    checkQueuedAndLogged(queued, messagesLogged);
    pause();
    messagesLogged += queued;
    checkQueuedAndLogged(0, messagesLogged);
  }

  private void checkQueuedAndLogged(int queued, int logged) {
    assertEquals(queued, logger.messagesInQueue());
    assertEquals(logged, logger.messagesLogged());
  }

  private void pause() throws Exception {
    Thread.sleep(50);
  }
}
```

Listing 4–6 `AsynchronousLogger.java`

```java
import java.util.ArrayList;
import java.util.List;
import java.util.Collections;
import java.io.PrintStream;

public class AsynchronousLogger {
  private List messages =
    Collections.synchronizedList(new ArrayList());
  private Thread t;
  private boolean running = false;
  private int logged = 0;
  private PrintStream logStream;

  public AsynchronousLogger(PrintStream stream) {
    logStream = stream;
    running = true;
    t = new Thread(new LoggerThread());
    t.setPriority(Thread.NORM_PRIORITY - 3);
    t.start();
  }

  private void mainLoggerLoop() {
    while (running) {
      logQueuedMessages();
      sleepTillMoreMessagesQueued();
    }
  }

  private void logQueuedMessages() {
    while (messagesInQueue() > 0)
      logOneMessage();
  }

  private void logOneMessage() {
    String msg;
    msg = (String) messages.remove(0);
```

Listing 4–6 (Continued) `AsynchronousLogger.java`

```java
      logStream.println(msg);
      logged++;
    }

    private void sleepTillMoreMessagesQueued() {
      try {
        synchronized (messages) {
          messages.wait();
        }
      } catch (InterruptedException e) {
      }
    }

    public void logMessage(String msg) {
      messages.add(msg);
      wakeLoggerThread();
    }

    public int messagesInQueue() {
      return messages.size();
    }

    public int messagesLogged() {
      return logged;
    }

    public void stop() throws InterruptedException {
      running = false;
      wakeLoggerThread();
      t.join();
    }

    private void wakeLoggerThread() {
      synchronized (messages) {
        messages.notifyAll();
      }
    }

    private class LoggerThread implements Runnable {
      public void run() {
        mainLoggerLoop();
      }
    }
  }
```

Multiple threads

Asynchronous messages imply multiple threads of control. We can show several different threads of control in a UML diagram by tagging the message name with a thread identifier, as shown in Figure 4–13.

   Notice that the name of the message is prefixed with an identifier such as T1, followed by a colon. This identifier names the thread that the message was sent from. In the diagram, the AsynchronousLogger object was created and manipulated by thread T1. The thread that actually does the message logging, running inside the Log object, is named T2.

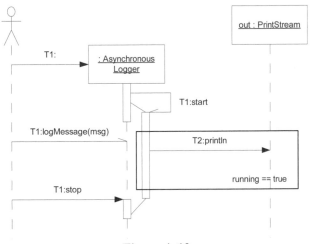

Figure 4–13
Multiple threads of control.

   As you can see, the thread identifiers don't necessarily correspond to names in the code. Listing 4–6 does not name the logging thread T2. Rather, the thread identifiers are for the benefit of the diagram.

Active objects

Sometimes we want to denote that an object has a separate internal thread. Such objects are known as *active objects*. They are shown with a bold outline, as in Figure 4–14.

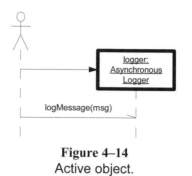

Figure 4–14
Active object.

Active objects are simply objects that instantiate and control their own thread. There arc no restrictions about their methods. Their methods may run in the object's thread, or they may run in the caller's thread.

Sending messages to interfaces

Our AsynchronousLogger class is just one way to log messages. What if we wanted our application to be able to use many different kinds of loggers? We'd probably create a Logger interface that declared the logMessage method, and derive our AsynchronousLogger class and all the other implementations from that interface. See Figure 4–15.

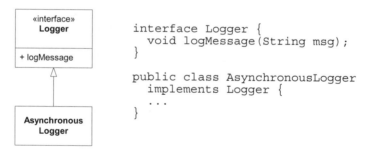

Figure 4–15
Simple logger design.

The application is going to be sending messages to the Logger interface. It won't know that the object is an AsynchronousLogger. How can we depict this in a sequence diagram?

The diagram in Figure 4–16 is the obvious approach. You just name the object for the interface and be done with it. This may seem to break the rules since it's impossible to have an instance of an interface. However, all we are saying here is that the logger object

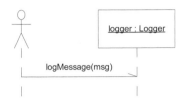

Figure 4–16
Sending to an interface.

conforms to the `Logger` type. We aren't saying that we somehow managed to instantiate an interface.

Sometimes, however, we know the type of the object and yet want to show the message being sent to an interface. For example, we might know that we have created an `AsynchronousLogger`, but we still want to show the application using only the `Logger` interface. Figure 4–17 shows how this is depicted. We use the interface lollipop on the lifeline of the object.

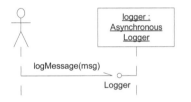

Figure 4–17
Sending to a derived type through an interface.

Conclusion

As we have seen, sequence diagrams are a powerful way to communicate the flow of messages in an object oriented application. We've also hinted about the fact that they are easy to abuse, and easy to overdo.

An occasional sequence diagram on the white board can be invaluable. A very short paper with five or six sequence diagrams denoting the most common interactions in a subsystem can be worth its weight in gold. On the other hand, a document filled with a thousand sequence diagrams is not likely to be worth the paper it's printed on.

One of the great fallacies of software development in the 1990s was the notion that developers should draw sequence diagrams for all methods *before* writing the code. This always proves to be a very expensive waste of time. Don't do it.

Instead, use sequence diagrams as the tool they were intended to be. Use them at a white board to communicate with others in real time. Use them in a document to capture the core salient collaborations of the system.

As far as sequence diagrams are concerned, too few is better than too many. You can always draw one later if you find you need it.

5
Use Cases

Think about if you need to include these or not !

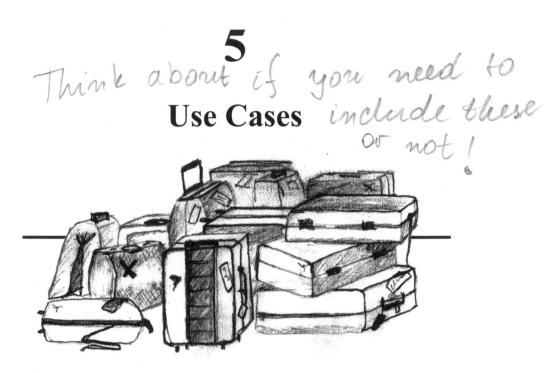

Use cases are a wonderful idea that has been vastly overcomplicated. Over and over again I have seen teams sitting and spinning in their attempts to write use cases. Typically they thrash on issues of form rather than substance. They argue and debate over preconditions, postconditions, actors, secondary actors, and a bevy of other things that *just don't matter.*

The real trick to use cases is to *keep them simple*. Don't worry about use case forms, just write them on *blank* paper, or on a *blank* page in a simple word processor, or on *blank* index cards. Don't worry about filling in all the details. Details aren't important until much later. Don't worry about capturing *all* the use cases; that's an impossible task.

The one thing to remember about use cases is: *tomorrow they are going to change.* No matter how diligently you capture them, no matter how fastidiously you record the details, no matter how thoroughly you think them through, no matter how much effort you apply to exploring and analyzing the requirements, *tomorrow* they are going to change.

If something is going to change tomorrow, you don't really need to capture its details today. Indeed, you want to postpone the capture of the details until the very last possible moment.

Think of use cases as *just in time requirements*.

Writing Use Cases

Notice the title of this section. We *write* use cases, we don't draw them. Use cases are not diagrams. Use cases are textual descriptions of behavioral requirements, written from a certain point of view.

"Wait!," you say. "I know UML has use case diagrams, I've seen them."

Yes, UML does have use case diagrams, and we'll study them in a few pages. However, those diagrams tell you nothing at all about the *content* of the use cases. They are devoid of information regarding the behavioral requirements that use cases are meant to capture. Use case diagrams in UML capture something else entirely. And we'll discuss them in due course.

What is a use case?

A use case is a description of the behavior of a system. That description is written from the point of view of a user who has just told the system to do something in particular. A use case captures the *visible* sequence of events that a system goes through in response to a *single* user stimulus.

A visible event is an event that the user can see. Use cases do not describe hidden behavior at all. They don't discuss the hidden mechanisms of the system. They only describe those things that a user can see.

The primary course

Typically, a use case is broken up into two sections. The first is the primary course. This section describes how the system responds to the stimulus of the user and assumes that nothing goes wrong.

For example, here is a typical use case for a point of sale system:

Check Out Item:

1. Cashier swipes product over scanner, scanner reads UPC code.

2. Price and description of item, as well as current subtotal appear on the display facing the customer. The price and description also appear on the cashier's screen.

3. Price and description are printed on receipt.

4. System emits an audible "acknowledgement" tone to tell the cashier that the UPC code was correctly read.

That's the primary course of a use case! Nothing more complex is necessary. Indeed, even the tiny sequence above might be too much detail if the use case isn't going to be implemented for awhile. We wouldn't want to record this kind of detail until the use case was within a few days or weeks of being implemented.

How can you estimate a use case if you don't record its detail? You talk to the stakeholders about the detail, without necessarily recording it. This will give you the information you need to give a rough estimate. Why not record the detail if we're going to talk to the stakeholders about it? Because tomorrow the details are going to change. Won't that change affect the estimate? Yes, but over many use cases those effects integrate out. Recording the detail too early just isn't cost effective.

If we aren't going to record the details of the use case just yet, then what *do* we record? How do we know that the use case even exists if we don't write something down? Write the name of the use case. Keep a list of them in a spreadsheet, or a word processor document. Better yet, write the name of the use case on an index card and maintain a stack of use case cards. Fill in the details as they get closer to implementation.

Alternate courses

Some of those details will concern things that can go wrong. During the conversations with the stakeholders you'll want to talk over failure scenarios. Later, as it gets closer and closer to the time when the use case will be implemented, you'll want to think through more and more of those alternate courses. They become addenda to the primary course of the use case. They can be written as follows:

> UPC Code Not Read:
>
> If the scanner fails to capture the UPC code, the system should emit the "re-swipe" tone telling the cashier to try again. If after three tries the scanner still does not capture the UPC code, the cashier should enter it manually.
>
> No UPC Code:
>
> If the item does not have a UPC code, the cashier should enter the price manually.

These alternate courses are interesting because they hint at other use cases that the stakeholders might not have identified initially. In this case it appears necessary to be able to enter the UPC or price manually.

What else?

What about actors, secondary actors, preconditions, postconditions, and the rest? What about all that stuff?

Don't worry about it. For the vast majority of the systems you will work on, you won't need to know about all those other things. Should the time come that you need to know more about use cases, then you can read Alistair Cockburn's definitive work on the topic: *Writing Effective Use Cases*, Addison-Wesley, 2001. For now, learn to walk before you learn to run. Get used to writing simple use cases as above. As you master them (defined as having successfully used them in a project), you can ever so carefully and parsimoniously adopt some of the more sophisticated techniques. But remember, don't sit and spin.

Use Case Diagrams

Of all the diagrams in UML, use case diagrams are the most confusing, and the least useful. With the exception of the system boundary diagram, which I'll describe in a minute, I recommend that you avoid them entirely.

System boundary diagram

Figure 5–1 shows a system boundary diagram. The large rectangle is the system boundary. Everything inside the rectangle is part of the system under development. Outside the rectangle we see the *actors* that *act* upon the system. Actors are entities outside the system that provide the stimuli for the system. Typically they are human users. They might also be other systems, or even devices such as real-time clocks.

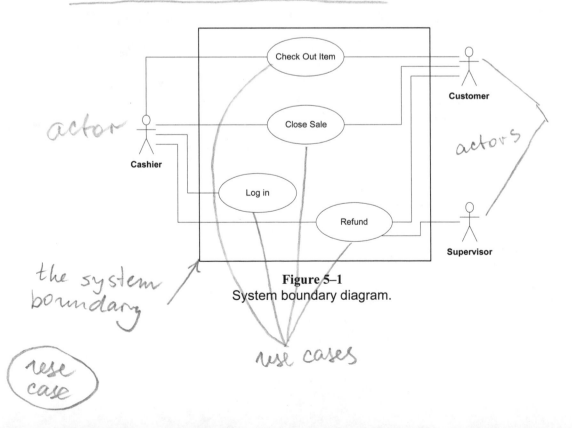

Figure 5–1
System boundary diagram.

Inside the boundary rectangle we see the use cases. These are the ovals with names inside. The lines connect the actors to the use cases that they stimulate. Avoid using arrows; nobody really knows what the direction of the arrowheads means.

This diagram is almost, but not quite, useless. It contains very little information of use to the Java programmer, but it makes a good cover page for a presentation to stakeholders.

Use case relationships

Use case relationships fall into the category of things that "seemed like a good idea at the time." I suggest that you actively ignore them. They'll add no value to your use cases or to your understanding of the system, and they will be the source of many never-ending debates about whether to use «extends» or «generalization».

Conclusion

This was a short chapter. That's fitting because the topic is simple. It is that simplicity that must be your attitude concerning use cases. If once you proceed down the dark path of use case complexity, forever will it dominate your destiny. Use the force, and keep your use cases simple.

yes, it is useful from software engineering point of view!

6

Principles of OOD

Angela Brooks

Reading chapters about notation is like a box of chocolate candy: After eating a few you start to crave meat. So let's dump the sugary notation for awhile and eat a nice, rare cheesburger.

When we look at a UML diagram, what are we looking for? How do we evaluate it? What are the principles of design that we should apply? In this chapter we will discuss five such principles that will help us evaluate whether a set of UML diagrams — or a batch of code, for that matter — are well designed.

Design Quality

What does it mean to be well designed? A system that is well designed is easy to understand, easy to change, and easy to reuse. It presents no particular development difficulties, is simple, terse, and economical. It is a pleasure to work with. Conversely, a bad design stinks like rotting meat.

terse =

69

Design smells

You know a programmer is working with a poor design if, while looking at the code, his facial expression reminds you of someone who has just opened a plastic sack of 12-day old kitchen garbage. Sometimes the smells can be overpowering. The smells of a poor design have many different components.

Angela Brooks

1. **Rigidity**: The system is hard to change because every time you change one thing, you have to change something else in a never-ending succession of changes.

2. **Fragility**: A change to one part of the system causes it to break in many other, completely unrelated, parts.

3. **Immobility**: It is hard to disentangle the system into components that can be reused in other systems.

4. **Viscosity**: The development environment is held together with duct tape and library paste. It takes forever to go around the edit–compile–test loop.

5. **Needless Complexity**: There are lots of very clever code structures that aren't actually necessary right now, but could be very useful one day.

6. **Needless Repetition**: The code looks like it was written by two programmers named Cut and Paste.

7. **Opacity**: Elucidation of the originator's intent presents certain difficulties related to convolution of expression.

It is our desire to rid the code of these smells. UML diagrams can often help with this because many of the smells can be found by examining the dependencies in the diagrams.

Dependency management

Many of these smells are a result of mismanaged dependencies. Mismanaged dependencies conjure the view of code that is a tangled mass of couplings. Indeed, it is this view of entanglement that was the origin of the term "spaghetti code."

Object oriented languages provide tools that aid in managing dependencies. Interfaces can be created that break or invert the direction of certain dependencies. Polymorphism allows modules to invoke functions without depending upon the modules that contain them. Indeed, an OOPL gives us lots of power to shape the dependencies the way we want.

So, how do we want them shaped? That's where the following principles come in. I have written a great deal about these principles. The definitive (and most long-winded) treatment is [Martin2002]. There are also quite a number of papers describing these principles on *www.objectmentor.com*. The remainder of this chapter provides a very brief summary.

The Single Responsibility Principle (SRP)

A CLASS SHOULD HAVE ONLY ONE REASON TO CHANGE.

You've probably read the nonsense about objects needing to know how to draw themselves in a GUI, or save themselves to disk, or convert themselves to XML, right? Beginning OO texts like to say things like that. I take a different view. Classes should know about only one thing. They should have a single responsibility. More to the point, there should only be one reason for a class to change.

Consider Figure 6–1. This class knows way too much. It knows how to calculate pay and taxes, how to read and write itself on disk, how to convert itself to XML and back, and how to print itself on various reports. Can you smell the **Fragility**? Change from SAX to JDOM and you have to change Employee. Change from Microsoft® Access to Oracle® and you have to change Employee. Change the format of the tax report and you have to change Employee. This design is badly coupled.

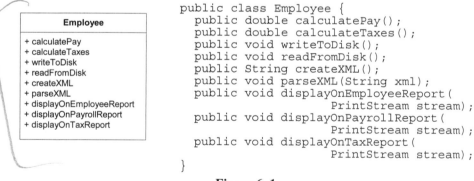

```
public class Employee {
    public double calculatePay();
    public double calculateTaxes();
    public void writeToDisk();
    public void readFromDisk();
    public String createXML();
    public void parseXML(String xml);
    public void displayOnEmployeeReport(
                    PrintStream stream);
    public void displayOnPayrollReport(
                    PrintStream stream);
    public void displayOnTaxReport(
                    PrintStream stream);
}
```

Figure 6–1
Class knows too many things.

In reality we want to separate all these concepts into their own classes so that each class has one, and only one, reason to change. We'd like the Employee class to deal with pay and taxes, an XML-related class to deal with converting Employee instances to and from XML, an EmployeeDatabase class to deal with reading and writing Employee instances to and from the database, and individual classes for each of the various reports. In short, we want a separation of concerns. A potential structure is shown in Figure 6–2.

or may be one Report class with methods to print all the each reports?

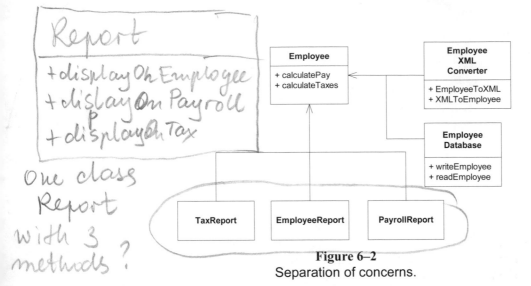

Handwritten notes:

Report
+ display On Employee
+ display On Payroll
+ display On Tax

One class
Report
with 3
methods ?

Figure 6–2
Separation of concerns.

Violation of this principle is pretty easy to spot in a UML diagram. Look for classes that have dependencies on more than one topic area. A dead giveaway is a class that implements one or more interfaces that endow it with certain properties. Careless use of an interface that endows an object with the ability to be stored on disk, for example, can lead to classes that couple business rules with issues of persistence.

Handwritten note: endow =

Consider the two diagrams in Figure 6–3. The one on the left couples Persistable tightly into Employee. All users of Employee will transitively depend upon Persistable. This dependence may not be great, but it will be there. Changes to the Persistable interface will have the potential of affecting all users of Employee.

Handwritten note: Couple =

The diagram on the right side of Figure 6–3 leaves Employee independent of Persistable, and yet allows for persistence just the same. Instances of PersistableEmployee can be passed around the system as Employees, without the rest of the system knowing about the coupling. The coupling exists, but is hidden to most of the system.

Handwritten note: I do not understand? that

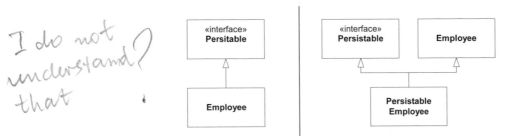

Figure 6–3
Two ways to use Persistable.

[handwritten: You can use as an example here the Student program (enquiry) from last year course work ! N.B. ! copy examples from student cw]

The Open–Closed Principle (OCP)

> *SOFTWARE ENTITIES (CLASSES, MODULES, FUNCTIONS, ETC.)*
> *SHOULD BE OPEN FOR EXTENSION, BUT CLOSED FOR*
> *MODIFICATION.*

[handwritten annotations: "methods" above FUNCTIONS; "method" below definition]

This principle has a high-falutin' definition, but a simple meaning: You should be able to change the environment surrounding a module without changing the module itself.

Consider, for example, Figure 6–4. It shows a simple application that deals with `Employee` objects through a database facade named `EmployeeDB`. The facade deals directly with the API of the database. This violates the OCP because a change to the implementation of the `EmployeeDB` class can force a rebuild of the `Employee` class. The `Employee` is transitively bound to the database API. Any system that contains the `Employee` class must also contain `TheDatabase` API.

[handwritten: Swing first ! / For this one you need to have explained MVC first !]

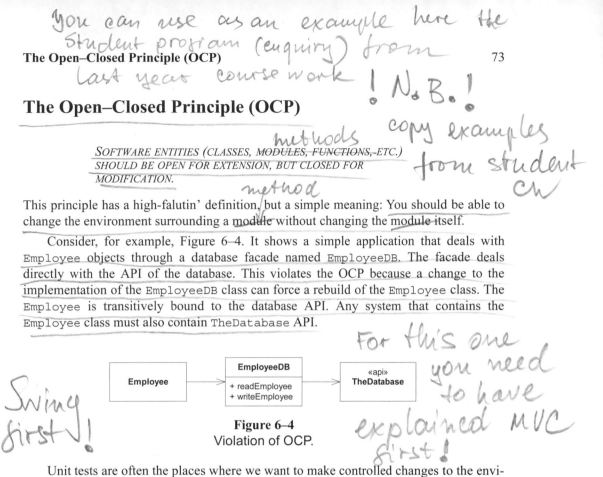

Figure 6–4
Violation of OCP.

Unit tests are often the places where we want to make controlled changes to the environment. Consider, for example, how we would test `Employee`. `Employee` objects make changes to the database. In a test environment we don't want the real database to change. We also don't want to create dummy databases just for the purposes of unit testing. Instead, we'd like to change the environment so that the test catches all the calls that `Employee` makes to the database, and verifies that those calls are made correctly.

We can do this by converting `EmployeeDB` to an interface, as in Figure 6–5. Then we can create derivatives that either invoke the true database API, or that support our tests. The interface separates `Employee` from the database API, and allows us the change the database environment that surrounds `Employee` without affecting `Employee` at all.

Among the systems that are plagued by violations of OCP are GUIs. Despite the fact that MODEL-VIEW-CONTROLLER has been known for nearly three decades, we often can't seem to get the design of GUI systems right. All too often the code that manipulates the GUI API is inextricably bound to the code that manages and manipulates the data being displayed.

Consider, for example, a very simple dialog box that displays a list of employees. The user selects an employee from the list and then clicks the Terminate button. We expect that if no employee is selected, then the Terminate button will be disabled. On the other hand, if we select an employee from the list, the Terminate button will be enabled. When the

[handwritten: Very good & relevent example ! / plague = draw similar for students]

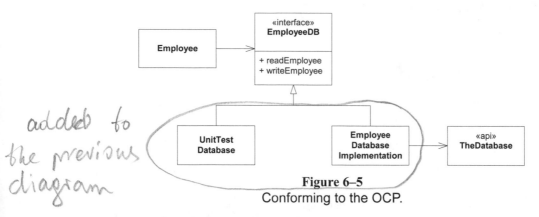

added to the previous diagram

Figure 6–5
Conforming to the OCP.

user clicks the Terminate button, the terminated employee disappears from the list, none of the remaining employees are shown as selected, and the Terminate button is disabled.

Implementations that violate the OCP would put all this behavior in the class that invokes the calls to the GUI API. OCP-compliant systems would separate the manipulation of the GUI from the manipulation of the data.

Figure 6–6 shows the structure of an OCP-compliant system. The Employee-TerminatorModel manages the list of employees, and is informed when the user selects or terminates an employee. The EmployeeTerminatorDialog manages the GUI. It is given the list of employees to display, and informs its controller when a selection changes or when the Terminate button is pressed.

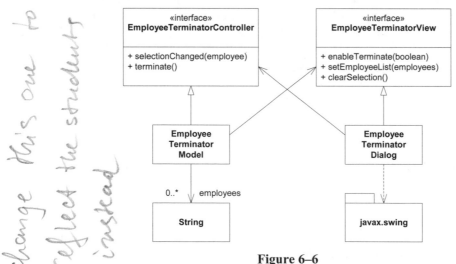

change this one to reflect the students instead

Figure 6–6
Isolating GUI from data manipulation.

The `EmployeeTerminatorModel` is responsible for actually deleting the selected employee from the list. It is also responsible for determining whether the terminate control is enabled or disabled. It doesn't know that this control is implemented with a button. It simply tells its associated view whether the user is allowed to terminate. Similarly, even though the model doesn't know anything about a list box, it can tell its view to clear the selection.

The `EmployeeTerminatorDialog` is brainless. It makes no decisions on its own and manages no data. The `EmployeeTerminatorModel` pulls its strings, and the dialog reacts. If the user interacts with the dialog, it simply tells its controller what's going on by calling methods on the `EmployeeTerminatorController` interface. These messages are passed to the `model`, which then interprets and acts upon them.[1]

The Java implementation of this structure is shown in Listings 6–1 through 6–4. The two interfaces don't hold any surprises. One might ask why `terminate` and `selectionChanged` are separate functions of `EmployeeTerminatorController`. Why not just have `terminate` take the `employee` argument? I did this because I didn't want the `EmployeeTerminatorDialog` making assumptions about what it means when the user clicks the Terminate button.

Listing 6–1 `EmployeeTerminatorView.java`

```
import java.util.Vector;

public interface EmployeeTerminatorView {
  void enableTerminate(boolean enable);
  void setEmployeeList(Vector employees);
  void clearSelection();
}
```

Listing 6–2 `EmployeeTerminatorController.java`

```
public interface EmployeeTerminatorController {
  public void selectionChanged(String employee);
  public void terminate();
}
```

`EmployeeTerminatorModel` is very straighforward. Upon construction it sends the list of employees to the view, clears the selection, and disables the terminate command. When the dialog reports a change in selection by calling `selectionChanged`, then the `model` appropriately enables the Terminate button and saves the selection. When the dialog calls terminate then the selected employee is removed from the list, the modified list is sent back to the view, the selection is cleared, and the Terminate button is disabled.

Listing 6–3 `EmployeeTerminatorModel.java`

```
import java.util.Vector;
```

---

1. Readers who know MVC will recognize this as a variation. In more complex situations the controller would be a true object rather than just being an interface for the model. In this case, however, the application is so simple that the controller simply acts as a pass through to the model.

Listing 6–3 (Continued) `EmployeeTerminatorModel.java`

```java
public class EmployeeTerminatorModel
            implements EmployeeTerminatorController {
  private EmployeeTerminatorView view;
  private Vector employees;
  private String selectedEmployee;

  public void initialize(Vector employees,
                         EmployeeTerminatorView view) {
    this.employees = employees;
    this.view = view;
    view.setEmployeeList(employees);
    view.clearSelection();
    view.enableTerminate(false);
  }

  // EmployeeTerminatorController interface

  public void selectionChanged(String employee) {
    view.enableTerminate(employee != null);
    selectedEmployee = employee;
  }

  public void terminate() {
    if (selectedEmployee != null)
      employees.remove(selectedEmployee);
    view.setEmployeeList(employees);
    view.clearSelection();
    view.enableTerminate(false);
  }
}
```

The `EmployeeTerminatorDialog` class is the most complex of the set. Fortunately, that complexity is related only to managing the GUI widgets and has nothing to do with the business rules of the system. It simply builds the Terminate button and list box, wires them up appropriately, and then gets them ready for display. The implementation of the `EmployeeTerminatorView` is trivial and unsurprising.

Listing 6–4 `EmployeeTerminatorDialog.java`

```java
import javax.swing.*;
import javax.swing.event.ListSelectionEvent;
import javax.swing.event.ListSelectionListener;
import java.awt.*;
import java.awt.event.ActionEvent;
import java.awt.event.ActionListener;
import java.util.Vector;

public class EmployeeTerminatorDialog
            implements EmployeeTerminatorView {
  private JFrame frame;
  private JList listBox;
  private JButton terminateButton;
  private EmployeeTerminatorController controller;
  private Vector employees;
```

Listing 6–4 (Continued) `EmployeeTerminatorDialog.java`

```java
public static final String
  EMPLOYEE_LIST_NAME = "Employee List";
public static final String
  TERMINATE_BUTTON_NAME = "Terminate";

public void
initialize(EmployeeTerminatorController controller) {
  this.controller = controller;
  initializeEmployeeListBox();
  initializeTerminateButton();
  initializeContentPane();
}

private void initializeEmployeeListBox() {
  listBox = new JList();
  listBox.setName(EMPLOYEE_LIST_NAME);
  listBox.addListSelectionListener(
    new ListSelectionListener() {
      public void valueChanged(ListSelectionEvent e) {
        if (!e.getValueIsAdjusting())
          controller.selectionChanged(
            (String) listBox.getSelectedValue());
      }
    }
  );
}

private void initializeTerminateButton() {
  terminateButton = new JButton(TERMINATE_BUTTON_NAME);
  terminateButton.disable();
  terminateButton.setName(TERMINATE_BUTTON_NAME);
  terminateButton.addActionListener(
    new ActionListener() {
      public void actionPerformed(ActionEvent e) {
        controller.terminate();
      }
    }
  );
}

private void initializeContentPane() {
  frame = new JFrame("Employee List");
  frame.getContentPane().setLayout(new FlowLayout());
  frame.getContentPane().add(listBox);
  frame.getContentPane().add(terminateButton);
  frame.getContentPane().setSize(300, 600);
  frame.pack();
}

public Container getContentPane() {
  return frame.getContentPane();
}

public JFrame getFrame() {
  return frame;
}
```

Listing 6–4 (Continued) `EmployeeTerminatorDialog.java`

```java
  // functions for EmployeeTerminatorView interface

  public void enableTerminate(boolean enable) {
    terminateButton.setEnabled(enable);
  }

  public void setEmployeeList(Vector employees) {
    this.employees = employees;
    listBox.setListData(employees);
    frame.pack();
  }

  public void clearSelection() {
    listBox.clearSelection();
  }
}
```

The `model` and `dialog` objects interact in an interesting way when it comes to selection. The `dialog` reports all changes in selection to the `model` by way of the controller interface. This includes changes caused when the `model` calls `clearSelection`. As you can see in Figure 6–7, when the model calls `clearSelection` on the `dialog`, the `dialog` responds by calling `setSelection` on the `model`.

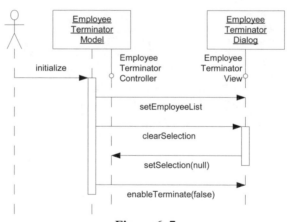

Figure 6–7
Interaction between the `model` and `dialog`.

The conformance to the OCP can be seen most clearly when you look at the unit tests for the `model` (Listing 6–5) and the `dialog` (Listing 6–6). These unit tests work without the tested modules knowing about their existence. The `TestEmployeeTerminator-Model` class tests the functionality of the `model`. The test pretends to be an `Employee-TerminatorView` and catches the messages that the `model` sends to the `view`, checking to be sure that they are called at the correct times and carry the appropriate information. This is known as the SELF SHUNT pattern[2] for unit testing.

Listing 6–5 `TestEmployeeTerminatorModel.java`

```java
import junit.framework.TestCase;
import junit.swingui.TestRunner;

import java.util.Vector;

public class TestEmployeeTerminatorModel extends TestCase
implements EmployeeTerminatorView {
  private boolean terminateEnabled = true;
  private String selectedEmployee;
  private Vector noEmployees = new Vector();
  private Vector threeEmployees = new Vector();
  private Vector employees = null;
  private EmployeeTerminatorModel m;

  public static void main(String[] args) {
    TestRunner.main(
      new String[]{"TestEmployeeTerminatorModel"});
  }

  public TestEmployeeTerminatorModel(String name) {
    super(name);
  }

  public void setUp() throws Exception {
    m = new EmployeeTerminatorModel();

    threeEmployees.add("Bob");
    threeEmployees.add("Bill");
    threeEmployees.add("Robert");
  }

  public void tearDown() throws Exception {
  }

  public void testNoEmployees() throws Exception {
    m.initialize(noEmployees, this);
    assertEquals(0, employees.size());
    assertEquals(false, terminateEnabled);
    assertEquals(null, selectedEmployee);
  }

  public void testThreeEmployees() throws Exception {
    m.initialize(threeEmployees, this);
    assertEquals(3, employees.size());
    assertEquals(false, terminateEnabled);
    assertEquals(null, selectedEmployee);
  }

  public void testSelection() throws Exception {
    m.initialize(threeEmployees, this);
```

---

2. [Feathers2001].

Listing 6–5 (Continued) `TestEmployeeTerminatorModel.java`

```java
    m.selectionChanged("Bob");
    assertEquals(true, terminateEnabled);
    m.selectionChanged(null);
    assertEquals(false, terminateEnabled);
  }

  public void testTerminate() throws Exception {
    m.initialize(threeEmployees, this);
    assertEquals(3, employees.size());
    selectedEmployee = "Bob";
    m.selectionChanged("Bob");
    m.terminate();
    assertEquals(2, employees.size());
    assertEquals(null, selectedEmployee);
    assertEquals(false, terminateEnabled);
    assert(employees.contains("Bill"));
    assert(employees.contains("Robert"));
    assert(!employees.contains("Bob"));
  }

  // EmployeeTerminatorView interface
  public void enableTerminate(boolean enable) {
    terminateEnabled = enable;
  }

  public void setEmployeeList(Vector employees) {
    this.employees = (Vector) employees.clone();
  }

  public void clearSelection() {
    selectedEmployee = null;
  }
}
```

The `TestEmployeeTerminatorDialog` class also uses the SELF-SHUNT pattern, pretending to be a `TestTerminatorController`. It catches the messages sent from the `dialog` to the `controller`, and verifies that they are called at the right times and contain the appropriate data. Most of this test just checks the wiring of the dialog box. It checks to make sure that the list box and button are created properly and that they function as they are supposed to.

Listing 6–6 `TestEmployeeTerminatorDialog.java`

```java
import junit.framework.TestCase;
import junit.swingui.TestRunner;

import javax.swing.*;
import java.awt.*;
import java.util.HashMap;
import java.util.Vector;

public class TestEmployeeTerminatorDialog
    extends TestCase
    implements EmployeeTerminatorController
{
```

Listing 6–6 (Continued) `TestEmployeeTerminatorDialog.java`

```java
  private EmployeeTerminatorDialog terminator;
  private JList list;
  private JButton button;
  private Container contentPane;
  private String selectedValue = null;
  private int selectionCount = 0;
  private int terminations = 0;

  public static void main(String[] args) {
    TestRunner.main(
      new String[]{"TestEmployeeTerminatorDialog"});
  }

  public TestEmployeeTerminatorDialog(String name) {
    super(name);
  }

  public void setUp() throws Exception {
    terminator = new EmployeeTerminatorDialog();
    terminator.initialize(this);
    putComponentsIntoMemberVariables();
  }

  private void putComponentsIntoMemberVariables() {
    contentPane = terminator.getContentPane();
    HashMap map = new HashMap();
    for (int i = 0; i < contentPane.getComponentCount(); i++) {
      Component c = contentPane.getComponent(i);
      map.put(c.getName(), c);
    }
    list = (JList) map.get(
      EmployeeTerminatorDialog.EMPLOYEE_LIST_NAME);
    button = (JButton) map.get(
      EmployeeTerminatorDialog.TERMINATE_BUTTON_NAME);
  }

  private void putThreeEmployeesIntoTerminator() {
    Vector v = new Vector();
    v.add("Bob");
    v.add("Bill");
    v.add("Boris");
    terminator.setEmployeeList(v);
  }

  public void testCreate() throws Exception {
    assertNotNull(contentPane);
    assertEquals(2, contentPane.getComponentCount());
    assertNotNull(list);
    assertNotNull(button);
    assertEquals(false, button.isEnabled());
  }

  public void testAddOneName() throws Exception {
    Vector v = new Vector();
    v.add("Bob");
    terminator.setEmployeeList(v);
```

Listing 6–6 (Continued) `TestEmployeeTerminatorDialog.java`

```java
    ListModel m = list.getModel();
    assertEquals(1, m.getSize());
    assertEquals("Bob", m.getElementAt(0));
  }

  public void testAddManyNames() throws Exception {
    putThreeEmployeesIntoTerminator();
    ListModel m = list.getModel();
    assertEquals(3, m.getSize());
    assertEquals("Bob", m.getElementAt(0));
    assertEquals("Bill", m.getElementAt(1));
    assertEquals("Boris", m.getElementAt(2));
  }

  public void testEnableTerminate() throws Exception {
    terminator.enableTerminate(true);
    assertEquals(true, button.isEnabled());
    terminator.enableTerminate(false);
    assertEquals(false, button.isEnabled());
  }

  public void testClearSelection() throws Exception {
    putThreeEmployeesIntoTerminator();
    list.setSelectedIndex(1);
    assertNotNull(list.getSelectedValue());
    terminator.clearSelection();
    assertEquals(null, list.getSelectedValue());
  }

  public void testSelectionChangedCallback() throws Exception {
    putThreeEmployeesIntoTerminator();
    list.setSelectedIndex(1);
    assertEquals("Bill", selectedValue);
    assertEquals(1, selectionCount);
    list.setSelectedIndex(2);
    assertEquals("Boris", selectedValue);
    assertEquals(2, selectionCount);
  }

  public void testTerminateButtonCallback() throws Exception {
    button.doClick();
    assertEquals(1, terminations);
  }

  // implement EmployeeTerminatorController
  public void selectionChanged(String employee) {
    selectedValue = employee;
    selectionCount++;
  }

  public void terminate() {
    terminations++;
  }
}
```

The tests demonstrate conformance to the OCP because it is possible to change the environment surrounding both the dialog and the model to a *test environment* without the dialog or model knowing it. Consider what this means in terms of the flexibility of the modules. We could easily replace the dialog with a command line UI, or a text menu UI. The model would never know the difference. We can put the model and dialog on different machines using RMI. We can change the environment of each module without affecting the other.

It's easy to see the mechanism of OCP conformance. Look again at Figure 6–6 on page 74. We see the familiar FLIP-FLOP pattern[3] of modules implementing one interface and communicating with another. Clearly we are free to change the environment surrounding the modules because of their use of abstract interfaces. Indeed, abstraction is the key to OCP conformance.

How do we identify the abstractions that help us to conform to the OCP? Most often I achieve OCP compliance simply by writing the unit tests before I write the actual code. Both of the preceding unit tests were written using this *test-first* method. Each of the test functions were written first, followed by just enough code in the module to make the test function pass.

For the sake of completeness, Listing 6–7 shows code that binds the dialog and model together and displays the dialog. I used this module as a final, manual, test. It allowed me to verify the (admittedly sparse) look and feel of the dialog. This is the only code I wrote that actually displays the dialog. The dialog unit test in Listing 6–6 simply checks the wiring and function of the dialog, but does not actually display it.

Listing 6–7 ShowEmployeeTerminator.java

```java
import java.awt.event.WindowAdapter;
import java.awt.event.WindowEvent;
import java.util.Vector;

public class ShowEmployeeTerminator {
  static Vector employees = new Vector();
  static EmployeeTerminatorDialog dialog;

  public static void main(String[] args) {
    initializeEmployeeVector();
    initializeDialog();
    runDialog();
  }

  private static void initializeEmployeeVector() {
    employees.add("Bob");
    employees.add("Bill");
    employees.add("Robert");
  }

  private static void initializeDialog() {
```

---

3. So named because of its resemblance to the circuit diagram of an Eccles-Jordan flip-flop. I know of no written description of this pattern, yet I run into it all the time.

```
Listing 6–7 (Continued) ShowEmployeeTerminator.java
    EmployeeTerminatorModel model =
      new EmployeeTerminatorModel();
    dialog = new EmployeeTerminatorDialog();
    dialog.initialize(model);
    model.initialize(employees, dialog);
  }

  private static void runDialog() {
    dialog.getFrame().addWindowListener(
      new WindowAdapter() {
        public void windowClosing(WindowEvent e) {
          for (int i = 0; i < employees.size(); i++) {
            String s = (String) employees.elementAt(i);
            System.out.println(s);
          }
          System.exit(0);
        }
      }
    );
    dialog.getFrame().setVisible(true);
  }
}
```

The Liskov Substitution Principle (LSP)

tricky

SUBTYPES MUST BE SUBSTITUTABLE FOR THEIR BASE TYPES.

Have you ever seen code that has lots of instanceof expressions in the clauses of if statements? Though there are some legitimate uses for expressions like this, they are few and far between. Usually they are a result of violating the LSP, and are themselves a violation of the OCP.

The LSP says that the users of base classes should not have to do anything special in order to use derivatives. Specifically, they should not have to use instanceof, or down-casts. Indeed, they should know nothing about the derivatives at all. Not even that they exist.

Consider the payroll application shown in Figure 6–8. The Employee class is abstract and has an abstract method named calcPay. It's pretty clear that SalariedEmployee will implement this to return the employee's salary. It's also pretty clear that Hourly-Employee will implement it to return the hourly rate times the sum of the hours on this week's time cards.

What would happen if we decided to add a VolunteerEmployee? How would we implement calcPay? At first this may seem obvious. We'd implement calcPay to return zero, as shown below.

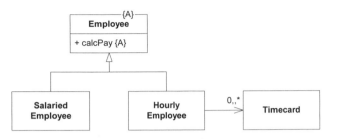

Figure 6–8
Simple payroll example.

```
public class VolunteerEmployee extends Employee {
   public double calcPay() {
      return 0;
   }
}
```

But is this right? Does it make any sense to even *call* calcPay on a Volunteer-Employee? After all, by returning zero we are implying that calcPay is a reasonable function to call, and payment is possible. We might find ourselves in the embarrassing situation of printing and mailing a paycheck with a gross pay of zero, or some other similar non sequitur.

So maybe the best thing to do is to throw an exception, indicating that this function really shouldn't have been called:

```
public class VolunteerEmployee extends Employee {
   public double calcPay() {
      throw new UnpayableEmployeeException();
   }
}
```

At first this seems like a reasonable thing to do. After all, it's *illegal* to call calcPay on a VolunteerEmployee. Exceptions are meant to be thrown for illegal situations like this.

Unfortunately, now every call to calcPay can throw an UnpayableEmployee-Exception, so either the exception must be caught or declared by the caller. Thus, a constraint upon a *derivative* has impacted the users of the base class.

To make matters worse, the following code is now illegal:

```
for (int i = 0; i < employees.size(); i++) {
   Employee e = (Employee) employees.elementAt(i);
   totalPay +=  e.calcPay();
}
```

To make it legal we have to wrap the call to calcPay in a try/catch block:

```
for (int i = 0; i < employees.size(); i++) {
   Employee e = (Employee) employees.elementAt(i);
   try {
      totalPay +=  e.calcPay();
   }
```

```
      catch (UnpayableEmployeeException el) {
      }
   }
   return totalPay;
}
```

This is ugly, complicated, and distracting. We might easily be tempted to change it to:

```
for (int i = 0; i < employees.size(); i++) {
   Employee e = (Employee) employees.elementAt(i);
   if (!(e instanceof VolunteerEmployee))
      totalPay += e.calcPay();
}
```

But this is even worse because now code that was supposed to operate on the Employee base class makes *explicit* reference to one of its derivatives.

All this confusion has come about because we have violated the LSP. VolunteerEmployee is not substitutable for Employee. Users of Employee are impacted by the very presence of VolunteerEmployee. And this results in strange exceptions and odd instanceof clauses in if statements, all of which violate the OCP.

You know you are violating the LSP whenever you try to make it illegal to invoke a function on a derivative. You may also be violating the LSP if you make a derivative method *degenerate*, that is, implemented with nothing. In both cases you are saying that this function makes no sense in this derivative. And that's a violation of LSP that can eventually lead to nasty exceptions and instanceof tests.

What's the solution to the VolunteerEmployee problem? Volunteers are not employees. It makes no sense to call calcPay on them, so they should not derive from Employee, and they should not be passed to functions that need to call calcPay.

The Dependency Inversion Principle (DIP)

> A. *HIGH-LEVEL MODULES SHOULD NOT DEPEND UPON LOW-LEVEL MODULES. BOTH SHOULD DEPEND UPON ABSTRACTIONS.*
>
> B. *ABSTRACTIONS SHOULD NOT DEPEND UPON DETAILS. DETAILS SHOULD DEPEND UPON ABSTRACTIONS.*

Better still: *Don't depend upon volatile concrete classes*. If you inherit from a class, make it an abstract class. If you hold a reference to a class, make it an abstract class. If you call a function, make it an abstract function.

In general, abstract classes and interfaces change far less often than their concrete derivatives. Therefore, we would rather depend upon the abstractions than the concretions. Following this principle reduces the impact that a change can have upon the system.

Does this mean we can't use Vector or String? After all, they are concrete classes. Does using them constitute a violation of DIP? No. It is perfectly safe to depend upon con-

Volatile =

crete classes that are not going to change. `Vector` and `String` are not going to change (much) in the next decade, so we can feel relatively safe using them.

It's the *volatile* concrete classes that we want to avoid depending upon. These are the concrete classes that are under active development, and that capture business rules that are likely to change. We want to create interfaces for these classes and be able to depend upon those interfaces.

From a UML standpoint, this principle is very easy to check. Follow every arrow in a UML diagram and check to make sure the target of the arrowhead is an interface or an abstract class. If not, and if the concrete class is volatile, then the DIP has been violated, and the system will be sensitive to change.

The Interface Segregation Principle (ISP)

> *CLIENTS SHOULD NOT DEPEND UPON METHODS THAT THEY DO NOT USE.*

Have you ever seen a fat class? A fat class is a class that has dozens or hundreds of methods. Typically we don't want to have such classes in our systems, but sometimes they are unavoidable.

The problem with fat classes, other than the fact that they are big and ugly, is that their users seldom use all their methods. That is, a user might call just two or three methods on a class that declares dozens. Unfortunately, those users are impacted when changes are made to the methods they *don't* call.

For example, consider the course enrollment system depicted in Figure 6–9. The diagram shows two clients of a class named `StudentEnrollment`. Clearly the `EnrollmentReportGenerator` does not invoke methods like `prepareInvoice` or `postPayment`. Let's also suppose that `AccountsReceivable` does not invoke the methods `getName` and `getDate`.

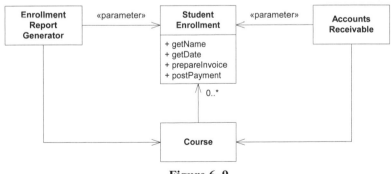

Figure 6–9
Unsegregated enrollment system.

Now, let's assume that the requirements change in a way that forces us to add a new argument to the `postPayment` method. This change to the declaration of `Student-Enrollment` may[4] force us to recompile and redeploy `EnrollmentReportGenerator`. This is unfortunate because `EnrollmentReportGenerator` does not care at all about the `postPayment` method.

We can prevent this unfortunate dependency by following a simple rule. Protect users from methods they don't need by giving them interfaces with just the methods they do need. Figure 6–10 shows how this rule can be applied.

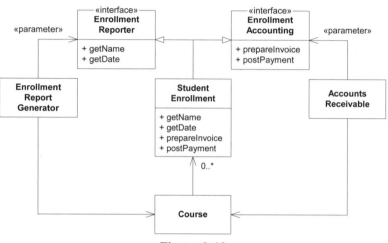

Figure 6–10
Segregated enrollment system.

Each user of a `StudentEnrollment` object is given an interface that provides just the methods that it is interested in. This protects the user from changes in methods that don't concern it. It also protects the user from knowing too much about the implementation of the object it is using.

Conclusion

So, five simple principles:

1. SRP — A class should have one and only one reason to change.

2. OCP — It should be possible to change the environment of a class without changing the class.

---

4. Some IDEs are smart enough to avoid such a recompile, but many are not.

3. LSP — Avoid making methods of derivatives illegal or degenerate. Users of base classes should not need to know about the derivatives.

4. DIP — Depend on interfaces and abstract classes instead of volatile concrete classes.

5. ISP — Give each user of an object an interface that has just the methods that user needs.

When should these principles be applied? At the first hint of pain. It is not wise to try to make all systems conform to all principles all the time, every time. You'll spend an eternity trying to imagine all the different environments to apply to the OCP, or all the different sources of change to apply to the SRP. You'll cook up dozens or hundreds of little interfaces for the ISP, and create lots of worthless abstractions for the DIP.

The best way to apply these principles is *reactively* as opposed to proactively. When you first detect that there is a structural problem with the code, or when you first realize that a module is being impacted by changes in another, *then* you should see whether one or more of these principles can be brought to bear to address the problem.

Of course, if you take a reactive approach to applying the principles, then you also need to take a *proactive* approach to putting the kinds of pressure on the system that will create pain early. If you are going to react to pain, then you need to be diligent about finding the sore spots.

One of the best ways to hunt for sore spots is to write lots and lots of unit tests. It works even better if you write the tests first, before you write the code that passes them. But that's a topic for the next chapter.

Notes

[Feathers2001]: Michael Feathers, "The 'Self'-Shunt Unit Testing Pattern." May 2001. Available at *www.objectmentor.com/resources/articles/SelfShunPtrn.pdf*

[Martin2002]: Robert C. Martin, *Agile Software Development—Principles, Patterns, and Practices.* Upper Saddle River, N.J.: Prentice Hall, 2002.

7

The Practices: *dX*

Angela Brooks

Now we're going to explore a set of practices that a team can use to get projects done. A group of practices like this is sometimes called a process. However, what I describe below is too lightweight to be called a process. It's just a set of simple disciplines that a team of developers can use to get a lot of work done in a short amount of time. I call this set of rules *dX*.[1]

Iterative Development

The key *dX* practice is to do *everything* in *short* iterations. By everything I mean requirements, analysis, design, implementation, testing, documentation... *Everything*. By short I mean one or two weeks. We do everything in one- or two-week cycles. Each cycle begins with a plan and ends with deliverables. After the initial exploration, the chief deliverable of each cycle, even the earliest of cycles, is working code.

---

1. A visual pun on XP that I adopted in the paper [Martin1999].

91

The initial exploration

Our first *dX* iteration begins with an exploration of the requirements. This is the only iteration that does not end in code, and is the only iteration that may be shorter than two weeks. Typically, exploration takes a few days. Sometimes it takes a week. On rare occasions it takes two weeks.

First we need someone who will be responsible for requirements and priorities. Call this person "the customer." In many projects this person may, in fact, be the real customer. In other projects the role of the customer may be played by a team of business analysts.

We sit down with the customer and talk over what the system has to do. For the first few days of the project we are just discussing how the system works and what behaviors it must have. We aren't necessarily writing much down. We are not trying to capture detailed requirements at this time, we are just trying to get an idea of the scope of the system.

As we discuss the system we identify use cases. We write the name of each use case down on an index card. We call these cards *user stories*. They don't contain the details of the use case, they contain only the name. You might write down a few other salient bits of information on the cards, but we aren't trying to be complete or thorough just yet. We're just trying to get our arms around the overall system.

This exploration process never ends. Even when we are in the depths of implementation, even after the Nth release of the system has been shipped, we are still going to be sitting down with the customer and regularly discussing new needs and features, and writing new stories.

Estimating the features

We write an estimate on each user story card. This estimate is a dimensionless number. We don't care what the units are at this point. All we care about is that the estimates are proportional to each other. That is, a story with an estimate of eight will take twice as long as a story with an estimate of four.

The best way to estimate is to base the estimate for a story on a previously implemented story. If you've done a story like the one you are currently estimating, and you know that the estimate on the previous story was six, you can make the estimate on the new story five, six, or seven depending upon how much simpler or harder the new story is.

If you don't have older stories to base your estimates on, then you can start estimating by using *perfect programming days*. Perfect programming days are days in which you went to bed on time the previous night, ate a hearty breakfast that morning, there was no traffic on the way to work, the phone never rings all day, there are no meetings, your computer never crashes, the network seems infinitely fast, and your co-workers are intelligent, patient, and considerate. How much could you get done on a day like that? How many days like that would it take to get the story you are estimating done? Write down that number and then forget that it had anything to do with real days — because it doesn't.

Stories that are too long should be split. Stories that are too short should be merged. A story should never be longer than three or four day's worth of effort for the whole team. They should never be shorter than about half a day's effort. Stories that are too short tend to be overestimated. Stories that are too long tend to be underestimated. So we merge and join stories until they sit near the sweet spot of accurate estimation.[2]

Spikes

As our last act of the initial exploration we might spend two or three days doing a quick and dirty implementation of two or three interesting stories. We are going to throw this implementation away. The goal is simply to calibrate our estimates. Say, for example, that it took five man-days to implement a story with a seven on it. That would imply that for quick and dirty implementations we can do seven points in five man-days. Perhaps it will take three times longer to do the same implementation in production quality. So, we'll reduce our calibration to seven points in 15 man-days. We'll round that down to half a point per man-day.

A two week iteration for a team of five contains 50 man-days. Our calibration implies that this team might get 25 points done in such an iteration. This number is the team's initial *velocity*.

Planning

Now that we have stories, estimates, and velocity, we can start planning our iterations. Planning is simply a matter of using the current velocity to figure out which stories will be done each iteration.

Planning releases

We begin by planning the first release. A release is typically six iterations or about three months. In six iterations, and at a velocity of 25, our team of five might get 150 story points done. So the customer picks stories with estimates that add up to 150. The customer picks the stories that are most important and cost effective. This batch of stories becomes the release plan.

Planning iterations

On the first day of each iteration we create a plan for that iteration. Since our initial velocity is 25, the customer selects stories from the release plan that add up to 25. Once again the customer selects these stories based both upon their business value, and their cost.

---

2. Accurate estimation. Now there's an oxymoron for you.

Cheap stories with high business value will be selected before expensive stories with low business value.

Next we take the stories that the customer selected and break them down into *tasks*. A task is much smaller than a story. It is a unit of work on the order of four to 10 man-hours in size. A task is a simple unit of work that a single developer can take responsibility for. It's a single dialog box, or a single database transaction, or something along those lines.

The customer helps us do the task breakdown, talking us through the details of the story. The customer also helps us make priority trade-offs. He points out which parts of a feature are important and which are not. He helps us identify whether a glitzy UI is important. He helps us keep the business value of the iteration high.

Usually it will take us two or three hours to break the stories down into tasks. During that time we write the tasks on a white board or a flip chart or the like. Next, we sign up to take responsibility for tasks.

Signup is a simple process. Each developer keeps a budget in the back of his or her head. This budget is the number of man-hours the developer will spend actually working on tasks during this iteration. As the developer signs up for a task, he estimates that task, and then subtracts that estimate from his budget. A developer can continue to sign up for tasks until his budget is zero.

We don't assign tasks to developers, we let them sign up. We find that the developers can usually work out the best distribution of tasks in this manner. We also let each developer estimate the tasks they are signing up for.

Ideally, at the end of the signup, every task will have an owner, and every developer's budget will be at zero. This seldom happens. Usually, especially during the first iterations, there are lots of tasks left on the board, and all the developers' budgets are at zero.

When this happens, the developers try to work out another way to divvy up the tasks. Perhaps someone signed up for a task that doesn't play to their strengths. Maybe that task should be done by someone else. The developers hash this out for a while in an effort to get more tasks signed up.

If there are still tasks left on the board, then the developers tell the customer that they can't get all 25 stories points done. The customer removes stories from the iteration until all the tasks can be signed up.

Ideally, the plan is finalized at about noon.

The midpoint

Let's say that we finally settled on 20 story points for the iteration. Now we start analyzing, designing, and implementing those stories. We'll talk about how to do that in the next few sections. Right now I want to jump forward to next Monday morning — the midpoint of the iteration.

On Monday morning we should have 10 story points done. We calculate the completed story points by adding up the estimates of the stories that are complete. This prevents us from getting all the stories half-done. What we want is to get half the *stories* done.

If we don't have 10 story points done, then we aren't going as fast as we thought. Let's say we only got eight story points done. Then we need to tell the customer that it's not likely that we'll get more than 16 story points done for the whole iteration. We ask the customer to remove a story or two so that the total is 16.

By the same token, if we have more than half of the stories done, then we ask the customer to add extra stories to the iteration. For example, if we have 15 story points done, then it looks like we might get a total of 30 done for the iteration. So we ask the customer to add more stories.

Velocity feedback

We stop the iteration on Friday afternoon whether we have completed all the stories or not. Then we recompute our velocity. If we completed 23 story points then our new velocity is 23 story points per iteration. The following Monday, when we do the plan for the next iteration, the customer will select stories that add up to 23.

This is how we continuously calibrate our estimates. We measure how many story points we got done each iteration and sign up only for that many in the next iteration. Each individual measures how many man-hours worth of tasks he completed in the last iteration and only signs up for that many tasks in the next iteration.

Organizing the Iterations into Management Phases

The *Unified Process*[3] suggests that projects go through four management phases. During the *Inception* phase we are trying to determine the feasibility and business case for the system. During the *Elaboration* phase we determine the architecture of the system and create a reliable plan for implementation. During the *Construction* phase we carry out the implementation of the system. Finally, during the *Transition* phase we install the system and work with the users to tune it.

Each of these phases of the Unified Process consists of one or more iterations, and each iteration produces working code. From the programmer's point of view, there is no difference between the phases. Each is simply composed of iterations, all of roughly the same structure. Each is a matter of identifying stories, estimating them, selecting them for implementation, and then implementing them.

---

3. [Kruchten1998].

What's in an Iteration?

During the two weeks of the iteration we carry out all the traditional tasks of software development. We analyze the requirements, design a solution, and implement that solution. However, we restrict our scope to *only* the stories selected for the current iteration. We do not consider any other stories that might be selected in future iterations. Our focus is on this iteration and only this iteration.

One might complain, that this leads to poor architectures, inflexible designs, or lots of rework. On the contrary it leads to the best architectures, very flexible designs, and very little rework. The reason is simple: We are always working on the most important features. The customer selects the features to be developed in each iteration based upon business value. Any feature scheduled for a later iteration is, by definition, not as important as the feature we are currently working on. Therefore our attention is always on the most important thing it can be one.

There are a set of practices that we like to follow while implementing stories. They help us to write clean, flexible code. They help us keep our defect rate down and create flexible and easy-to-understand designs. They help us communicate with the customer and eliminate surprises.

Developing in pairs

When using *dX*, we develop all software in pairs. Two developers work together at a single workstation implementing a task that one of them signed up for. Both programmers are fully engaged in writing the code. Both have their eyes locked on the screen. One may control the keyboard, but both know exactly what is about to happen. Indeed, the keyboard moves rapidly back and forth between them. I've even seen instances where one developer uses the keyboard while another uses the mouse.

We change partners once per day. The owner of the task stays with his task, and recruits others to work with him. On average each programmer will spend about half his time working on the tasks he signed up for. The other half of his time will be spent helping other people with their tasks.

You might think this cuts productivity in half. After all, the owner of each task is only spending half his time on that task. However, the loss of productivity does not seem to happen. It turns out that pairing is a very efficient way to write software.

Acceptance tests

At the start of each *dX* iteration, once the customer has selected the stories to be implemented, the customer and QA folks work together to flesh the selected user stories into use cases and to write executable acceptance tests for the stories. These tests are delivered to the programmers before the iteration is half over.[4] These tests are the true requirements document. It is in these tests that the details of the requirements are truly documented.

Once the developers receive the tests, they *know* what their stories and tasks must accomplish. They run the tests continuously throughout development, making sure that they never break any that have passed. A good iteration ends in a kind of anticlimax, with everybody going home early Friday afternoon, all acceptance tests passing.

The acceptance tests are usually written in a high level testing language that is easily automatable. An acceptance testing framework or tool executes the tests at the whim of the programmers or customers. See *http://fitnesse.org* for such a tool.

Unit tests

In a *dX* project we write unit tests. Lots and lots of unit tests. Moreover, we write them first, before we write the code that passes them. Indeed, the rule is that we will not write any production code until we have a unit test that is failing. Every line of production code is written to make a particular failing unit test pass.

The technique is extremely iterative. We write a tiny fragment of a unit test, no more than five or 10 lines of code. Then we compile it. Usually it won't compile because it uses code that hasn't been written yet. So we write just enough of the production code to get the test to compile. Typically this will be less than half a dozen lines of code. Then we run the test. It will fail because we did not finish writing the production code. Seeing it fail we then write just enough production code to make that one fragment of the test pass. Once it passes we add another fragment to the test and start over.

This cycle lasts between one and 10 minutes depending upon the language or the environment. The faster you can go around the loop the better. And each time around the loop you run *all* the tests you have written for that module. This means that, no matter what is going on at the moment, the code was working a just a few minutes ago. We don't have dozens of windows open with dozens of modules torn to shreds hoping we can wire them all back together again. *A minute or so ago all our tests passed.*

As we work from day to day we continue to add more and more tests to the growing body of unit tests. Dozens per day, hundreds per week, thousands per month. We organize them into a body that is convenient to run. We run them all the time. We are confident in the state of our code.

The tests are a form of documentation. If you want to know how to invoke a particular API function, there is a test that does it. If you want to know how to create a certain object, there is a test that does it. The tests act as a set of examples for nearly every programming task in the system. This kind of documentation is unambiguous, accurate, compilable, and executable.

---

4. At least one QA manager I know of made it his goal to deliver the acceptance tests *during* the iteration planning meeting. He worked with the customer a few days before the iteration began to get an idea of which stories were most important. He then developed acceptance tests for those stories "on spec."

Refactoring[5]

The ability to run some or all of the suite of unit and acceptance tests provides a simple way to determine if we've done something to break the system. If we desire to make a change, we can make it fearlessly, because the tests will tell us if we've broken anything important.

This means that we can make changes to the code with near impunity. If we see a variable that could have a better name, we can rename it. If we see a class that has too many methods, we can split it. If we see a method that is in the wrong class, we can move it. Indeed, so long as we are supported by a bevy of unit and acceptance tests, we can fearlessly make any change we like.

Thus, we incorporate refactoring — the act of improving a program's structure without changing its behavior — into the practices of *dX*. Every hour or so of active programming is followed by a period of refactoring. We look at the code we've written and *improve* it. We make these improvements in tiny steps, each just a few minutes long, running the tests after each step. We gradually improve the structure of the system, never letting it degrade. The rule is, *never let the sun set on bad code.*

Open office

The best environment for dX is an open office or laboratory. We put tables in the middle with workstations for pairs. We all work together in the same room, including the customer. Our goal is to work together as a team, frequently interacting with each other, able to ask quick questions of each other, get quick advice, or lean over and look at some code.

Continual integration

The source code control system used in *dX* is nonblocking. That means that anyone can check out a module, no matter who else might have it checked out. First one to check in wins. Second one to check in merges.

The possibility of merging creates an interesting tension. The longer you have a module checked out the greater the likelihood of having to do a merge. Nobody likes to merge, no matter how good the tool support is, therefore there is a pressure to check in early and often. This is a good thing.

However, *dX* has a rule about checking in. When you check in code you must first demonstrate that *all* of the unit and acceptance tests pass. That means you have to fully integrate your changes into the system, build the system, and test the system before you finish the check in.

---

5. [Fowler1999b].

In a *dX* project, this happens many times per day per pair. Therefore integration is happening continually. There is never a big final integration to be performed.

Conclusion

Gosh, did I forget to mention UML? No, I didn't forget. I also didn't mention Java. That's because these tools are irrelevant to the practices. UML is not a method, UML is a notation. Java is not a method, Java is a programming language. We use these notations and languages only when we need them. They are tools to be used, not methods to be followed.

Well, what about documentation? Don't we need to use UML to create useful documents? Yes, we do. However, we don't need to make them as part of a process. Documentation produced by default is almost always useless. There is a rule in *dX* known as Martin's First Law of Documentation. It says, *produce only those documents for which you have a significant and immediate need*. This means that we do not draw UML diagrams as a matter of course. We do not specifically capture all requirements in class diagrams. We do not capture all use cases in sequence diagrams. We use these tools when there is an immediate and significant need, otherwise we don't use them.

In a *dX* project you will see people using UML. You'll see them at white boards scratching diagrams while debating different design options with each other. You'll see them producing hardcopy diagrams as road maps for others to follow. What you won't see are people producing diagrams because a process told them to. The only diagrams they produce are the ones they know for sure that they need right now.

The practices I described above as part of *dX* are drawn from the practices of *Extreme Programming*[6] (XP). Indeed, if you look closely you'll see that *dX* is just *XP* turned upsidedown.

Notes

[Beck1999]: Kent Beck, *Extreme Programming Explained: Embrace Change.* Reading, Mass.: Addison-Wesley, 1999.

[Fowler1999b]: Martin Fowler, *Refactoring.* Reading, Mass.: Addison-Wesley, 1999.

[Jeffries2000]: Ron Jeffries, Ann Anderson, Chet Hendrickson, *Extreme Programming Installed.* Reading, Mass.: Addison-Wesley, 2000.

---

6. [Beck1999], [Jeffries2000]

[Kruchten1998]: Philippe Kruchten, *The Rational Unified Process*. Reading, Mass.: Addison-Wesley, 1998.

[Martin1999]: Robert C. Martin, "RUP vs. XP." 1999. Available at *www.objectmentor.com/resources/articles/RUPvsXP.pdf*

8

Packages

The Legacy System

Angela Brooks

There are two different kinds of packages that are important to Java programmers. The first is the source code package represented by the Java `package` keyword. The second is the binary component represented by a `.jar` file.

Java Packages

Java packages are namespaces. They allow programmers to create small private areas in which to declare classes. The names of those classes will not collide with identically named classes in different packages.

Java compilation systems keep the generated binary `.class` files in directory structures that mimic the package structure of the source code. Thus, the `.class` file for the class `A.B.C` will likely be stored on disk in a file whose path is something like `A/B/C.class`. Since Java compilers read foreign declarations from `.class` files instead of

101

.java files, it is critical that both the compiler and runtime system know the appropriate classpaths for the packages included in the application.

Because of these issues it is important to give due consideration to the package structure of the system. UML has notational tools that can help with that consideration.

Packages

There are several ways to denote a package in UML. Figure 8–1 shows the simplest. The package icon is simply a rectangle with a tab on the top to make it look a bit like a file folder. The fully qualified name of the package is shown within the rectangle.

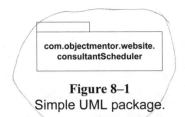

Figure 8–1
Simple UML package.

If you so desire, you can put the name of the package in the tab of the rectangle. This leaves the large rectangle free so that you can list some or all of the classes within the package. Figure 8–2 shows what this looks like.

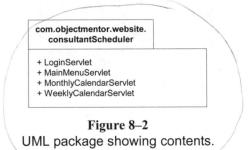

Figure 8–2
UML package showing contents.

Finally, you can show package nesting structure using the *contains* relationship, as shown in Figure 8–3.

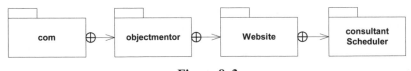

Figure 8–3
UML package nesting.

Dependencies

The code within a package often depends upon the code within other packages. In Java we see this when we import a class, or a group of classes, into our source code. We also see it if we use the qualified name of a class. In UML we depict this dependency by using the *dependency* relationship, as shown in Figure 8–4.

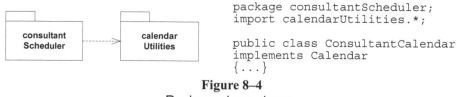

```
package consultantScheduler;
import calendarUtilities.*;

public class ConsultantCalendar
implements Calendar
{...}
```

Figure 8–4
Package dependency.

   Note that the dependency is not the result of the `import` statement. Rather it is the result of the actual use of `calendarUtilities.Calendar` from within `consultant-Scheduler.ConsultantCalendar`. In Java, `import` statements do not create a true dependency, though compilers are within their rights to complain if the imported class or package does not exist.

Binary Components — `.jar` Files

While packages are convenient groupings for source code, they do not always make convenient groupings for binary code. Often we want to bundle larger chunks of binary code together into components in the form of a `.jar` file. Such a component can be conveniently deployed to the systems in which it will execute.

   Components are depicted in UML as shown in Figure 8–5. The interface icon shown on the top is optional. It denotes that one of the interfaces available within the `CalendarRenderer` component is named `Calendar`.

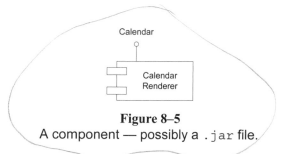

Figure 8–5
A component — possibly a `.jar` file.

   As with packages, components can also be related with dependency relationships. Indeed, usually a component contains one or more whole packages, so the dependencies between the components will usually be a subset of the dependencies between the packages.

Principles of Package Design

Over the years I've come to depend upon a simple set of principles to help me organize the large-scale structure of a software application. These principles are not rules, and they are not "the right way." Rather, they are simple heuristics that help me make the trade-offs necessary to partition a system.

You will find that these principles do not lead you to a functional decomposition. The packages that these principles lead you to create are meant to gather volatile classes together, and keep apart those classes that change for different reasons. They try to isolate those classes that change frequently from those that don't. They try to separate the high-level architecture of the system from the low-level details, and keep the high-level architecture independent.

These principles are discussed in great detail in [Martin2002]. I cover them very briefly here.

The Release/Reuse Equivalency Principle (REP)

People don't usually reuse classes. Usually they reuse groups of classes together. Such reusable groupings should be placed into a package. That package should then be tracked and released for the benefit of those who would reuse it.

This principle says that one of the criteria for placing classes into a package is to create a package that is convenient for others to reuse.

A package that is being reused by others must be treated with a certain care and respect by the author. Reusers must be notified, in advance, of changes the author intends to make to the package. The author should consider maintaining older versions of the package for a time, to give the reusers opportunity to incorporate changes gradually. This implies a certain clerical overhead and logistics that is hard to apply on a per-class basis. Thus, creating reusable classes is convenient for both the author and the reuser.

In the end, the smallest thing you can reuse is the smallest thing that someone else is willing to put the effort into releasing and tracking. The granule of reuse is the granule of release.

The Common Closure Principle (CCP)

The Single Responsibility Principle (SRP) told us to give each class one and only one reason to change. The CCP extends this to packages. We want all the classes in a package closed against the same kinds of changes. We want changes to be focused into single packages.

Most systems are built from many, perhaps dozens or even hundreds, of packages. Those packages depend upon each other, creating a large graph of dependencies. The goal of the CCP is to group classes together by their susceptibility to change. Those classes that change for the same reason are placed in the same package. Thus, when a particular change occurs, very few of the packages in the dependency structure will have to be changed.

The Common Reuse Principle (CRP)

The Interface Segregation Principle (ISP) told us to create specific interfaces for each client of a class. The CRP does the same for packages. A package that has many clients is responsible to all those packages. A change in that package can have a large impact upon all the packages that depend upon it. Therefore, as much as is possible, we want to separate those classes that are used by a client from those that are used by other clients.

When a package contains classes that are used by different clients, changes to one class in the package can have an impact even upon those packages that don't use the changed class. The fact that the package has changed may be enough to cause the client packages to be rereleased and redeployed.

The Acyclic Dependencies Principle (ADP)

Cycles in the package dependency graph can lead to build problems and developability problems. When are cycles, it is impossible to determine which classes and which packages should be built first, and which should be built next.

Dependencies are transitive. If package A depends upon package B, and package B depends upon package C, then package A depends transitively upon package C. This means that when there is a cycle in the package dependency graph, every package in the cycle depends upon every other package in the cycle. Such fully connected dependency graphs can make it very hard to keep the packages isolated from each other so that the developers can work on them without impacting other developers.

The solution is to keep the dependency cycles out of the package dependency graph. This can be done manually, or you can use a tool like JDepend (see *www.clarkware.com*) to help.

The Stable Dependencies Principle (SDP)

Some packages are meant to be easy to change. Other packages are meant to have many incoming dependencies, making them hard to change. If a package that has many incoming dependencies hangs a dependency of its own upon a package that was meant to be easy to change, then it will make that package hard to change. See Figure 8–6.

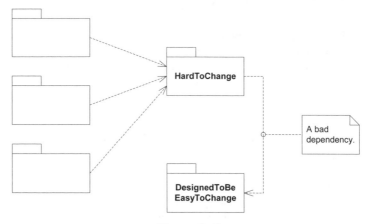

Figure 8–6
A violation of the SDP.

The SDP says that packages should not depend on packages that are less stable (easier to change) than themselves. The target of every package dependency will be harder to change than the depending package.

There are some simple metrics discussed in [Martin2002] that allow teams to calculate the stability of each package, and then evaluate whether dependencies flow in the direction of stability.

The Stable Abstractions Principle (SAP)

Since stable packages are hard to change, we need a way to keep them flexible. The Open–Closed Principle (OCP) told us that a module could be extended without modifying it. Stable packages are hard to modify, but they need not be hard to extend. Thus, the SAP says that in order to keep stable packages easy to extend, stable packages should be abstract. The more stable a package is, the more abstract it should be.

The abstractness of a package is related to the number of abstract classes and interfaces it contains. The higher the ratio of abstract classes and interfaces, the more abstract the package is. According to the SAP, a package with many incoming dependencies is very stable, and should therefore also be very abstract.

The SDP and SAP combined are the package version of the Dependency Inversion Principle (DIP). The DIP told us that class relationships should point at abstract classes or interfaces. The SDP/SAP combination says that stability increases with incoming dependencies, and that abstraction should increase with stability. Therefore the abstraction of a package should increase with incoming dependencies.

Again, [Martin2002] presents a set of metrics to measure the abstractness of a package, and to manage the relationship between stability and abstractness.

Conclusion

How important is it to draw package and component diagrams? It turns out that they are reasonably useful diagrams. The ADP showed us that dependency cycles between packages and components are problematic and need to be resolved. Drawing a picture of the current structure is often useful for resolving such cycles.

Package dependency diagrams are also reasonably useful for showing the order in which packages should be compiled. Compiling packages in the wrong order can lead to bizarre build problems. The dependency diagram tells you which packages depend upon which others, and therefore which should be compiled first.

Of course the best way to create these diagrams is to generate them from the code. Diagrams of the package structure that don't contain *every* dependency that exists within the code are not particularly useful for resolving cycles or determining build order. Thus, it is not a bad idea to employ a tool that detects the dependencies and either creates the dependency diagrams, or at least provides a list of the dependencies so you can make your own diagram.[1]

Notes

[**Martin2002**]: Robert C. Martin, *Agile Software Development—Principles, Patterns, and Practices*. Upper Saddle River, N.J.: Prentice Hall, 2002.

---

1. see JDepend at *www.clarkware.com* for just such a tool.

9

Object Diagrams

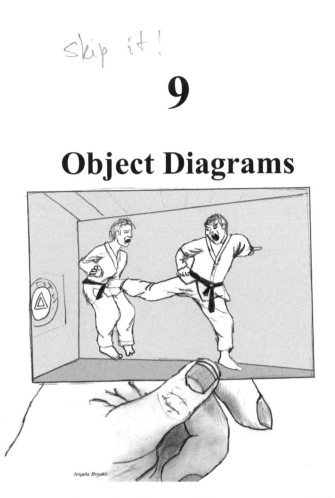

Angela Brooks

Sometimes it can be useful to show the state of the system at a particular point in time. Like a snapshot of a running system, a UML object diagram shows the objects, relationships, and attribute values that obtain at a given instant.

A Snapshot in Time

Some time ago I was involved with an application that allowed users to draw the floor plan of a building on a GUI. The program captured the rooms, doors, windows, and wall openings in the data structure, as shown in Figure 9–1. While this diagram shows you what kinds of data structures are possible, it does not tell you exactly what objects and relationships are instantiated at any given instant of time.

Let's assume that a user of our program draws two rooms, a kitchen, and a lunch room, connected by a wall opening. Both the kitchen and the lunch room have a window to the outside. The lunch room also has a door to the outside, and it opens outward. This scenario is depicted by the object diagram in Figure 9–2.

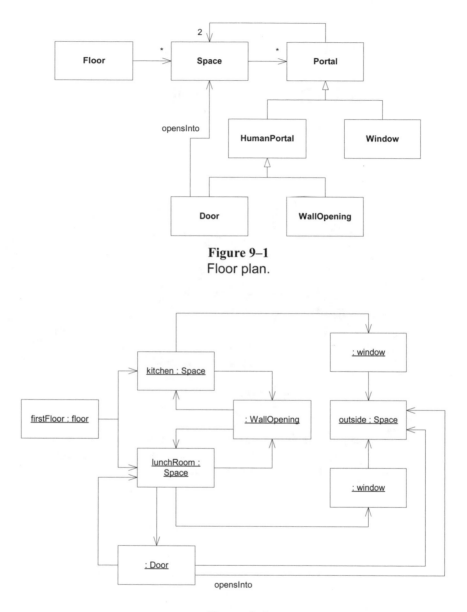

Figure 9–1
Floor plan.

Figure 9–2
Lunch room and kitchen.

This diagram shows the objects that are currently in the system, and what other objects they are connected to. It shows `kitchen` and the `lunchRoom` as separate instances of `Space`. It shows how these two rooms are connected by a wall opening. It shows that the outside is actually represented by another instance of space. And it shows all the other objects and relationships that must exist.

Object diagrams like this are useful when you need to show what the internal structure of a system looks like at a particular point in time, or when the system is in a particular state. An object diagram shows the intent of the designer. It shows the way that certain classes and relationships are actually going to be used. It can help to show how the system will change as different inputs are given to it.

But be careful, it is easy to get carried away. In the last decade I think I have drawn less than a dozen object diagrams of this kind. The need for them simply has not arisen very frequently. When they are needed, they are indispensable, and that's why I'm including them in this book. However, you aren't going to need them very often, and you should definitely not assume that you need to draw them for every scenario in the system, or even for every system.

Active Objects

Another place where object diagrams are useful is in multithreaded systems. Consider, for example, the `Socket-Service` code in Listing 9–1. This program implements a simple framework that allows you to write socket servers without having to deal with all the nasty threading and synchronization issues that accompany sockets.

```
Listing 9–1   SocketService.java
import java.io.IOException;
import java.net.ServerSocket;
import java.net.Socket;
import java.util.LinkedList;

public class SocketService {
  private ServerSocket serverSocket = null;
  private Thread serviceThread = null;
  private boolean running = false;
  private SocketServer itsService = null;
  private LinkedList threads = new LinkedList();

  public SocketService(
        int port, SocketServer service) throws Exception {
    itsService = service;
```

Listing 9–1 (Continued) SocketService.java

```
    serverSocket = new ServerSocket(port);
    serviceThread = new Thread(
      new Runnable() {
        public void run() {
          serviceThread();
        }
      }
    );
    serviceThread.start();
  }

  public void close() throws Exception {
    running = false;
    serviceThread.interrupt();
    serverSocket.close();
    serviceThread.join();
    waitForServerThreads();
  }

  private void serviceThread() {
    running = true;
    while (running) {
      try {
        Socket s = serverSocket.accept();
        startServerThread(s);
      }
      catch (IOException e) {
      }
    }
  }

  private void startServerThread(Socket s) {
    Thread serverThread = new Thread(new ServerRunner(s));
    synchronized (threads) {
      threads.add(serverThread);
    }
    serverThread.start();
  }

  private void
  waitForServerThreads() throws InterruptedException {
    while (threads.size() > 0) {
      Thread t;
      synchronized (threads) {
        t = (Thread) threads.getFirst();
      }
      t.join();
    }
  }

  private class ServerRunner implements Runnable {
    private Socket itsSocket;

    ServerRunner(Socket s) {
      itsSocket = s;
    }
```

Listing 9–1 (Continued) `SocketService.java`

```java
public void run() {
    try {
        itsService.serve(itsSocket);
        synchronized (threads) {
            threads.remove(Thread.currentThread());
        }
        itsSocket.close();
    }
    catch (IOException e) {
    }
}
}
```

The class diagram for this code is shown in Figure 9–3. It's not very inspiring, and it's difficult to see what the intent of this code is from the class diagram. It shows all the classes and relationships all right, but somehow the big picture doesn't come through.

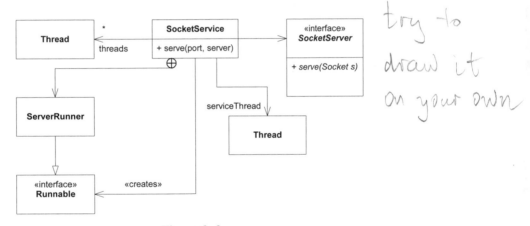

Figure 9–3
`SocketService` class diagram.

However, look at the object diagram in Figure 9–4. This shows the structure much better than the class diagram. It shows that the `SocketService` holds onto the `serviceThread`, and that the `serviceThread` runs in an anonymous inner class. It shows that the `serviceThread` is responsible for creating all the `ServerRunner` instances.

Note the heavy bold lines around the `Thread` instances. Objects with heavy bold borders represent *active objects*. Active objects act as the head of a thread of control. They contain the methods that control the thread, such as `start`, `stop`, `setPriority`, and so on. In this diagram all the active objects are instances of `Thread` because all the processing is done in derivatives of `Runnable` that the `Thread` instances hold references to. The

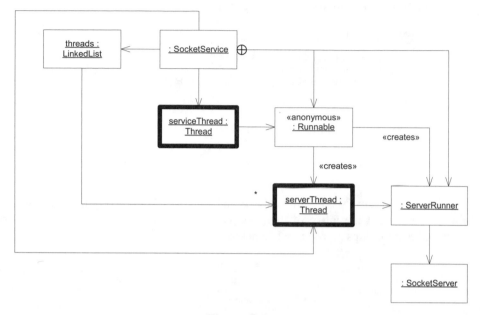

Figure 9–4
`SocketService` object diagram.

`Runnable` derivatives aren't active because they don't control the thread. Rather, the thread invokes them.

Why is the object diagram more expressive than the class diagram? Because the structure of this application is built at runtime. The structure is more about objects than it is about classes.

Conclusion

Object diagrams show you a snapshot of the state of the system at a particular instant of time. This can be a useful way to depict a system, especially when the system's structure is built dynamically instead of imposed by the static structure of its classes. However, one should be leery of drawing many object diagrams. Most of them can be inferred directly from corresponding class diagrams, and therefore serve little purpose.

10

State Diagrams

Angela Brooks

UML has a very rich set of notations for describing finite state machines (FSMs). We'll look at the most useful bits of that notation in this chapter. FSMs are an enormously useful tool for writing all kinds of software. I use them for GUIs, communication protocols, and any other type of event-based system. Unfortunately, I find that too many developers are unfamiliar with the concepts of FSMs and are therefore missing many opportunities to simplify. I'll do my small part to correct that in this chapter.

The Basics

Figure 10–1 shows a simple *state transition diagram* (STD) that describes a finite state machine that controls the way a user logs in to a system. The rounded rectangles represent *states*. The name of each state is in its upper compartment. In the lower compartment are special actions that tell us what to do when the state is entered or exited. For example, as

115

we enter the `Prompting for Login` state, we invoke the `showLoginScreen` action. When we exit that state, we invoke the `hideLoginScreen` action.

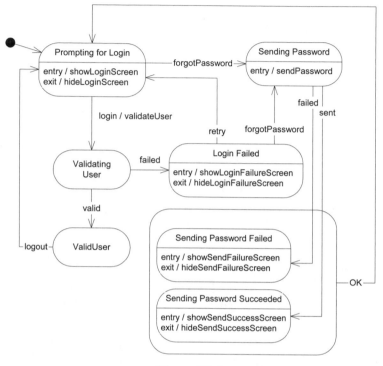

Figure 10–1
Simple login state machine.

The arrows between the states are called *transitions*. Each is labeled with the name of the event that triggers the transition. Some are also labeled with an action to be performed when the transition is triggered. For example, if we are in the `Prompting for Login` state, and we get a `login` event, then we transition to the `Validating User` state and invoke the `validateUser` action.

The black circle in the upper left of the diagram is called an *initial pseudo state*. An FSM begins its life following the transition out of this pseudo state. Thus, our state machine starts out transitioning into the `Prompting for Login` state.

I drew a *superstate* around the `Sending Password Failed` and `Sending Password Succeeded` states because both states react to the OK event by transitioning to the `Prompting for Login` state. I didn't want to draw two identical arrows, so I used the convenience of a superstate.

This finite state machine makes it clear how the login process works. It also breaks the process down into nice compact little functions. If we implement all the action func-

tions like `showLoginScreen`, `validateUser`, and
`sendPassword`, and wire them up with the logic shown
in the diagram, then we can be sure that the login process
will work.

Special events

The lower compartment of a state contains event / action
pairs. The `entry` and `exit` events are standard, but as
you can see from Figure 10–2 you can supply your own
events if you like. If one of these special events occurs
while the FSM is in that state, then the corresponding
action is invoked.

Figure 10–2
States and special events in UML.

Before UML, I used to represent a special event like this as a transition arrow that
looped around back to the same state, as in Figure 10–3. However, in UML this has a
slightly different meaning. Any transition that exits a state will invoke the `exit` action (if
any). Likewise, any transition that enters a state will invoke the `entry` action (if any).
Thus, in UML, a reflexive transition like Figure 10–3 invokes not only `myAction`, but
also the `exit` and `entry` actions.

Figure 10–3
Reflexive transition.

Superstates

As you saw in the login FSM in Figure 10–1, superstates are convenient when you have many states that respond to some of the same events in the same way. You can draw a superstate around those similar states and simply draw the transition arrows leaving the superstate instead of leaving the individual states. Thus, the two diagrams in Figure 10–4 are equivalent.

Superstate transitions can be overridden by drawing explicit transition from the substates. Thus, in Figure 10–5, the `pause` transition for `S3` overrides the default `pause` transition for the `Cancelable` superstate. In this sense, a super-state is rather like a base class. Substates can override their superstate transitions the same way that derived classes can override their base class

Angela Brooks

methods. However, it is inadvisable to push this metaphor too far. The relationship between superstates and substates is not really equivalent to inheritance.

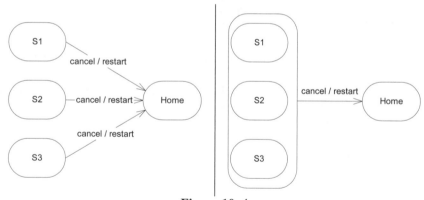

Figure 10–4
Transition: Multiple states and superstate.

Superstates can have `entry`, `exit`, and special events the same way that normal states can have them. Figure 10–6 shows an FSM in which there are `exit` and `entry` actions in both superstates and substates. As the FSM transitions from `Some State` into `Sub` it first invokes the `enterSuper` action, followed by the `enterSub` action. Likewise, if the FSM transitions out of `Sub2` back to `Some State`, it first invokes `exitSub2` and then `exitSuper`. However, since the `e2` transition from `Sub` to `Sub2` does not exit the superstate, it simply invokes `exitSub` and `enterSub2`.

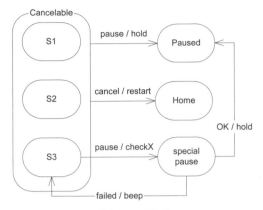

Figure 10–5
Overriding superstate transitions.

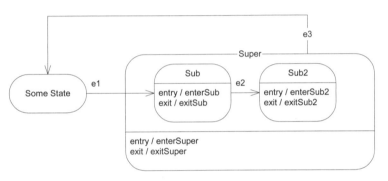

Figure 10–6
Hierarchical invocation of `entry` and `exit` actions.

Initial and final pseudostates

Figure 10–7 shows two pseudostates that are commonly used in UML. FSMs come into existence *in the process of* transitioning out of the initial pseudostate. The transition leading out of the initial pseudostate cannot have an event, since the event is the creation of the state machine. It can, however, have an action. This action will be the first action invoked after the creation of the FSM.

Similarly, a FSM dies in the process of transitioning into the *final pseudostate*. The final pseudostate is never actually reached. If there is an action on the transition into the final pseudostate, it will be the last action invoked by the FSM.

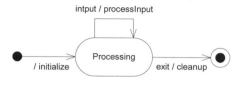

Figure 10–7
Initial and final pseudo states.

Using FSM Diagrams

I find diagrams like this to be immensely useful for figuring out state machines for sub-systems whose behavior is well known. On the other hand, most systems that are amenable to FSMs do not have behaviors that are well known in advance. Rather, the behaviors of most systems grow and evolve over time. Diagrams aren't a conducive medium for systems that must change frequently. Issues of layout and space intrude upon the content of the diagrams. This intrusion can sometimes prevent designers from making needed changes to a design. The spectre of reformatting the diagram prevents them from adding a needed class or state, and causes them to use a substandard solution that doesn't impact the diagram layout.

Text, on the other hand, is a very flexible medium for dealing with change. Layout issues are at a minimum, and there is always room to add lines of text. Therefore, for systems that evolve, I create *state transition tables* (STTs) in text files rather than STDs. Consider the STD of the subway turnstile in Figure 10–8. This can be easily represented as an STT, as shown in Figure 10–9.

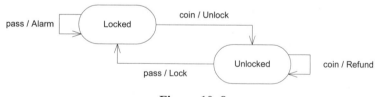

Figure 10–8
Subway turnstile STD.

The STT is a simple table with four columns. Each row of the table represents a transition. Look at each transition arrow on the diagram. You'll see that the table rows contain the two endpoints of each arrow, and the event and action of the arrow. You read the STT using the following sentence template: "If we are in the `Locked` state, and we get a `coin` event, then we go to the `Unlocked` state and invoke the `Unlock` function."

Current State	Event	New State	Action
Locked	coin	Unlocked	Unlock
Locked	pass	Locked	Alarm
Unlocked	coin	Unlocked	Refund
Unlocked	pass	Locked	Lock

Figure 10–9
Subway turnstile STT.

This table can be converted into a text file very simply:

```
Locked    coin Unlocked Unlock
Locked    pass Locked   Alarm
Unlocked coin Unlocked Refund
Unlocked pass Locked    Lock
```

These 16 words contain all the logic of the FSM, and it occurred to me that it should be possible to write a simple compiler that reads the text file and generates code that implements that logic.

SMC

So, about 15 years ago, I wrote a simple compiler, named SMC[1], that reads STTs and generates C++ code to implement the logic. Since then SMC has grown and changed to emit code for different languages. SMC is freely available from the resources section of *www.objectmentor.com*.

The input to SMC for the turnstile example is shown in Listing 10–1. Most of this syntax is pretty easy to understand. The details are explained in the smc.txt document that you can download from the previously mentioned URL. The FSMName header supplies the name of the class that SMC will generate. The Context header tells SMC the name of a class that the FSM should inherit from.

```
Listing 10–1  Turnstile.sm
Context TurnStileContext
FSMName TurnStile
Initial Locked
{
    Locked
    {
        Coin      Unlocked    Unlock
        Pass      Locked      Alarm
    }
    Unlocked
    {
        Coin      Unlocked    Thankyou
        Pass      Locked      Lock
    }
}
```

1. SMC stands for State Machine Compiler.

The code generated from this input is shown in Listing 10–2. It makes use of the STATE pattern. One generated, this code never needs to be edited, or even examined. It simply implements the logic, allowing the action functions to be implemented in the Context class.

Listing 10–2 TurnStile.java **(Generated)**

```java
public class TurnStile extends TurnStileContext {
    private State itsState;
    private static String itsVersion = "";
    private static Locked itsLockedState;
    private static Unlocked itsUnlockedState;

    public TurnStile() {
        itsLockedState = new Locked();
        itsUnlockedState = new Unlocked();
        itsState = itsLockedState;
    }

    public String getVersion() {
        return itsVersion;
    }

    public String getCurrentStateName() {
        return itsState.stateName();
    }

    public void Pass() {
        itsState.pass();
    }

    public void Coin() {
        itsState.coin();
    }

    private abstract class State {
        public abstract String stateName();

        public void pass() {
            FSMError("Pass", itsState.stateName());
        }

        public void coin() {
            FSMError("Coin", itsState.stateName());
        }

    }

    private class Locked extends State {
        public String stateName() {
            return "Locked";
        }

        public void pass() {
            Alarm();
            itsState = itsLockedState;
        }
```

Listing 10–2 (Continued) `TurnStile.java` (Generated)

```
        public void coin() {
            Unlock();
            itsState = itsUnlockedState;
        }
    }

    private class Unlocked extends State {
        public String stateName() {
            return "Unlocked";
        }

        public void pass() {
            Lock();
            itsState = itsLockedState;
        }

        public void coin() {
            Thankyou();
            itsState = itsUnlockedState;
        }
    }
}
```

Creating and maintaining FSMs in this form is much easier than trying to maintain diagrams, and generating the code saves lots of time. So, though diagrams can be very useful to help you think through or present an FSM to others, the text form is much more convenient for development.

ICE: A case study

Several years ago I was involved in a workstation project named ICE. Users sat at GUIs and worked through a sequence of screens using a fairly simple workflow. The logic of the GUI is shown in Figure 10–10. This diagram was never drawn while the project was being developed; I just drew it here to show you how a complex FSM would be drawn in UML.

The SMC input for this diagram is shown in Listing 10–3. This source file grew from humble beginnings to the full description you see now. This file was easy to create, easy to maintain, and fit very nicely into our build procedure.

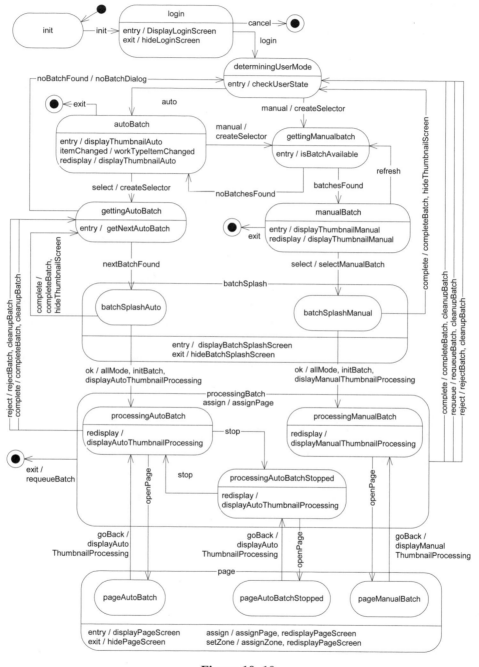

Figure 10–10
ICE FSM.

Conclusion

Finite state machines are a powerful concept for structuring software. UML provides a very powerful notation for visualizing FSMs. However, it is often easier to develop and maintain an FSM using a textual language than diagrams.

The UML state diagram notation is much richer than I have described. There are several other pseudostates, icons, and widgets that you can apply. However, I rarely find them useful. The notation I have described in this chapter is all I really ever use.

Listing 10–3   `ice.sm`

```
Context RootFSM
Initial init
FSMName RootFSMGen
Version 042399 1528 rcm
FSMGenerator smc.generator.java.SMJavaGenerator
Pragma Package root
{
    init
    {
        init        login       {}
    }

    login <displayLoginScreen >hideLoginScreen
    {
        login       determiningUserMode {}
        cancel      end                 {}
    }


    determiningUserMode < { cleanupThumbnails checkUserState }
    {
        auto        autoBatch           {}
        manual      gettingManualBatch { createSelector }
    }

    autoBatch   < { setUserAuto displayThumbnailAuto }
    {
        manual      gettingManualBatch { createSelector }
        select      gettingAutoBatch   { createSelector }
        itemChanged *                  workTypeItemChanged
        redisplay   *                  displayThumbnailAuto
        exit        end                {}
    }


    gettingAutoBatch <getNextAutoBatch
    {
        nextBatchFound  batchSplashAuto     {}
        noBatchFound    determiningUserMode { noBatchDialog }
    }


    gettingManualBatch <isBatchAvailable
```

Listing 10–3 (Continued) `ice.sm`

```
{
    batchesFound    manualBatch                 {}
    noBatchFound    autoBatch                   {}
}

manualBatch < { setUserManual displayThumbnailManual }
{
    auto         autoBatch              {}
    refresh      gettingManualBatch     {}
    select       batchSplashManual      selectManualBatch
    redisplay    *                      displayThumbnailManual
    exit         end                    {}
}

(processingBatch) >hideThumbnailScreen
{
    ok           *                      {}
    cancel       *                      {}


    complete     determiningUserMode { completeBatch
                                       cleanupBatch }
    requeue      determiningUserMode { requeueBatch
                                       cleanupBatch }
    reject       determiningUserMode { rejectBatch
                                       cleanupBatch }
    assign       *                      assignPage
    exit         end                    requeueBatch
}

processingAutoBatch : processingBatch
{
    stop         processingAutoBatchStopped  {}
    complete     gettingAutoBatch       { completeBatch
                                         cleanupBatch }
    reject       gettingAutoBatch       { rejectBatch
                                         cleanupBatch }
    openPage     pageAutoBatch              {}
    redisplay    *                 displayAutoThumbnailProcessing
}


processingAutoBatchStopped : processingBatch
{
    complete     determiningUserMode   { completeBatch
                                         cleanupBatch }
    reject       determiningUserMode   { rejectBatch
                                         cleanupBatch }
    openPage     pageAutoBatchStopped      {}
    stop         processingAutoBatch       {}
    redisplay    *                 displayAutoThumbnailProcessing
}

processingManualBatch : processingBatch
{
    openPage     pageManualBatch            {}
```

Listing 10–3 (Continued) `ice.sm`

```
        redisplay    *              displayManualThumbnailProcessing
    }


    (batchSplash) <displayBatchSplashScreen >hideBatchSplashScreen
    {
    }


    batchSplashAuto : batchSplash
    {
        ok          processingAutoBatch {allMode initBatch
                                displayAutoThumbnailProcessing}
        complete    gettingAutoBatch    {completeBatch
                                        hideThumbnailScreen}
    }

    batchSplashManual : batchSplash
    {
        ok          processingManualBatch  {allMode initBatch
                                displayManualThumbnailProcessing}
        complete    determiningUserMode    {completeBatch
                                        hideThumbnailScreen}

    }

    (page) <displayPageScreen >hidePageScreen
    {
        assign      *      {assignPage redisplayPageScreen}
        setZone     *      {assignZone redisplayPageScreen}
    }

    pageAutoBatch : page
    {
        goBack  processingAutoBatch displayAutoThumbnailProcessing
    }

    pageAutoBatchStopped : page
    {
        goBack  processingAutoBatchStopped
                                    displayAutoThumbnailProcessing
    }

    pageManualBatch : page
    {
        goBack  processingManualBatch displayManualThumbnailProcessing
    }

    end <exitProgram
    {
    }
}
```

11

Heuristics and Coffee

Angela Brooks

Over the past dozen years I have taught, and continue to teach, OO design to professional software developers. My courses are divided into morning lectures and afternoon exercises. For the exercises I will divide the class up into teams and have them solve a design problem using UML. The next morning we choose one or two teams to present their solutions on a white board, and we critique their designs.

I have taught these courses hundreds of times and have noticed that there is a group of design mistakes that are commonly made by the students. This chapter presents a few of the most common errors, shows why they are errors, and addresses how they can be corrected. Then it goes on to solve the problem in a way that I think resolves all the design forces nicely.

The Mark IV Special Coffee Maker

During the first morning of an OOD class I present the basic definitions of classes, objects, relationships, methods, polymorphism, and so on. At the same time I present the basics of UML. Thus, the students learn the fundamental concepts, vocabulary, and tools of object oriented design.

During the afternoon I give the class the following exercise to work on: I ask them to design the software that controls a simple coffee maker. Here is the specification I give them.[1]

The Mark IV Special Coffee Maker

The Mark IV Special makes up to 12 cups of coffee at a time. The user places a filter in the filter holder, fills the filter with coffee grounds, and slides the filter holder into its receptacle. The user then pours up to 12 cups of water into the water strainer and presses the Brew button. The water is heated until boiling. The pressure of the evolving steam forces the water to be sprayed over the coffee grounds, and coffee drips through the filter into the pot. The pot is kept warm for extended periods by a warmer plate, which only turns on if there is coffee in the pot. If the pot is removed from the warmer plate while water is being sprayed over the grounds, the flow of water is stopped so that brewed coffee does not spill on the warmer plate. The following hardware needs to be monitored or controlled:

- The heating element for the boiler. It can be turned on or off.

- The heating element for the warmer plate. It can be turned on or off.

- The sensor for the warmer plate. It has three states: `warmerEmpty`, `potEmpty`, `potNotEmpty`.

- A sensor for the boiler, which determines whether there is water present. It has two states: `boilerEmpty` or `boilerNotEmpty`.

- The Brew button. This is a momentary button that starts the brewing cycle. It has an indicator that lights up when the brewing cycle is over and the coffee is ready.

- A pressure-relief valve that opens to reduce the pressure in the boiler. The drop in pressure stops the flow of water to the filter. It can be opened or closed.

The hardware for the Mark IV has been designed and is currently under development. The hardware engineers have even provided a low-level API for us to use, so we don't have to write any bit-twiddling I/O driver code. The code for these interface functions is shown in Listing 11–1. If this code looks strange to you, just keep in mind that it was written by hardware engineers.

---

1. This problem comes from my first book: [Martin1995], p. 60.

Listing 11–1 `CofeeMakerAPI.java`

```java
public interface CoffeeMakerAPI {
  public static CoffeeMakerAPI api = null; // set by main.

  /**
   * This function returns the status of the warmer-plate
   * sensor. This sensor detects the presence of the pot
   * and whether it has coffee in it.
   */
  public int getWarmerPlateStatus();

  public static final int WARMER_EMPTY = 0;
  public static final int POT_EMPTY = 1;
  public static final int POT_NOT_EMPTY = 2;

  /**
   * This function returns the status of the boiler switch.
   * The boiler switch is a float switch that detects if
   * there is more than 1/2 cup of water in the boiler.
   */
  public int getBoilerStatus();

  public static final int BOILER_EMPTY = 0;
  public static final int BOILER_NOT_EMPTY = 1;

  /**
   * This function returns the status of the brew button.
   * The brew button is a momentary switch that remembers
   * its state. Each call to this function returns the
   * remembered state and then resets that state to
   * BREW_BUTTON_NOT_PUSHED.
   *
   * Thus, even if this function is polled at a very slow
   * rate, it will still detect when the brew button is
   * pushed.
   */
  public int getBrewButtonStatus();

  public static final int BREW_BUTTON_PUSHED = 0;
  public static final int BREW_BUTTON_NOT_PUSHED = 1;

  /**
   * This function turns the heating element in the boiler
   * on or off.
   */
  public void setBoilerState(int boilerStatus);

  public static final int BOILER_ON = 0;
  public static final int BOILER_OFF = 1;

  /**
   * This function turns the heating element in the warmer
   * plate on or off.
   */
  public void setWarmerState(int warmerState);

  public static final int WARMER_ON = 0;
```

```
Listing 11–1 (Continued) CofeeMakerAPI.java
  public static final int WARMER_OFF = 1;

  /**
   * This function turns the indicator light on or off.
   * The indicator light should be turned on at the end
   * of the brewing cycle. It should be turned off when
   * the user presses the brew button.
   */
  public void setIndicatorState(int indicatorState);

  public static final int INDICATOR_ON = 0;
  public static final int INDICATOR_OFF = 1;

  /**
   * This function opens and closes the pressure-relief
   * valve. When this valve is closed, steam pressure in
   * the boiler will force hot water to spray out over
   * the coffee filter. When the valve is open, the steam
   * in the boiler escapes into the environment, and the
   * water in the boiler will not spray out over the filter.
   */
  public void setReliefValveState(int reliefValveState);

  public static final int VALVE_OPEN = 0;
  public static final int VALVE_CLOSED = 1;
}
```

A challenge

If you want a challenge, stop reading here and try to design this software yourself. Remember that you are designing the software for a simple, embedded real-time system. What I expect of my students is a set of class diagrams, sequence diagrams, and state machines.

A common, but hideous, coffee maker solution

By far the most common solution that my students present is the one in Figure 11–1. In this diagram we see the central CoffeeMaker class surrounded by minions that control the various devices. The CoffeeMaker contains a Boiler, a WarmerPlate, a Button, and a Light. The Boiler contains a BoilerSensor and a BoilerHeater. The WarmerPlate contains a PlateSensor and a PlateHeater. Finally there are two base classes, Sensor and Heater, that act as parents to the Boiler and WarmerPlate elements, respectively.

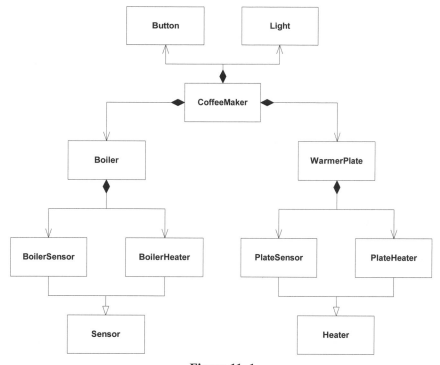

Figure 11–1
Hyper-concrete coffee maker.

It is hard for beginners to appreciate just how hideous this structure is. There are quite a few rather serious errors lurking in this diagram. Many of these errors would not be noticed until you actually tried to code this design and found that the code was absurd.

But before we get to the problems with the design itself, let's look at the problems with the way the UML is created.

Missing methods

The biggest problem that Figure 11–1 exhibits is a complete lack of methods. We are writing a *program* here, and programs are about behavior! Where is the behavior in this diagram?

When designers create diagrams without methods they may be partitioning the software on something other than behavior. Partitionings that are not based upon behavior are almost always significant errors. It is the behavior of a system that is the first clue to how the software should be partitioned.

Vapor classes

We can see how poorly partitioned this particular design is, if we consider the methods we might put in the class `Light`. Clearly the `Light` object just wants to be turned on or turned off. Thus we might put an `on()` and `off()` method in class `Light`. What would the implementation of those function look like? See Listing 11–2.

Listing 11–2 `Light.java`

```
public class Light {
  public void on() {
    CoffeeMakerAPI.api.
      setIndicatorState(CoffeeMakerAPI.INDICATOR_ON);
  }

  public void off() {
    CoffeeMakerAPI.api.
      setIndicatorState(CoffeeMakerAPI.INDICATOR_OFF);
  }
}
```

There are some peculiar things about class `Light`. First, it has no variables. This is odd since an object usually has some kind of state that it manipulates. What's more, the `on()` and `off()` methods simply delegate to the `setIndicatorState` method of the `CoffeeMakerAPI`. So apparently the `Light` class is nothing more than a call translator. It's not really doing anything useful.

This same reasoning can be applied to the `Button`, `Boiler`, and `WarmerPlate` classes. They are nothing more than adapters that translate a function call from one form to another. Indeed, they could be removed from the design altogether without changing any of the logic in the `CoffeeMaker` class. That class would simply have to call the `CoffeeMakerAPI` directly instead of through the adapters.

By considering the methods, and then the code, we have demoted these classes from the prominent position the hold in Figure 11–1, to mere place holders without much reason to exist. For this reason, I call them *vapor classes*.

Imaginary abstraction

Notice the `Sensor` and `Heater` base classes in Figure 11–1. The previous section should have convinced you that their derivatives were mere vapor, but what about base classes themselves? On the surface they seem to make a lot of sense. And yet, there doesn't seem to be any place for them.

Abstractions are tricky things. We humans see them everywhere, but many are not appropriate to be turned into base classes. These, in particular, have no place in this design. We can see this by asking ourselves who uses them.

No class in the system actually makes use of the `Sensor` or `Heater` class. If nobody uses them, what reason do they have to exist? Sometimes we might tolerate a base class that nobody uses if it supplied some common code to the derivatives, but these bases have no code in them at all. At best their methods are abstract. Consider, for example, the `Heater` interface in Listing 11–3. A class with nothing but abstract functions and that no other class uses is officially useless.

Listing 11–3 `Heater.java`

```
public interface Heater {
  public void turnOn();
  public void turnOff();
}
```

The `Sensor` class (Listing 11–4) is worse! Like `Heater`, it has abstract methods and no users. What's worse is that the return value of its sole method is ambiguous. What does the `sense()` method return? In the `BoilerSensor` it returns two possible values, but in `WarmerPlateSensor` it returns three possible values. In short, we cannot specify the contract of the *Sensor* in the interface. The best we can do is say that sensors may return `ints`. This is pretty weak.

Listing 11–4 `Sensor.java`

```
public interface Sensor {
  public int sense();
}
```

What really happened here is that we read through the specification, found a bunch of likely nouns, made some inferences about their relationships, and then created a UML diagram based on that reasoning. If we accepted these decisions as an architecture and implemented them the way they stand, then we'd wind up with an all-powerful `CoffeeMaker` class surrounded by vaporous minions. We might as well program it in C!

God classes

Everybody knows that god classes are a bad idea. We don't want to concentrate all the intelligence of a system into a single object or a single function. One of the goals of OOD is the partitioning and distribution of behavior into many classes and many functions. It turns out, however, that many object models that appear to be distributed are really the abode of gods in disguise. Figure 11–1 is a prime example. At first glance it looks like there are lots of classes with interesting behavior. But as we drill down into the code that would imple-

ment those classes we find that only one of those classes, `CoffeeMaker`, has any interesting behavior, and the rest are all imaginary abstractions or vapor classes.

A Coffee Maker Solution

Solving the coffee maker problem is an interesting exercise in abstraction. Most developers new to OO find themselves quite surprised by the result.

The trick to solving this problem is to step back and separate its details from its essential nature. Forget about boilers, valves, heaters, sensors, and all the little details and concentrate on the underlying problem. What is that problem? The problem is, how do you make coffee?

How *do* you make coffee? The simplest, and most common solution to this problem, is to pour hot water over coffee grounds, and to collect the resulting infusion in some kind of vessel. Where do we get the hot water from? Let's call it a `HotWaterSource`. Where do we collect the coffee? Let's call it a `ContainmentVessel`[2].

Are these two abstractions really classes? Does a `HotWaterSource` have behavior that could be captured in software? Does a `ContainmentVessel` do something that software could control? If we think about the Mark IV unit, we could imagine the boiler, valve, and boiler sensor playing the role of the `HotWaterSource`. The `HotWaterSource` would be responsible for heating the water and delivering it over the coffee grounds to drip into the `ContainmentVessel`. We could also imagine the warmer plate and its sensor playing the role of the `ContainmentVessel`. It would be responsible for keeping the contained coffee warm, and also for letting us know whether there was any coffee left in the vessel.

Crossed wires

How would you capture the previous discussion in a UML diagram? Figure 11–2 shows one possible schema. `HotWaterSource` and `ContainmentVessel` are both represented as classes, and are associated by the flow of coffee.

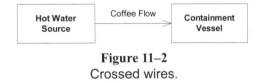

Figure 11–2
Crossed wires.

---

2. That name is particularly appropriate for the kind of coffee that *I* like to make.

The association shows an error that OO novices commonly make. The association is made with something physical about the problem instead of with the control of software behavior. The fact that coffee flows from the `HotWaterSource` to the `Containment-Vessel` is completely irrelevant to the association between those two classes.

For example, what if the software in the `ContainmentVessel` told the `HotWater-Source` when to start and stop the flow of hot water into the vessel? This might be depicted as shown in Figure 11–3. Notice that the `ContainmentVessel` is sending the start message to the `HotWaterSource`. This means that the association in Figure 11–2 is backwards. `HotWaterSource` does not depend upon the `ContainmentVessel` at all. Rather, the `ContainmentVessel` depends upon the `HotWaterSource`.

Figure 11–3
Starting the flow of hot water.

The lesson here is simply this: Associations are the pathways through which messages are sent between objects. They have nothing to do with the flow of physical objects. The fact that hot water flows from the boiler to the pot does not mean that there should be an association from the `HotWaterSource` to the `ContainmentVessel`.

I call this particular mistake *crossed wires* because the wiring between the classes has gotten crossed between the logical and physical domains.

The coffee maker user interface

It should be clear that something is missing from our coffee maker model. We have a `HotWaterSource` and a `ContainmentVessel`, but we don't have any way for a human to interact with the system. Somewhere our system has to listen for commands from a human. Likewise the system must be able to report its status to its human owners. Certainly the Mark IV had hardware dedicated to this purpose. The button and the light served as the user interface.

Thus, we'll add a `UserInterface` class to our coffee maker model. This gives us a triad of classes interacting to create coffee under the direction of a user.

Use Case 1: User pushes brew button

OK, given these three classes, how do their instances communicate? Let's look at several use cases to see if we can find out what the behavior of these classes is.

Which one of our objects detects the fact that the user has pressed the Brew button? Clearly, it must be the `UserInterface` object. What should this object do when the Brew button is pushed?

Our goal is to start the flow of hot water. However, before we can do that, we'd better make sure that the `ContainmentVessel` is ready to accept coffee. We'd also better make sure that the `HotWaterSource` is ready. If we think about the Mark IV, we're making sure that the boiler is full, and that the pot is empty and in place on the warmer.

So the first thing our `UserInterface` object does is to send a message to the `HotWaterSource` and the `ContainmentVessel` to see if they are ready. This is shown in Figure 11–4.

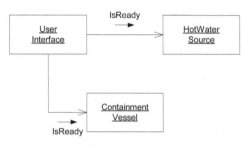

Figure 11–4
Brew button pressed, checking for ready.

If either of these queries returns false, then we refuse to start brewing coffee. The `UserInterface` object can take care of letting the user know that his request was denied. In the Mark IV case, we might flash the light a few times.

If both queries return true, then we need to start the flow of hot water. Probably the `UserInterface` object should send a `Start` message to the `HotWaterSource`. The `HotWaterSource` will then start doing whatever it needs to do to get hot water flowing. In the case of the Mark IV, it will close the valve and turn on the boiler. Figure 11–5 shows the completed scenario.

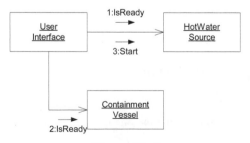

Figure 11–5
Brew button pressed, complete.

Use Case 2: Containment vessel not ready

In the Mark IV we know that the user can take the pot off the warmer while coffee is brewing. Which one of our objects would detect the fact that the pot had been removed? Certainly it would be the `ContainmentVessel`. The requirements for the Mark IV tell us that we need to stop the flow of coffee when this happens. Thus the `Containment-Vessel` must be able to tell the `HotWaterSource` to stop sending hot water. Likewise, it needs to be able to tell it to start again when the pot is replaced. Figure 11–6 adds the new methods.

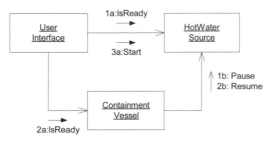

Figure 11–6
Pausing and resuming the flow of hot water.

Use Case 3: Brewing complete

At some point we will be done brewing coffee, and we'll have to turn off the flow of hot water. Which one of our objects knows when brewing is complete? In the Mark IV's case the sensor in the boiler tells us that the boiler is empty. So our `HotWaterSource` would detect this. However, it's not hard to envision a coffee maker in which the `Containment-Vessel` would be the one to detect that brewing was done. For example, what if our coffee maker was plumbed into the water mains and therefore had an infinite supply of water? What if the water was heated by an intense microwave generator[3] as it flowed through the pipes into a thermally isolated vessel? What if that vessel had a spigot from which users got their coffee? In this case it would be a sensor in the vessel that would know that it was full, and that hot water should be shut off.

The point is that in the abstract domain of the `HotWaterSource` and `Containment-Vessel`, neither is an especially compelling candidate for detecting completion of the brew. My solution to that is to ignore the issue. I'll assume that either object can tell the others that brewing is complete.

Which objects in our model need to know that brewing is complete? Certainly the `UserInterface` needs to know since, in the Mark IV, it must turn the light on. It should

---

3. OK...I'm having a bit of fun. But, what if?

also be clear that the `HotWaterSource` needs to know that brewing is over, because it'll need to stop the flow of hot water. In the Mark IV it'll shut down the boiler and open the valve. Does the `ContainmentVessel` need to know that brewing is complete? Is there anything special that the `ContainmentVessel` needs to do, or to keep track of, once the brewing is complete? In the Mark IV it's going to detect an empty pot being put back on the plate, signalling that the user has poured the last of the coffee. This causes the Mark IV to turn the light *out*. So, yes, the `ContainmentVessel` needs to know that brewing is complete. Indeed, the same argument can be used to say that the `UserInterface` should send the `Start` message to the `ContainmentVessel` when brewing starts. Figure 11–7 shows the new messages. Note that I've shown that either `HotWaterSource` or `ContainmentVesslel` can send the `Done` message.

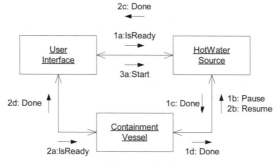

Figure 11–7
Detecting when brewing is complete.

Use Case 4: Coffee all gone

The Mark IV shuts off the light when brewing is complete *and* an empty pot is placed on the plate. Clearly, in our object model, it is the `ContainmentVessel` that should detect this. It will have to send a `Complete` message to the `UserInterface`. Figure 11–8 shows the completed collaboration diagram.

From this diagram we can draw a class diagram with all the associations intact. This diagram holds no surprises. You can see it in Figure 11–9.

Implementing the abstract model

Our object model is reasonably well partitioned. We have three distinct areas of responsibility, and each seems to be sending and receiving messages in a balanced way. There does not appear to be a god object anywhere. Nor do there appear to be any vapor classes.

So far, so good, but how do we implement the Mark IV in this structure? Do we just implement the methods of these three classes to invoke the `CoffeeMakerAPI`? This

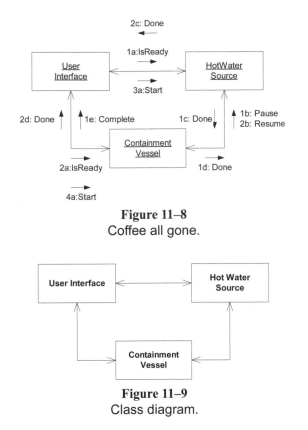

Figure 11–8
Coffee all gone.

Figure 11–9
Class diagram.

would be a real shame! We've captured the essence of what it takes to make coffee. It would be pitifully poor design if we were to now tie that essence to the Mark IV.

In fact, I'm going to make a rule right now. None of the three classes we have created must ever know anything about the Mark IV. This is the Dependency Inversion Principle (DIP). We are not going to allow the high-level coffee making policy of this system to depend upon the low-level implementation.

OK, then how will we create the Mark IV implementation? Let's look at all the use cases again, but this time, let's look at them from the Mark IV point of view.

Use Case 1: User pushes Brew button

Looking at our model, how does the UserInterface know that the Brew button has been pushed? Clearly, it must call the CoffeeMakerAPI.getBrewButtonStatus() function. Where should it call this function? We've already decreed that the UserInterface class itself cannot know about the CoffeeMakerAPI. So where does this call go?

We'll apply the DIP and put the call in a derivative of UserInterface. See Figure 11–10 for details.

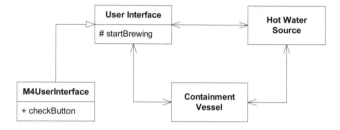

Figure 11–10
Detecting the Brew button.

We've derived M4UserInterface from UserInterface, and we've put a check-Button() method in M4UserInterface. When this function is called, it will call the CoffeeMakerAPI.getBrewButtonStatus() function. If the button has been pressed, it will invoke the protected startBrewing() method of UserInterface. Listings 11–5 and 11–6 show how this would be coded.

Listing 11–5 M4UserInterface.java

```java
public class M4UserInterface extends UserInterface {
  private void checkButton() {
    int buttonStatus =
        CoffeeMakerAPI.api.getBrewButtonStatus();
    if (buttonStatus == CoffeeMakerAPI.BREW_BUTTON_PUSHED) {
      startBrewing();
    }
  }
}
```

Listing 11–6 UserInterface.java

```java
public class UserInterface {
  private HotWaterSource hws;
  private ContainmentVessel cv;

  public void done() {}
  public void complete() {}
  protected void startBrewing() {
    if (hws.isReady() && cv.isReady()) {
      hws.start();
      cv.start();
    }
  }
}
```

You might be wondering why I created the protected `startBrewing()` method at all. Why didn't I just call the `start()` functions from `M4UserInterface`? The reason is simple, but significant. The `isReady()` tests, and the consequential calls to the `start()` methods of the `HotWaterSource` and the `ContainmentVessel` are high-level policy that the `UserInterface` class should possess. That code is valid irrespective of whether we are implementing a Mark IV and should therefore not be coupled to the Mark IV derivative. You will see me make this same distinction over and over again in this example. I keep as much code as I can in the high-level classes. The only code I put into the derivatives is code that is directly, and inextricably, associated with the Mark IV.

Implementing the *isReady()* functions

How are the `isReady()` methods of `HotWaterSource` and `ContainmentVessel` implemented? It should be clear that these are really just abstract methods, and that these classes are therefore abstract classes. The corresponding derivatives `M4HotWaterSource` and `M4ContainmentVessel` will implement them by calling the appropriate `Coffee-MakerAPI` functions. Figure 11–11 shows the new structure, and Listings 11–7 and 11–8 show the implementation of the two derivatives.

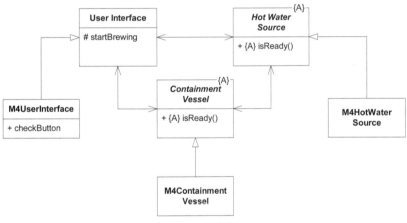

Figure 11–11
Implementing the `isReady` methods.

```
Listing 11–7  M4HotWaterSource.java
public class M4HotWaterSource extends HotWaterSource {
  public boolean isReady() {
    int boilerStatus =
      CoffeeMakerAPI.api.getBoilerStatus();
    return boilerStatus == CoffeeMakerAPI.BOILER_NOT_EMPTY;
  }
}
```

Listing 11–8 `M4ContainmentVessel.java`

```
public class M4ContainmentVessel extends ContainmentVessel {
  public boolean isReady() {
    int plateStatus =
      CoffeeMakerAPI.api.getWarmerPlateStatus();
    return plateStatus == CoffeeMakerAPI.POT_EMPTY;
  }
}
```

Implementing the *start()* functions

The `start()` method of `HotWaterSource` is just an abstract method that is implemented by `M4HotWaterSource` to invoke the `CoffeeMakerAPI` functions that close the valve and turn on the boiler. As I wrote these functions I began to get tired of all the `CoffeeMakerAPI.api.XXX` structures I was writing, so I did a little refactoring at the same time. The result is in Listing 11–9.

Listing 11–9 `M4HotWaterSource.java`

```
public class M4HotWaterSource extends HotWaterSource {
  CoffeeMakerAPI api;

  public M4HotWaterSource(CoffeeMakerAPI api) {
    this.api = api;
  }

  public boolean isReady() {
    int boilerStatus = api.getBoilerStatus();
    return boilerStatus == api.BOILER_NOT_EMPTY;
  }

  public void start() {
    api.setReliefValveState(api.VALVE_CLOSED);
    api.setBoilerState(api.BOILER_ON);
  }
}
```

The `start()` method for the `ContainmentVessel` is a little more interesting. The only action that the `M4ContainmentVessel` needs to take is to remember the brewing state of the system. As we'll see later, this will allow it to respond correctly when pots are placed on, or removed from, the plate. Listing 11–10 shows the code.

Listing 11–10 `M4ContainmentVessel.java`

```
public class M4ContainmentVessel extends ContainmentVessel {
  private CoffeeMakerAPI api;
  private boolean isBrewing;

  public M4ContainmentVessel(CoffeeMakerAPI api) {
    this.api = api;
    isBrewing = false;
  }

  public boolean isReady() {
```

Listing 11–10 (Continued) `M4ContainmentVessel.java`

```
    int plateStatus = api.getWarmerPlateStatus();
    return plateStatus == api.POT_EMPTY;
}

public void start() {
    isBrewing = true;
}
}
```

How does M4UserInterface.checkButton get called?

This is an interesting point. How does the flow of control ever get to a place at which the `CoffeeMakerAPI.getBrewButtonStatus()` function can be called? For that matter, how does the flow of control get to where *any* of the sensors can be detected?

Many of the teams who try to solve this problem get completely hung up on this point. Some don't want to assume that there's a multithreading operating system in the coffee maker, and so they want to use a polling approach to the sensors. Others want to put multithreading in so that they don't have to worry about polling. I've seen this particular argument go back and forth for an hour or more in some teams.

The mistake that these teams are making (which I eventually point out to them after letting them sweat a bit) is that the choice between threading and polling is completely irrelevant. This decision can be made at the very last minute without harm to the design. Therefore it is always best to assume that messages can be sent asynchronously, as though there were independent threads, and then put the polling or threading in at the last minute.

The design so far has assumed that somehow the flow of control will asynchronously get into the `M4UserInterface` object so that it can call `CoffeeMakerAPI.getBrew-ButtonStatus()`. Now let's assume that we are working in a very minimal JVM that does not support threading. This means we're going to have to poll. How can we make this work?

Consider the `Pollable` interface in Listing 11–11. This interface has nothing but a `poll()` method. Now, what if `M4UserInterface` implemented this interface? What if the `main()` program hung in a hard loop just calling this method over and over again? Then the flow of control would continuously be reentering `M4UserInterface` and we could detect the Brew button.

Listing 11–11 `Pollable.java`

```
public interface Pollable {
    public void poll();
}
```

Indeed, we can repeat this pattern for all three of the M4 derivatives. Each has its own sensors it needs to check. So, as shown in Figure 11–12, we can derive all of the M4 derivatives from `Pollable` and call them all from `main()`.

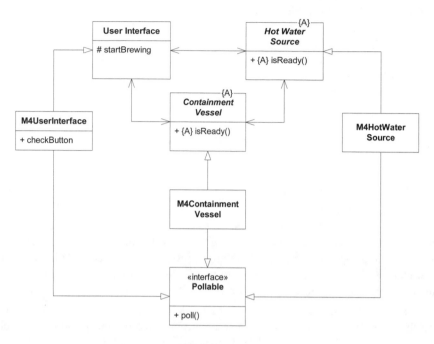

Figure 11–12
Pollable coffee maker.

Listing 11–12 shows what the main function might look like. It is placed in a class called CoffeeMaker. The main() function creates the implemented version of the api, and then creates the three M4 components. It calls init() functions to wire the components up to each other. Finally it hangs in an infinite loop calling poll() on each of the components in turn.

```
Listing 11–12 CoffeeMaker.java
public class CoffeeMaker {
  public static void main(String[] args) {
    CoffeeMakerAPI api = new M4CoffeeMakerAPIImplementation();

    M4UserInterface ui = new M4UserInterface(api);
    M4HotWaterSource hws = new M4HotWaterSource(api);
    M4ContainmentVessel cv = new M4ContainmentVessel(api);

    ui.init(hws,cv);
    hws.init(ui,cv);
    cv.init(ui,hws);

    while(true) {
      ui.poll();
      hws.poll();
      cv.poll();
```

Listing 11–12 (Continued) `CoffeeMaker.java`

```
      }
    }
  }
```

Now it should be clear how the `M4UserInterface.checkButton()` function gets called. Indeed, it should be clear that this function is really not called `checkButton()`. It is called `poll()`. Listing 11–13 shows what `M4UserInterface` looks like now.

Listing 11–13 `M4UserInterface.java`

```
public class M4UserInterface extends UserInterface
                             implements Pollable {
  private CoffeeMakerAPI api;
  private HotWaterSource hws;
  private ContainmentVessel cv;

  public void init(HotWaterSource hws, ContainmentVessel cv) {
    this.hws = hws;
    this.cv = cv;
  }

  public M4UserInterface(CoffeeMakerAPI api) {
    this.api = api;
  }

  private void poll() {
    int buttonStatus = api.getBrewButtonStatus();
    if (buttonStatus == api.BREW_BUTTON_PUSHED) {
      startBrewing();
    }
  }
}
```

Completing the Coffee Maker

The reasoning used in the previous sections can be repeated for each of the other components of the coffee maker. The result is shown in Listings 11–14 through 11–21.

The benefits of this design

Despite the trivial nature of the problem, this design shows some very nice characteristics. Figure 11–13 shows the structure. I have drawn a line around the three abstract classes. These are the classes that hold the high-level policy of the coffee maker. Notice that all dependencies that cross the line point inward. Nothing inside the line depends upon anything outside. Thus, the abstractions are completely separated from the details.

The abstract classes know nothing of buttons, lights, valves, sensors, nor any other of the detailed elements of the coffee maker. By the same token, the derivatives are dominated by those details.

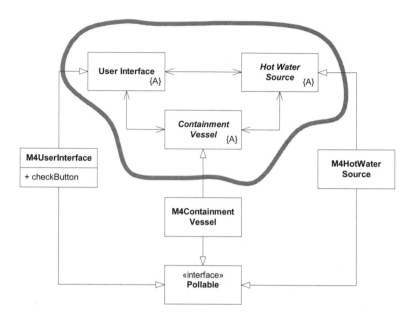

Figure 11–13
Coffee maker components.

Note that the three abstract classes could be reused to make many different kinds of coffee machines. We could easily use them in a coffee machine that is connected to the water mains and uses a tank and spigot. It seems likely that we could also use them for a coffee vending machine. Indeed, I think we could use it in an automatic tea brewer or even a chicken soup maker. This segregation between high-level policy and detail is the essence of object oriented design.

How did I really come up with this design?

I did not just sit down one day and develop this design in a nice straightfoward manner. Indeed, my very first design for the coffee maker looked much more like Figure 11–1. However, I have written about this problem many times, and have used it as an exercise while teaching class after class. So this design has been refined over time.

The code you see below was created, test first, using the unit tests in Listing 11–22. I created the code based upon the structure in Figure 11–13, but put it together incrementally, one failing test case at a time.[4]

---

4. [Beck2002].

I am not convinced that the test cases are complete. If this were more than an example program, I'd do a more exhaustive analysis on the test cases. However, I felt that such an analysis would have been overkill for this book.

Listing 11–14 `UserInterface.java`

```java
public abstract class UserInterface {
  private HotWaterSource hws;
  private ContainmentVessel cv;
  protected boolean isComplete;

  public UserInterface() {
    isComplete = true;
  }

  public void init(HotWaterSource hws, ContainmentVessel cv) {
    this.hws = hws;
    this.cv = cv;
  }

  public void complete() {
    isComplete = true;
    completeCycle();
  }

  protected void startBrewing() {
    if (hws.isReady() && cv.isReady()) {
      isComplete = false;
      hws.start();
      cv.start();
    }
  }

  public abstract void done();
  public abstract void completeCycle();
}
```

Listing 11–15 `M4UserInterface.java`

```java
public class M4UserInterface extends UserInterface
                             implements Pollable {
  private CoffeeMakerAPI api;

  public M4UserInterface(CoffeeMakerAPI api) {
    this.api = api;
  }

  public void poll() {
    int buttonStatus = api.getBrewButtonStatus();
    if (buttonStatus == api.BREW_BUTTON_PUSHED) {
      startBrewing();
    }
  }

  public void done() {
    api.setIndicatorState(api.INDICATOR_ON);
  }
```

Listing 11–15 (Continued) `M4UserInterface.java`

```
public void completeCycle() {
  api.setIndicatorState(api.INDICATOR_OFF);
}
}
```

Listing 11–16 `HotWaterSource.java`

```
public abstract class HotWaterSource {
  private UserInterface ui;
  private ContainmentVessel cv;
  protected boolean isBrewing;

  public HotWaterSource() {
    isBrewing = false;
  }

  public void init(UserInterface ui, ContainmentVessel cv) {
    this.ui = ui;
    this.cv = cv;
  }

  public void start() {
    isBrewing = true;
    startBrewing();
  }

  public void done() {
    isBrewing = false;
  }

  protected void declareDone() {
    ui.done();
    cv.done();
    isBrewing = false;
  }

  public abstract boolean isReady();
  public abstract void startBrewing();
  public abstract void pause();
  public abstract void resume();
}
```

Listing 11–17 `M4HotWaterSource.java`

```
public class M4HotWaterSource extends HotWaterSource
                              implements Pollable {
  private CoffeeMakerAPI api;

  public M4HotWaterSource(CoffeeMakerAPI api) {
    this.api = api;
  }

  public boolean isReady() {
    int boilerStatus = api.getBoilerStatus();
    return boilerStatus == api.BOILER_NOT_EMPTY;
```

Listing 11–17 (Continued) `M4HotWaterSource.java`

```java
  }

  public void startBrewing() {
    api.setReliefValveState(api.VALVE_CLOSED);
    api.setBoilerState(api.BOILER_ON);
  }

  public void poll() {
    int boilerStatus = api.getBoilerStatus();
    if (isBrewing) {
      if (boilerStatus == api.BOILER_EMPTY) {
          api.setBoilerState(api.BOILER_OFF);
          api.setReliefValveState(api.VALVE_CLOSED);
          declareDone();
      }
    }
  }

  public void pause() {
    api.setBoilerState(api.BOILER_OFF);
    api.setReliefValveState(api.VALVE_OPEN);
  }

  public void resume() {
    api.setBoilerState(api.BOILER_ON);
    api.setReliefValveState(api.VALVE_CLOSED);
  }
}
```

Listing 11–18 `ContainmentVessel.java`

```java
public abstract class ContainmentVessel {
  private UserInterface ui;
  private HotWaterSource hws;
  protected boolean isBrewing;
  protected boolean isComplete;

  public ContainmentVessel() {
    isBrewing = false;
    isComplete = true;
  }

  public void init(UserInterface ui, HotWaterSource hws) {
    this.ui = ui;
    this.hws = hws;
  }

  public void start() {
    isBrewing = true;
    isComplete = false;
  }

  public void done() {
    isBrewing = false;
  }
```

Listing 11–18 (Continued) `ContainmentVessel.java`

```java
protected void declareComplete() {
  isComplete = true;
  ui.complete();
}

protected void containerAvailable() {
  hws.resume();
}

protected void containerUnavailable() {
  hws.pause();
}

public abstract boolean isReady();
}
```

Listing 11–19 `M4ContainmentVessel.java`

```java
public class M4ContainmentVessel extends ContainmentVessel
  implements Pollable {
  private CoffeeMakerAPI api;
  private int lastPotStatus;

  public M4ContainmentVessel(CoffeeMakerAPI api) {
    this.api = api;
    lastPotStatus = api.POT_EMPTY;
  }

  public boolean isReady() {
    int plateStatus = api.getWarmerPlateStatus();
    return plateStatus == api.POT_EMPTY;
  }

  public void poll() {
    int potStatus = api.getWarmerPlateStatus();
    if (potStatus != lastPotStatus) {
      if (isBrewing) {
        handleBrewingEvent(potStatus);
      } else if (isComplete == false) {
        handleIncompleteEvent(potStatus);
      }
      lastPotStatus = potStatus;
    }
  }

  private void handleBrewingEvent(int potStatus) {
    if (potStatus == api.POT_NOT_EMPTY) {
      containerAvailable();
      api.setWarmerState(api.WARMER_ON);
    } else if (potStatus == api.WARMER_EMPTY) {
      containerUnavailable();
      api.setWarmerState(api.WARMER_OFF);
    } else { // potStatus == api.POT_EMPTY
      containerAvailable();
      api.setWarmerState(api.WARMER_OFF);
```

Listing 11–19 (Continued) `M4ContainmentVessel.java`

```
      }
    }

    private void handleIncompleteEvent(int potStatus) {
      if (potStatus == api.POT_NOT_EMPTY) {
        api.setWarmerState(api.WARMER_ON);
      } else if (potStatus == api.WARMER_EMPTY) {
        api.setWarmerState(api.WARMER_OFF);
      } else { // potStatus == api.POT_EMPTY
        api.setWarmerState(api.WARMER_OFF);
        declareComplete();
      }
    }
  }
}
```

Listing 11–20 `Pollable.java`

```
public interface Pollable {
  public void poll();
}
```

Listing 11–21 `CoffeeMaker.java`

```
public class CoffeeMaker {
  public static void main(String[] args) {
    CoffeeMakerAPI api = new M4CoffeeMakerAPIImplementation();

    M4UserInterface ui = new M4UserInterface(api);
    M4HotWaterSource hws = new M4HotWaterSource(api);
    M4ContainmentVessel cv = new M4ContainmentVessel(api);

    ui.init(hws,cv);
    hws.init(ui,cv);
    cv.init(ui,hws);

    while(true) {
      ui.poll();
      hws.poll();
      cv.poll();
    }
  }
}
```

Listing 11–22 `TestCoffeeMaker.java`

```
import junit.framework.TestCase;
import junit.swingui.TestRunner;

class CoffeeMakerStub implements CoffeeMakerAPI {
  public boolean buttonPressed;
  public boolean lightOn;
  public boolean boilerOn;
  public boolean valveClosed;
  public boolean plateOn;
  public boolean boilerEmpty;
  public boolean potPresent;
  public boolean potNotEmpty;
```

Listing 11–22 (Continued) `TestCoffeeMaker.java`

```java
  public CoffeeMakerStub() {
    buttonPressed = false;
    lightOn = false;
    boilerOn = false;
    valveClosed = true;
    plateOn = false;
    boilerEmpty = true;
    potPresent = true;
    potNotEmpty = false;
  }

  public int getWarmerPlateStatus() {
    if (!potPresent)
      return WARMER_EMPTY;
    else if (potNotEmpty)
      return POT_NOT_EMPTY;
    else
      return POT_EMPTY;
  }

  public int getBoilerStatus() {
    return boilerEmpty ? BOILER_EMPTY : BOILER_NOT_EMPTY;
  }

  public int getBrewButtonStatus() {
    if (buttonPressed) {
      buttonPressed = false;
      return BREW_BUTTON_PUSHED;
    } else {
      return BREW_BUTTON_NOT_PUSHED;
    }
  }

  public void setBoilerState(int boilerStatus) {
    boilerOn = boilerStatus == BOILER_ON;
  }

  public void setWarmerState(int warmerState) {
    plateOn = warmerState == WARMER_ON;
  }

  public void setIndicatorState(int indicatorState) {
    lightOn = indicatorState == INDICATOR_ON;
  }

  public void setReliefValveState(int reliefValveState) {
    valveClosed = reliefValveState == VALVE_CLOSED;
  }
}

public class TestCoffeeMaker extends TestCase {
  public static void main(String[] args) {
    TestRunner.main(new String[]{"TestCoffeeMaker"});
  }
```

Listing 11–22 (Continued) `TestCoffeeMaker.java`

```java
  public TestCoffeeMaker(String name) {
    super(name);
  }

  private M4UserInterface ui;
  private M4HotWaterSource hws;
  private M4ContainmentVessel cv;
  private CoffeeMakerStub api;

  public void setUp() throws Exception {
    api = new CoffeeMakerStub();
    ui = new M4UserInterface(api);
    hws = new M4HotWaterSource(api);
    cv = new M4ContainmentVessel(api);
    ui.init(hws, cv);
    hws.init(ui, cv);
    cv.init(ui, hws);
  }

  private void poll() {
    ui.poll();
    hws.poll();
    cv.poll();
  }

  public void tearDown() throws Exception {
  }

  public void testInitialConditions() throws Exception {
    poll();
    assert(api.boilerOn == false);
    assert(api.lightOn == false);
    assert(api.plateOn == false);
    assert(api.valveClosed == true);
  }

  public void testStartNoPot() throws Exception {
    poll();
    api.buttonPressed = true;
    api.potPresent = false;
    poll();
    assert(api.boilerOn == false);
    assert(api.lightOn == false);
    assert(api.plateOn == false);
    assert(api.valveClosed == true);
  }

  public void testStartNoWater() throws Exception {
    poll();
    api.buttonPressed = true;
    api.boilerEmpty = true;
    poll();
    assert(api.boilerOn == false);
    assert(api.lightOn == false);
    assert(api.plateOn == false);
    assert(api.valveClosed == true);
```

Listing 11–22 (Continued) `TestCoffeeMaker.java`

```java
  }

  public void testGoodStart() throws Exception {
    normalStart();
    assert(api.boilerOn == true);
    assert(api.lightOn == false);
    assert(api.plateOn == false);
    assert(api.valveClosed == true);
  }

  private void normalStart() {
    poll();
    api.boilerEmpty = false;
    api.buttonPressed = true;
    poll();
  }

  public void testStartedPotNotEmpty() throws Exception {
    normalStart();
    api.potNotEmpty = true;
    poll();
    assert(api.boilerOn == true);
    assert(api.lightOn == false);
    assert(api.plateOn == true);
    assert(api.valveClosed == true);
  }

  public void testPotRemovedAndReplacedWhileEmpty()
  throws Exception {
    normalStart();
    api.potPresent = false;
    poll();
    assert(api.boilerOn == false);
    assert(api.lightOn == false);
    assert(api.plateOn == false);
    assert(api.valveClosed == false);
    api.potPresent = true;
    poll();
    assert(api.boilerOn == true);
    assert(api.lightOn == false);
    assert(api.plateOn == false);
    assert(api.valveClosed == true);
  }

  public void testPotRemovedWhileNotEmptyAndReplacedEmpty()
  throws Exception {
    normalFill();
    api.potPresent = false;
    poll();
    assert(api.boilerOn == false);
    assert(api.lightOn == false);
    assert(api.plateOn == false);
    assert(api.valveClosed == false);
    api.potPresent = true;
    api.potNotEmpty = false;
    poll();
```

Listing 11–22 (Continued) `TestCoffeeMaker.java`

```java
      assert(api.boilerOn == true);
      assert(api.lightOn == false);
      assert(api.plateOn == false);
      assert(api.valveClosed == true);
    }

    private void normalFill() {
      normalStart();
      api.potNotEmpty = true;
      poll();
    }

    public void testPotRemovedWhileNotEmptyAndReplacedNotEmpty()
    throws Exception {
      normalFill();
      api.potPresent = false;
      poll();
      api.potPresent = true;
      poll();
      assert(api.boilerOn == true);
      assert(api.lightOn == false);
      assert(api.plateOn == true);
      assert(api.valveClosed == true);
    }

    public void testBoilerEmptyPotNotEmpty() throws Exception {
      normalBrew();
      assert(api.boilerOn == false);
      assert(api.lightOn == true);
      assert(api.plateOn == true);
      assert(api.valveClosed == true);
    }

    private void normalBrew() {
      normalFill();
      api.boilerEmpty = true;
      poll();
    }

    public void testBoilerEmptiesWhilePotRemoved()
    throws Exception {
      normalFill();
      api.potPresent = false;
      poll();
      api.boilerEmpty = true;
      poll();
      assert(api.boilerOn == false);
      assert(api.lightOn == true);
      assert(api.plateOn == false);
      assert(api.valveClosed == true);
      api.potPresent = true;
      poll();
      assert(api.boilerOn == false);
      assert(api.lightOn == true);
      assert(api.plateOn == true);
      assert(api.valveClosed == true);
```

Listing 11–22 (Continued) `TestCoffeeMaker.java`

```
    }

  public void testEmptyPotReturnedAfter() throws Exception {
    normalBrew();
    api.potNotEmpty = false;
    poll();
    assert(api.boilerOn == false);
    assert(api.lightOn == false);
    assert(api.plateOn == false);
    assert(api.valveClosed == true);
  }
}
```

OOverkill

This example has certain pedagogical advantages. It is small, easy to understand, and shows how the principles of OOD can be used to manage dependencies and separate concerns. On the other hand, its very smallness means that the benefits of that separation probably do not outweigh the costs.

If we were to write the Mark IV coffee maker as a finite state machine, we'd find that it had seven states and 18 transitions.[5] We could encode this into 18 lines of SMC code. A simple main loop that polls the sensors would be another ten lines or so, and the action functions that the FSM would invoke would be another couple of dozen. In short, we could write the whole program in less than a page of code.

If we don't count the tests, the OO solution of the coffee maker is *five* pages of code. There is no way that we can justify this disparity. In larger applications the benefits of dependency management and the separation of concerns clearly outweigh the costs of OOD. However, in this example the reverse is true.

---

5. [Martin1995], p. 65.

Notes

[Martin1995]: Robert C. Martin, *Designing Object Oriented C++ Applications using the Booch Method.* Upper Saddle River, NJ.: Prentice Hall, 1995.

[Beck2002]: Kent Beck, *Test-Driven Development.* Reading, Mass.: Addison-Wesley, 2002.

12

SMC Remote Service: Case Study

Some time ago I decided to write a pair of programs that would allow users to compile SMC[1] input files remotely. On the client side the program would be invoked just like SMC. However, instead of compiling a state map file it would take the file and ship it across the Internet to a central server. This server would compile the state map file into Java or C++ and then ship the resulting files back to the client. Except for the network delay, the remote user would not see much difference between compiling locally and compiling remotely.

The reason I developed the remote compiler was to get some idea of how many people are using SMC, and how often they are using it. Another reason is to make sure that all SMC users are using the most current version of the compiler.

Caveat Emptor

In this chapter I describe these programs using text, UML, and code. I do this to show you how UML and code are related, and the many options for documenting a system using UML. However, you should *not* take this chapter as a recommendation for how systems should be documented. Indeed I am purposely over documenting this software so that I can show you all the various UML diagrams in a well-controlled context.

These programs were designed without the use of any UML at all. They started from very humble beginnings and were refactored through no less than 20 revisions to get to where they are in this book.[2] At no point did I need or want a UML diagram to help me with the design. Nor do I think that the use of UML diagrams would have made the development more efficient or would have resulted in a superior design.

If I were documenting this software for other developers to maintain, I would certainly create some UML diagrams to show them. However, I would not create anywhere near the amount of UML diagrams I am going to show here. Again, what you see here is *severely* over documented in UML.

---

1. See "SMC" on page 121.
2. I am thinking about publishing a book that chronicles that development. It would have one chapter for each revision of the system, showing how it evolved from state to state.

You have been warned.

Unit Tests

Among the best documents for describing a software system are the unit tests for that system. Usually I would show you the unit tests first, before showing you the production code. However, in this case I am trying to expose UML, not the system itself. So I have put the tests at the end of the chapter, instead of giving them the prominence that they deserve. Still, you'll likely find that you'll understand the code much better if you read through those tests, so I strongly recommend looking through them.

The SMCRemote System

Figure 12–1 shows the physical deployment of the system. There are two executable programs, each contained within its own node. The two programs communicate using a socket connection.

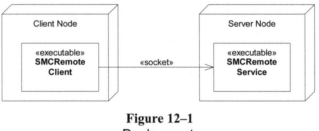

Figure 12–1
Deployment.

SMCRemoteClient

First, let's look at the client side of the program. The next several pages will present text, diagrams, and code that show how the SMCRemoteClient works, and how it is structured.

SMCRemoteClient Command Line

Users invoke the SMCRemoteClient for one of two purposes:

- To register to use the SMCRemote system
- To use the SMCRemote system to compile a .sm file

The difference between the two is specified on the command line. To register to use SMCRemote the user types the following:

```
SMCRemote -r <email-address>
```

The SMCRemote registers the email address, calculates a password, and emails that password back to the email address. From then on, the user will use that email address and password in order to run compiles.

To run a compile the user types the following:

```
SMCRemote -u <email-address> -w <password> <file>
```

This command sends the file to the remote compiler. The remote compiler verifies that the email and password are valid. Then it compiles the file. The compiled file is then sent back to the client and written in the user's directory. Any stdout or stderr messages produced by the compiler are also sent back to the client and will appear on the user's console.

There are other command line options as well:

- -p <port> - specifies the port number of the remote server.
- -h <host> - specifies the hostname of the remote server.
- -g <generator> - for a compile, specifies the code generator to use. <generator> may be either java or C++.
- -v - Verbose output. Prints lots of messages on the console to tell you the progress and what kind of errors the SMCRemoteClient has encountered.

SMCRemote Communication Protocols

The two different functions of the SMCRemoteClient use two different communications protocols. The protocol for registration is shown in Figure 12–2, and the protocol for compilation is shown in Figure 12–3.

Both protocols begin with the client creating a connection to the server. The server responds with a simple identification string that includes the SMCRemoteServer's version number. Then it sends a message of the day, if one exists. The client will print that message on its console.

Registration is simply a matter of sending the email address from the client to the server. In the normal case the server generates a password for the user, creates a user record, and then emails the password to the email address. The server sends a response back to the client telling the user that he'll find his password in an email message.

Compilation is a bit more complex. After the initial connection, the client collects the email and password from the command line and issues a login request to the server. The server validates the email and password and sends a login response back. If the response is

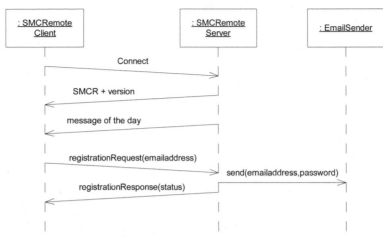

Figure 12–2
Registration protocol.

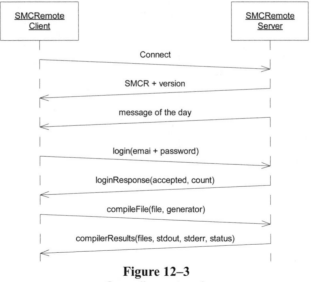

Figure 12–3
Compile protocol.

positive, then the client gathers up the file to compile and sends it to the server. The server runs the compiler, gathers up the output files and the `stdout` and `stderr` streams, and sends them back to the client. The client writes the output files in the user's directory and emits the `stdout` and `stderr` streams on his console.[3]

SMCRemoteClient

The structure of the SMCRemote client program is shown in Figure 12–4. SMCRemote-Client has the main program. It holds a reference to ClientCommandLine and MessageLogger. ClientCommandLine knows how to parse the command line arguments. MessageLogger knows how to format and dispose of the various status messages that come from the different parts of the client program.

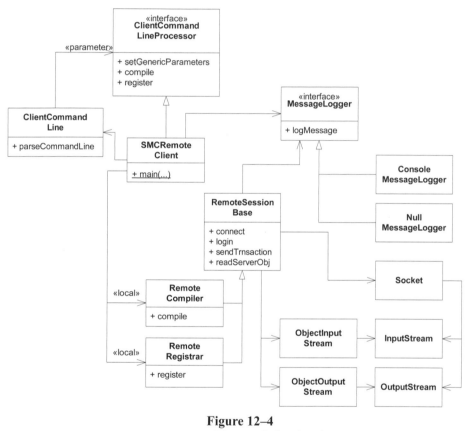

Figure 12–4
SMCRemoteClient static structure.

---

3. Readers experienced with distributed systems should be shaking their heads in frustration. By creating a separate transaction for login, I have violated the old maxim, "Round trips are the enemy." It would be much more efficient to piggyback the login protocol on top of the compile protocol. The compileFile message could carry the email and password, and the compileResults message could carry back a login failure response. I didn't do this for two reasons. First, none of my trials indicated that the round trip time was significant. Second, this program was written for teaching purposes, and I wanted a two-stage protocol in the example.

Figure 12–5 shows what happens when the client boots up. First it constructs an instance of the SMCRemoteClient and passes the command line arguments to it. The SMCRemoteClient constructor creates the ClientCommandLine object and directs it to parse the arguments. It then asks the ClientCommandLine to set the generic parameters like host, port, and verbose. The ClientCommandLine calls back to the SMC-RemoteClient instance through the ClientCommandLineProcessor interface. Next the SMCRemoteClient creates the appropriate derivative of the MessageLogger, depending upon the state of the verbose flag. Finally, the SMCRemoteClient constructor returns, and main calls run upon the newly created SMCRemoteClient object.

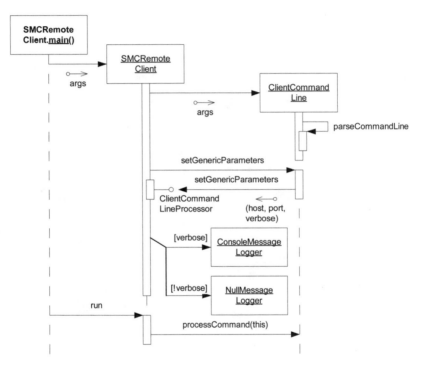

Figure 12–5
SMCRemoteClient.main().

The run method of SMCRemoteClient checks the validity of the command line. If the command line is malformed, it prints a usage message and exits. Otherwise it sends the processCommand message to the ClientCommandLine object. The ClientCommand-Line responds by inspecting the command line arguments in order to determine whether they represent a registration or a compilation. Then, as shown in Figure 12–6 and Figure 12–7, the ClientCommandLine sends a message back to the SMCRemoteClient through the `ClientCommandLineProcessor` interface. The message it sends is either `register` or `compile`.

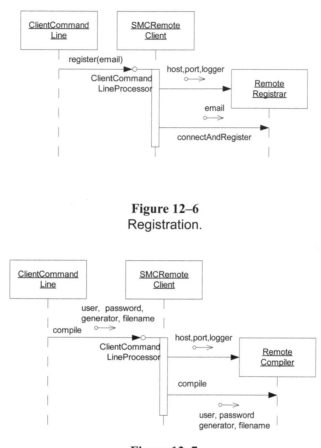

Figure 12–6
Registration.

Figure 12–7
Compilation.

The code for `SMCRemoteClient`, `ClientCommandLine`, and `ClientCommand-LineProcessor` is in Listings 12–1, 12–2, and 12–3, respectively. You should be able to match the interaction diagram in Figure 12–5 to the code in those listings.

Listing 12–1   `SMCRemoteClient.java`

```
package com.objectmentor.SMCRemote.client;

public class SMCRemoteClient implements ClientCommandLineProcessor {
  public static final String VERSION = "$Id$";
```

Listing 12–1 (Continued) `SMCRemoteClient.java`

```java
private ClientCommandLine commandLine;
private String itsHost;
private int itsPort;
private boolean isVerbose = false;
private MessageLogger itsLogger;

public static void main(String[] args) {
  SMCRemoteClient client = new SMCRemoteClient(args);
  client.run();
}

public SMCRemoteClient(String[] args) {
  commandLine = new ClientCommandLine(args);
  commandLine.setGenericParameters(this);
  if (isVerbose)
    itsLogger = new ConsoleMessageLogger();
  else
    itsLogger = new NullMessageLogger();
}

private void run() {
  if (commandLine.isValid()) {
    logHeader();
    commandLine.processCommand(this);
  } else {
    System.out.println("usage: ");
    System.out.println(
      "  to compile: java SMCRemoteClient -u <emailaddress> -w <password> <filename>");
    System.out.println("  to register: java SMCRemoteClient -r <emailaddress>");
    System.out.println("options: -h <hostname>   override default hostname.");
    System.out.println("         -p <port>       override default port");
    System.out.println("         -v              verbose console output");
  }
}

public void setGenericParameters(String host, int port, boolean verbose) {
  itsHost = host;
  itsPort = port;
  isVerbose = verbose;
}

public void compile(String username, String password,
                    String generator, String filename) {
  RemoteCompiler compiler = new RemoteCompiler(itsHost, itsPort, itsLogger);
  compiler.compile(username, password, generator, filename);
}

public void register(String registrant) {
  RemoteRegistrar registrar = new RemoteRegistrar(itsHost, itsPort, itsLogger);
  registrar.connectAndRegister(registrant);
}

private void logHeader() {
  logMessage("SMCRemoteClient-----------------------------------");
  logMessage(VERSION);
```

Listing 12–1 (Continued) `SMCRemoteClient.java`

```
    logMessage("host =      " + itsHost);
    logMessage("port =      " + itsPort);
    logMessage("--------------------------------------------------");
  }

  private void logMessage(String msg) {
    itsLogger.logMessage(msg);
  }
}
```

Listing 12–2 `ClientCommandLine.java`

```
package com.objectmentor.SMCRemote.client;

import com.neoworks.util.Getopts;

public class ClientCommandLine {
  public static final String DEFAULT_HOST = "localhost";
  public static final String DEFAULT_PORT = "9000";
  public static final String DEFAULT_GENERATOR = "java";

  private String itsFilename = null;
  private String itsHost = DEFAULT_HOST;
  private int itsPort = Integer.parseInt(DEFAULT_PORT);
  private String itsGenerator = DEFAULT_GENERATOR;
  private boolean isVerbose = false;
  private String itsRegistrant;
  private String itsUsername;
  private String itsPassword;
  private boolean isValid = false;
  private Getopts opts;

  public ClientCommandLine(String[] args) {
    isValid = parseCommandLine(args);
  }

  public boolean isValid() {
    return isValid;
  }

  public boolean parseCommandLine(String[] args) {
    opts = new Getopts("r:h:p:g:u:w:v", args);
    if (opts.error()) return false;

    try {
      itsFilename = opts.argv(0);
      itsHost = opts.option('h', DEFAULT_HOST);
      itsPort = Integer.parseInt(opts.option('p', DEFAULT_PORT));
      itsGenerator = opts.option('g', DEFAULT_GENERATOR);
      itsRegistrant = opts.option('r', null);
      itsUsername = opts.option('u', null);
      itsPassword = opts.option('w', null);
      isVerbose = opts.hasOption('v');
    } catch (NumberFormatException e) {
      return false;
    }
```

Listing 12–2 (Continued) `ClientCommandLine.java`

```java
    return isCompileCommand() || isRegistrationCommand();
  }

  public void setGenericParameters(ClientCommandLineProcessor processor) {
    processor.setGenericParameters(itsHost, itsPort, isVerbose);
  }

  public void processCommand(ClientCommandLineProcessor processor) {
    if (isCompileCommand()) {
      processor.compile(itsUsername, itsPassword, itsGenerator, itsFilename);
    } else if (isRegistrationCommand()) {
      processor.register(itsRegistrant);
    }
  }

  private boolean hasFileName() {
    return opts.argc() == 1;
  }

  private boolean isCompileCommand() {
    return opts.hasOption('u') &&
      opts.hasOption('w') &&
      !opts.hasOption('r') &&
      hasFileName();
  }

  private boolean isRegistrationCommand() {
    return opts.hasOption('r') &&
      (itsRegistrant != null) &&
      !opts.hasOption('u') &&
      !opts.hasOption('w') &&
      !opts.hasOption('g') &&
      !hasFileName();
  }

  public boolean isVerbose() {
    return isVerbose;
  }

  public String getHost() {
    return itsHost;
  }

  public String getFilename() {
    return itsFilename;
  }

  public int getPort() {
    return itsPort;
  }

  public String getGenerator() {
    return itsGenerator;
  }
```

Listing 12–2 (Continued) `ClientCommandLine.java`

```java
  public String getUsername() {
    return itsUsername;
  }

  public String getPassword() {
    return itsPassword;
  }
}
```

Listing 12–3 `ClientCommandLineProcessor.java`

```java
package com.objectmentor.SMCRemote.client;

public interface ClientCommandLineProcessor {
  public void setGenericParameters(String host, int port, boolean verbose);
  public void compile(String username, String password, String generator, String filename);
  public void register(String registrant);
}
```

The Loggers

You can see the implementation of the logger files in Listings 12–4 through 12–6. The `MessageLogger` interface allows the `SMCRemoteClient` and all its minions to log messages. `NullMessageLogger` simply ignores those messages, whereas `Console-MessageLogger` prints the messages on standard out, along with time and date information.

Listing 12–4 `MessageLogger.java`

```java
package com.objectmentor.SMCRemote.client;

public interface MessageLogger {
  public void logMessage(String msg);
}
```

Listing 12–5 `NullMessageLogger.java`

```java
package com.objectmentor.SMCRemote.client;

public class NullMessageLogger implements MessageLogger {
  public void logMessage(String msg) {
  }
}
```

Listing 12–6 `ConsoleMessageLogger.java`

```java
package com.objectmentor.SMCRemote.client;

import java.text.SimpleDateFormat;
import java.util.Date;

public class ConsoleMessageLogger implements MessageLogger {
  public void logMessage(String msg) {
    Date logTime = new Date();
    SimpleDateFormat fmt = new SimpleDateFormat("yyyy.MM.dd hh:mm:ss");
```

Listing 12–6 (Continued) `ConsoleMessageLogger.java`

```
    String logTimeString = fmt.format(logTime);
    System.out.println(logTimeString + " | " + msg);
  }
}
```

The Remote Sessions

Figure 12–8 shows more of the static structure of the `RemoteRegistrar` and `Remote-Compiler`. Both derive from the base class `RemoteSessionBase`, which supplies them with some common utilities. These classes use the DATA TRANSFER OBJECT[4] pattern in order to communicate with the server. The `LoginTransaction`, `LoginResponse-Transaction`, `RegistrationTransaction`, `RegistrationResponseTransac-tion`, `CompileFileTransaction`, and `CompilerResultsTransaction` are the data transfer objects used by the remote sessions. These objects are data packets that are sent back and forth between the client and server. Indeed, you can see that these names are very similar to those used to name the messages in the protocol sequence diagrams in Figures 12–2 and 12–3.

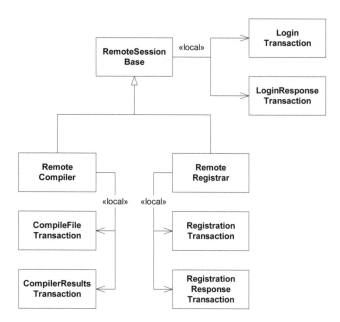

Figure 12–8
Remote sessions.

---

4. [Fowler2002], p. 401.

RemoteSessionBase

The code for the `RemoteSessionBase` and the two login transactions is shown in Listings 12–7 through 12–9. `RemoteSessionBase` contains a set of utility functions that `RemoteRegistrar` and `RemoteCompiler` both use. It also contains the functions that perform the login protocol used by the `RemoteCompiler`.

Listing 12–7 `RemoteSessionBase.java`

```java
package com.objectmentor.SMCRemote.client;

import com.objectmentor.SMCRemote.transactions.*;

import java.io.*;
import java.net.Socket;

public class RemoteSessionBase {
  private String itsHost;
  private int itsPort;
  private MessageLogger itsLogger;
  private Socket smcrSocket;
  private ObjectInputStream is;
  private ObjectOutputStream os;

  public RemoteSessionBase(String itsHost, int itsPort, MessageLogger logger) {
    this.itsHost = itsHost;
    this.itsPort = itsPort;
    this.itsLogger = logger;
  }

  public String getHost() {
    return itsHost;
  }

  public int getPort() {
    return itsPort;
  }

  protected void logMessage(String msg) {
    itsLogger.logMessage(msg);
  }

  protected boolean connect() {
    logMessage("Trying to connect to: " + getHost() + ":" + getPort() + "...");
    boolean connectionStatus = false;
    try {
      smcrSocket = new Socket(getHost(), getPort());
      is = new ObjectInputStream(smcrSocket.getInputStream());
      os = new ObjectOutputStream(smcrSocket.getOutputStream());
      String headerLine = (String) readServerObject();
      connectionStatus = headerLine != null && headerLine.startsWith("SMCR");
      String message = (String) readServerObject();
      if (message != null) {
        System.out.println(message);
      }
```

Listing 12–7 (Continued) `RemoteSessionBase.java`

```
      if (connectionStatus)
        logMessage("Connection acknowledged: " + headerLine);
      else
        logMessage("Bad Acknowledgement: " + headerLine);
    } catch (Exception e) {
      connectionStatus = false;
      logMessage("Connection failed: " + e.getMessage());
    }
    return connectionStatus;
  }

  public void close() {
    if (is != null || os != null || smcrSocket != null) {
      logMessage("Closing Connection.");
      try {
        if (is != null) is.close();
        if (os != null) os.close();
        if (smcrSocket != null) smcrSocket.close();
      } catch (IOException e) {
        logMessage("Couldn't close : " + e.getMessage());
      }
    }
  }

  protected boolean login(String username, String password) {
    try {
      LoginTransaction lt = new LoginTransaction(username, password);
      sendTransaction(lt);
      LoginResponseTransaction lrt = (LoginResponseTransaction) readServerObject();
      if (lrt.isAccepted()) {
        logMessage("login (" + lrt.getLoginCount() + ") accepted.");
        return true;
      } else {
        logMessage("Login Rejected");
        return false;
      }
    } catch (Exception e) {
      logMessage("login failed: " + e);
      return false;
    }
  }

  protected boolean sendTransaction(SocketTransaction t) {
    boolean sent = false;
    try {
      os.writeObject(t);
      os.flush();
      sent = true;
    } catch (IOException e) {
      sent = false;
    }
    return sent;
  }
```

Listing 12–7 (Continued) `RemoteSessionBase.java`

```
protected Object readServerObject() throws Exception {
    return is.readObject();
}
}
```

Listing 12–8 `LoginTransaction.java`

```
package com.objectmentor.SMCRemote.transactions;

public class LoginTransaction implements SocketTransaction {
    private String itsUserName;
    private String itsPassword;

    public LoginTransaction(String itsUserName, String itsPassword) {
        this.itsUserName = itsUserName;
        this.itsPassword = itsPassword;
    }

    public String getUserName() {
        return itsUserName;
    }

    public String getPassword() {
        return itsPassword;
    }

    public void accept(SocketTransactionProcessor processor) throws Exception {
        processor.process(this);
    }
}
```

Listing 12–9 `LoginResponseTransaction.java`

```
package com.objectmentor.SMCRemote.transactions;

public class LoginResponseTransaction implements SocketTransaction {
    private boolean isAccepted;
    private int loginCount;

    public LoginResponseTransaction(boolean accepted, int loginCount) {
        this.loginCount = loginCount;
        this.isAccepted = accepted;
    }

    public boolean isAccepted() {
        return isAccepted;
    }

    public int getLoginCount() {
        return loginCount;
    }

    public void accept(SocketTransactionProcessor processor) throws Exception {
        processor.process(this);
    }
}
```

The first three lines of the `RemoteSesionBase.login()` function are particularly illustrative:

```
LoginTransaction lt = new LoginTransaction(username, password);
sendTransaction(lt);
LoginResponseTransaction lrt =
  (LoginResponseTransaction) readServerObject();
```

These lines show how all the communication across the sockets is achieved. As you can see from Listing 12–10, all the transactions are serializable, so it is absurdly simple to write them to, and read them from, a socket.

Listing 12–10 shows one other thing. There is the hint of a VISITOR[5] pattern lurking in the `SocketTransaction` class. We won't see why until we study the `SMCRemote-Server` later on in this chapter.

Listing 12–10 `SocketTransaction.java`

```
package com.objectmentor.SMCRemote.transactions;

import java.io.Serializable;

public interface SocketTransaction extends Serializable {
  public void accept(SocketTransactionProcessor processor) throws Exception;
}
```

RemoteRegistrar

The `RemoteRegistar` and the two registration transactions are shown in Listings 12–11 through 12–13. The process is very simple. It simply connects to the server and sends the `RegistrationTransaction`. Then it receives the `RegistrationResponseTrans-action` and makes sure that it was accepted by the server.

Listing 12–11 `RemoteRegistrar.java`

```
package com.objectmentor.SMCRemote.client;

import com.objectmentor.SMCRemote.transactions.*;

public class RemoteRegistrar extends RemoteSessionBase {

  public RemoteRegistrar(String itsHost, int itsPort, MessageLogger logger) {
    super(itsHost, itsPort, logger);
  }

  public void connectAndRegister(String registrant) {
    if (connect()) {
      RegistrationResponseTransaction rrt;
      if ((rrt = register(registrant)) != null) {
        if (rrt.isConfirmed()) {
          logMessage(registrant + " was registered");
```

---

5. [Gamma1995], p. 331.

Listing 12–11 (Continued) `RemoteRegistrar.java`

```
          System.out.println("User: " + registrant + " registered.  Email sent.");
        } else {
          logMessage(registrant + " was NOT registered: " + rrt.getFailureReason());
          System.out.println(
            registrant + " was NOT registered: " + rrt.getFailureReason());
        }
      } else { // rrt == null
        System.out.println("Something bad happened.  Sorry.");
      }
      close();
    } else {  // conect
      System.out.println("failed to connect to " + getHost() + ":" + getPort());
    }
  }

  RegistrationResponseTransaction register(String registrant) {
    logMessage("Attempting to register " + registrant);
    RegistrationTransaction t = new RegistrationTransaction(registrant);
    sendTransaction(t);
    RegistrationResponseTransaction rrt = null;
    try {
      rrt = (RegistrationResponseTransaction) readServerObject();
    } catch (Exception e) {
      logMessage("Could not send registration response: " + e.getMessage());
      return null;
    }
    return rrt;
  }
}
```

Listing 12–12 `RegistrationTransaction.java`

```
package com.objectmentor.SMCRemote.transactions;

public class RegistrationTransaction implements SocketTransaction {
  private String username;

  public String getUsername() {
    return username;
  }

  public RegistrationTransaction(String username) {
    this.username = username;
  }

  public void accept(SocketTransactionProcessor processor) throws Exception {
    processor.process(this);
  }
}
```

Listing 12–13 `RegistrationResponseTransaction.java`

```
package com.objectmentor.SMCRemote.transactions;

public class RegistrationResponseTransaction implements SocketTransaction {
  private boolean confirmed;
  private String failureReason;
```

Listing 12–13 (Continued) `RegistrationResponseTransaction.java`

```
public RegistrationResponseTransaction(boolean confirmed) {
  this.confirmed = confirmed;
}

public String getFailureReason() {
  return failureReason;
}

public void setFailureReason(String failureReason) {
  this.failureReason = failureReason;
}

public boolean isConfirmed() {
  return confirmed;
}

public void accept(SocketTransactionProcessor processor) throws Exception {
  processor.process(this);
}
}
```

RemoteCompiler

The `RemoteCompiler` is a bit more complicated than the `RemoteRegistrar`, though the idea is the same. Figure 12–9 is a rough model of the sequence. The diagram does not completely conform to the code, but it's pretty close. Making it conform completely to the code would have made the diagram more cluttered than it should have been. By the same token, making the code correspond to the diagram would have made the code more cluttered than it should have been. This kind of mismatch between the code and diagram is not uncommon. The clarity of each is satisfied in different ways.

In the code (Listing 12–14), compilation begins when the `ClientCommandLine` instance calls the `compile()` method of `SMCRemoteCompiler`, which in turn creates the `RemoteCompiler` and calls its `compile()` method.

The `compile()` method of `RemoteCompiler` logs a header message and then calls `connectAndRequestCompile()`. This method makes sure that the file to be compiled exists, connects to the server, and then invokes the `login()` method. The `login()` method executes the login protocol. If the login succeeds, the `compileFile()` method is invoked. This method builds the `CompileFileTransaction` (Listing 12–15) object and sends it to the server. It then reads the `CompilerResultsTransaction` (Listing 12–16) from the server and writes any files it contains onto the local filesystem.

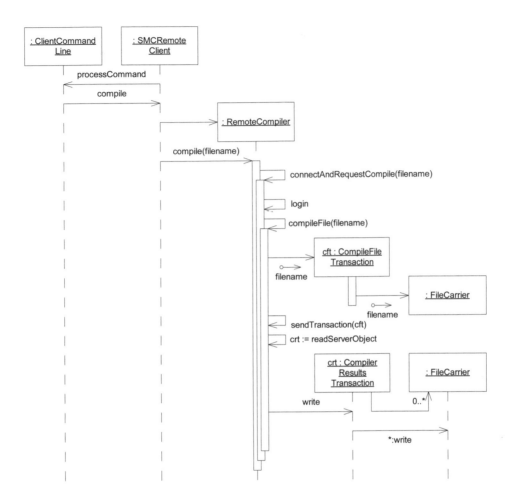

Figure 12–9
Compile process.

Listing 12–14 RemoteCompiler.java

```
package com.objectmentor.SMCRemote.client;

import com.objectmentor.SMCRemote.transactions.*;

import java.io.*;
import java.util.Vector;

public class RemoteCompiler extends RemoteSessionBase {

  private String itsFilename = null;
  private String itsGenerator = ClientCommandLine.DEFAULT_GENERATOR;
  private String itsRegistrant;
```

Listing 12–14 (Continued) `RemoteCompiler.java`

```java
public RemoteCompiler(String itsHost, int itsPort, MessageLogger itsLogger) {
  super(itsHost, itsPort, itsLogger);
}

public void compile(String username, String password,
                    String generator, String filename) {
  itsFilename = filename;
  itsGenerator = generator;
  logCompileHeader();
  connectAndRequestCompile(username, password);
}

private void connectAndRequestCompile(String username, String password) {
  if (prepareFile()) {
    if (connect()) {
      if (login(username, password)) {
        if (compile() == false) {
          System.out.println("Internal error, something awful.  Sorry.");
        }
      } else { // login
        System.out.println("failed to log in.");
      }
      close();
    } else { // connect
      System.out.println("failed to connect to " + getHost() + ":" + getPort());
    }
  } else { // prepareFile
    System.out.println("could not open: " + itsFilename);
  } // prepareFile
}

private boolean compile() {
  CompilerResultsTransaction crt = compileFile();
  if (crt == null)
    return false;
  writeCompilerOutputLines(crt);
  return true;
}

public void setFilename(String itsFilename) {
  this.itsFilename = itsFilename;
}

public boolean prepareFile() {
  File f = new File(itsFilename);
  return f.exists();
}

public CompilerResultsTransaction compileFile() {
  CompilerResultsTransaction crt = null;
  logMessage("Sending file and requesting compilation.");
  try {
    CompileFileTransaction t = new CompileFileTransaction(itsFilename, itsGenerator);
    if (sendTransaction(t) == true) {
      crt = (CompilerResultsTransaction) readServerObject();
```

Listing 12–14 (Continued) `RemoteCompiler.java`

```java
        logCompilerResultsMessage(crt);
        crt.write();
      }
    } catch (Exception e) {
      logMessage("Compilation process failed: " + e.getMessage());
    }

    return crt;
  }

  private static void writeCompilerOutputLines(CompilerResultsTransaction crt) {
    Vector stdout = crt.getStdoutLines();
    writeLineVector(System.out, crt.getStdoutLines());
    writeLineVector(System.err, crt.getStderrLines());
  }

  private static void writeLineVector(PrintStream ps, Vector stdout) {
    for (int i = 0; i < stdout.size(); i++) {
      String s = (String) stdout.elementAt(i);
      ps.println(s);
    }
  }

  private void logCompileHeader() {
    logMessage("Compiling...");
    logMessage("file =      " + itsFilename);
    logMessage("generator = " + itsGenerator);
  }

  private void logCompilerResultsMessage(CompilerResultsTransaction crt) {
    logMessage("Compilation results received.");
    String filenames[] = crt.getFilenames();
    for (int i = 0; i < filenames.length; i++) {
      String s = (String) filenames[i];
      logMessage("..file: " + s + " received.");
    }
  }
}
```

Listing 12–15 `CompileFileTransaction.java`

```java
package com.objectmentor.SMCRemote.transactions;

import com.objectmentor.SocketUtilities.FileCarrier;

import java.io.File;

public class CompileFileTransaction implements SocketTransaction {
  private FileCarrier itsCarrier;
  private String itsGenerator;

  public CompileFileTransaction(String filename, String generator) {
    itsCarrier = new FileCarrier(null, filename);
    itsGenerator = generator;
  }
```

Listing 12–15 (Continued) `CompileFileTransaction.java`

```java
  public String getFilename() {
    return itsCarrier.getFilename();
  }

  public String getGenerator() {
    return itsGenerator;
  }

  public void write(File subDirectory) {
    itsCarrier.write(subDirectory);
  }

  public void accept(SocketTransactionProcessor processor) throws Exception {
    processor.process(this);
  }
}
```

Listing 12–16 `CompilerResultsTransaction.java`

```java
package com.objectmentor.SMCRemote.transactions;

import com.objectmentor.SocketUtilities.FileCarrier;

import java.io.File;
import java.util.Vector;

public class CompilerResultsTransaction implements SocketTransaction {
  public static final int OK = 0;
  public static final int NOT_LOGGED_IN = 1;

  private FileCarrier[] files;
  private String[] filenames;
  private Vector stdout;
  private Vector stderr;
  private int status;

  public int getStatus() {
    return status;
  }

  public void setStatus(int status) {
    this.status = status;
  }

  public Vector getStdoutLines() {
    return stdout;
  }

  public Vector getStderrLines() {
    return stderr;
  }

  public String[] getFilenames() {
    return filenames;
  }
```

Listing 12–16 (Continued) `CompilerResultsTransaction.java`

```java
  public CompilerResultsTransaction() {
    stdout = new Vector();
    stderr = new Vector();
  }

  public void loadFiles(File subDirectory, String[] filenames) {
    this.filenames = filenames;
    files = new FileCarrier[filenames.length];
    for (int fileIndex = 0; fileIndex < filenames.length; fileIndex++) {
      files[fileIndex] = new FileCarrier(subDirectory, filenames[fileIndex]);
    }
  }

  public void write() {
    for (int fileIndex = 0; fileIndex < files.length; fileIndex++) {
      FileCarrier carrier = files[fileIndex];
      carrier.write();
    }
  }

  public void accept(SocketTransactionProcessor processor) throws Exception {
    processor.process(this);
  }
}
```

FileCarrier

Both the `CompileFileTransaction` and the `CompilerResultsTransaction` need to carry text files across the client/server boundary. They do this by using a helper class called `FileCarrier`. `FileCarrier` holds the name of the file being carried and a list of strings that correspond to the lines of text in the file. It contains methods for loading the `FileCarrier` from a file and for creating a new file from the `FileCarrier`.

Listing 12–17 `FileCarrier.java`

```java
package com.objectmentor.SocketUtilities;

import java.io.*;
import java.util.*;

public class FileCarrier implements Serializable {
  private String itsFilename;
  private LinkedList itsLines = new LinkedList();
  private boolean loaded = false;
  private boolean error = false;

  public FileCarrier(File subDirectory, String filename) {
    File inputFile = new File(subDirectory, filename);
    itsFilename = new String(filename);
    BufferedReader br = null;
    try {
      br = new BufferedReader(new InputStreamReader(new FileInputStream(inputFile)));
      String line;
      while ((line = br.readLine()) != null) {
```

Listing 12–17 (Continued) `FileCarrier.java`

```
          itsLines.add(line);
      }
      br.close();
      loaded = true;
    } catch (Exception e) {
      error = true;
    }
  }

  public void write() {
    write(null);
  }

  public void write(File subDirectory) {
    File f = new File(subDirectory, itsFilename);
    if (f.exists()) f.delete();
    try {
      PrintStream w = new PrintStream(new FileOutputStream(f));
      for (Iterator i = itsLines.iterator(); i.hasNext();) {
        String line = (String) i.next();
        w.println(line);
      }
      w.close();
    } catch (IOException e) {
      error = true;
    }
  }

  public boolean isLoaded() {
    return loaded;
  }

  public boolean isError() {
    return error;
  }

  public String getFilename() {
    return itsFilename;
  }
}
```

SMCRemoteClient Conclusion

That's pretty much all there is to say about the SMCRemoteClient. It's a pretty simple process. It reads its command line arguments, figures out whether to perform a registration or a compilation, builds the appropriate transactions and sends them to the server, and reads the response transactions back. Not rocket science.

SMCRemoteServer

The server is a bit more complex than the client. It must run continuously, accepting connections and responding to them. It must also be able to deal with many concurrent transactions. It must maintain a database of registrations, and must know how to invoke, control, and capture the output of the SMC compiler.

The story of the server begins with a bit of framework that I, and my son Micah, put together some months back.

SocketService

While we were working on a Ruby Web server named ROPE, Micah and I wrote a simple Ruby framework to accept incoming socket requests. It worked very nicely and was so generic that I later translated it into a simple Java framework for socket servers.[6] This framework creates the server socket, waits for connections on that socket, and spawns a new thread for each incoming connection. Figure 12–10 shows its structure.

Figure 12–10
SocketService.

The idea is pretty simple. If you want to write a program that serves incoming socket connections, you derive your program from `SocketServer`. Then you create an instance of the `SocketService` and pass your derivative into the constructor, along with the number of the port where you want your server to listen. From then on, whenever a connection comes into that port, a new thread will be created and the `serve` method of your derivative will be invoked in that new thread.

For example, `HelloService` in Listing 12–18 is a simple socket service that responds to an incoming connection by sending "Hello" and then closing the connection. The program in Listing 12–19 tests that `HelloService` does what it is supposed to.

Listing 12–18   Socket Service That Says "Hello".
```
class HelloService implements SocketServer {
  public void serve(Socket s) {
    try {
```

---

6. Yes, this is the same framework that I've been using for fodder in my "Craftsman" column in *Software Development* magazine.

Listing 12–18 (Continued)   Socket Service That Says "Hello".

```
        OutputStream os = s.getOutputStream();
        PrintStream ps = new PrintStream(os);
        ps.println("Hello");
    } catch (IOException e) {
    }
  }
}
```

Listing 12–19 A client that tests `HelloService`.

```
public void testSendMessage() throws Exception {
    ss = new SocketService(999, new HelloService());
    Socket s = new Socket("localhost", 999);
    BufferedReader br = TestUtility.GetBufferedReader(s);
    String answer = br.readLine();
    s.close();
    ss.close();
    assertEquals("Hello", answer);
  }
```

The complete implementation of the `SocketService` framework is shown in Listings 12–20 through 12–21. The gist of its operation is shown in Figure 12–11. The `SocketService` begins its life by spawning the `serviceThread` and then returning. The `serviceThread` hangs in a loop calling `accept` on the `serverSocket`. The call to `accept` returns with a new socket each time there is an incoming connection. The `serviceThread` then spawns a new `serverThread` and loops back to call `accept` on the `ServerSocket` again. The `serverThread` calls `serve` on the `SocketServer` derivative supplied by the user.

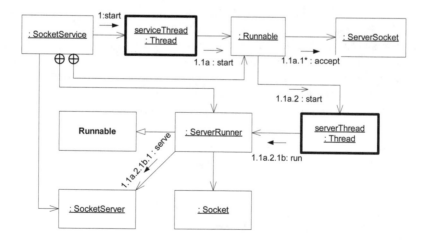

Figure 12–11
`SocketService` object diagram.

As an aside, the diagram in Figure 12–11 shows how rapidly message sequence numbers can become unworkable in UML collaboration diagrams. This particular sequence of messages is much better shown as a collaboration diagram than as a sequence diagram, since exposing the topology of the relationships is more important than exposing the sequence of events. Unfortunately, even mildly complex scenarios lead to sequence numbers that look more like organic chemistry than software.

Listing 12–20 `SocketServer.java`

```
package com.objectmentor.SocketService;

import java.net.Socket;

public interface SocketServer
{
  public void serve(Socket s);
}
```

Listing 12–21 `SocketService.java`

```
package com.objectmentor.SocketService;

import java.io.IOException;
import java.net.*;
import java.util.LinkedList;

public class SocketService {
  private ServerSocket serverSocket = null;
  private Thread serviceThread = null;
  private boolean running = false;
  private SocketServer itsService = null;
  private LinkedList threads = new LinkedList();

  public SocketService(int port, SocketServer service)
  throws Exception {
    itsService = service;
    serverSocket = new ServerSocket(port);
    serviceThread = new Thread(
      new Runnable() {
        public void run() {
          serviceThread();
        }
      }
    );
    serviceThread.start();
  }

  public void close() throws Exception {
    waitForServiceThreadToStart();
    running = false;
    serverSocket.close();
    serviceThread.join();
    waitForServerThreads();
  }

  private void waitForServiceThreadToStart() {
```

Listing 12–21 (Continued) `SocketService.java`

```java
      while (running == false) Thread.yield();
  }

  private void serviceThread() {
    running = true;
    while (running) {
      try {
        Socket s = serverSocket.accept();
        startServerThread(s);
      } catch (IOException e) {
      }
    }
  }

  private void startServerThread(Socket s) {
    Thread serverThread = new Thread(new ServerRunner(s));
    synchronized (threads) {
      threads.add(serverThread);
    }
    serverThread.start();
  }

  private void waitForServerThreads()
  throws InterruptedException {
    while (threads.size() > 0) {
      Thread t;
      synchronized (threads) {
        t = (Thread) threads.getFirst();
      }
      t.join();
    }
  }

  private class ServerRunner implements Runnable {
    private Socket itsSocket;

    ServerRunner(Socket s) {
      itsSocket = s;
    }

    public void run() {
      try {
        itsService.serve(itsSocket);
        synchronized (threads) {
          threads.remove(Thread.currentThread());
        }
        itsSocket.close();
      } catch (IOException e) {
      }
    }
  }
}
```

SMCRemoteService

Clearly we can build upon the SocketService framework to create the SMCRemote-Service program. The diagram in Figure 12–12 shows the structure. SMCRemote-Service has a SocketService instance that it initializes with an anonymous inner class that implements the SocketServer interface. This class delegates to SMCRemote-Server, which handles the protocols for each connection.

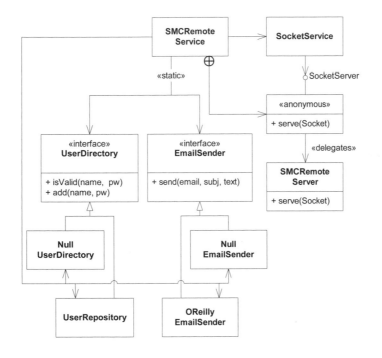

Figure 12–12
High-level structure of SMCRemoteService.

SMCRemoteService also holds a reference to a UserDirectory and an Email-Sender. These two classes have two derivatives each; one is a NULLOBJECT[7] and the other provides a functional implementation. The functional implementation of User-Directory is named UserRepository. This class manages the user database. It allows users to be added to the database. It also provides methods for checking the password of a user. The functional implementation of EmailSender is OReillyEmailSender. This class makes use of a third-party SMTP agent to send email.

---

7. See the NULLOBJECT pattern in [Martin2002], p. 189.

The listings for SMCRemoteService and the two interfaces are shown in Listings 12–22 through 12–24. For the most part, SMCRemoteService contains a set of utilities that SMCRemoteServer uses.

Listing 12–22 SMCRemoteService.java

```java
package com.objectmentor.SMCRemote.server;

import com.objectmentor.SocketService.*;

import com.neoworks.util.Getopts;

import java.io.*;
import java.text.SimpleDateFormat;
import java.util.*;
import java.net.Socket;

class NullUserDirectory implements UserDirectory {
  public boolean isValid(String username, String password) {
    return true;
  }

  public String getPassword(String username) {
    return null;
  }

  public int incrementLoginCount(String username) {
    return 0;
  }

  public boolean add(String username, String password) {
    return true;
  }
}

class NullEmailSender implements EmailSender {
  public boolean send(String emailAddress, String subject, String text) {
    return true;
  }
}

public class SMCRemoteService {
  public static final String DEFAULT_PORT = "9000";
  public static final String VERSION = "0.99";
  public static final String COMPILE_COMMAND = "java -cp c:\\SMC\\smc.jar smc.Smc -f";

  static boolean isVerbose = false;
  static boolean isEmailQuiet = false;
  static int servicePort;
  static String messageFile;

  private static UserDirectory userDirectory = new NullUserDirectory();
  private static EmailSender emailSender = new NullEmailSender();
  private SocketService service;

  SocketServer server = new SocketServer() {
    public void serve(Socket socket) {
```

Listing 12–22 (Continued) `SMCRemoteService.java`

```java
      new SMCRemoteServer().serve(socket);
    }
  };

  public SMCRemoteService(int port) throws Exception {
    service = new SocketService(port, server);
  }

  public void close() throws Exception {
    service.close();
  }

  static void setUserDirectory(UserDirectory userDirectory) {
    SMCRemoteService.userDirectory = userDirectory;
  }

  public static void setEmailSender(EmailSender emailSender) {
    SMCRemoteService.emailSender = emailSender;
  }

  public static void main(String[] args) {
    if (parseCommandLine(args)) {
      verboseHeader();
      setUserDirectory(new UserRepository("users"));
      if (!isEmailQuiet) setEmailSender(new OReillyEmailSender());
      try {
        SMCRemoteService service = new SMCRemoteService(servicePort);
      } catch (Exception e) {
        System.err.println("Could not connect");
      }
    } else {
      System.out.println("usage: java SMCRemoteService -p <port> -v");
    }
  }

  static boolean validate(String username, String password) {
    return userDirectory.isValid(username, password);
  }

  static boolean addUser(String username, String password) throws Exception {
    return userDirectory.add(username, password);
  }

  static String getPassword(String username) {
    return userDirectory.getPassword(username);
  }

  static int incrementLoginCount(String username) throws Exception {
    return userDirectory.incrementLoginCount(username);
  }

  static boolean sendEmail(String emailAddress, String subject, String text) {
    return emailSender.send(emailAddress, subject, text);
  }

  static boolean parseCommandLine(String[] args) {
```

Listing 12–22 (Continued) `SMCRemoteService.java`

```java
    Getopts opts = new Getopts("m:p:ve", args);
    if (opts.error())
      return false;

    try {
      servicePort = Integer.parseInt(opts.option('p', DEFAULT_PORT));
      isVerbose = opts.hasOption('v');
      messageFile = opts.option('m', null);
      isEmailQuiet = opts.hasOption('e');
    } catch (NumberFormatException e) {
      return false;
    }

    return true;
  }

  static String buildCommand(String filename, String generator) {
    String generatorClass;

    if (generator.equals("java"))
      generatorClass = "smc.generator.java.SMJavaGenerator";
    else if (generator.equals("C++"))
      generatorClass = "smc.generator.cpp.SMCppGenerator";
    else
      return "echo bad generator " + generator;

    return COMPILE_COMMAND + " -g " + generatorClass + " " + filename;
  }

  static int executeCommand(String command, Vector stdout, Vector stderr)
  throws Exception {
    Runtime rt = Runtime.getRuntime();
    Process p = rt.exec(command);
    flushProcessOutputs(p, stdout, stderr);
    p.waitFor();

    return p.exitValue();
  }

  private static void flushProcessOutputs(Process p, Vector stdout, Vector stderr)
  throws IOException {
    BufferedReader stdoutReader =
      new BufferedReader(new InputStreamReader(p.getInputStream()));
    BufferedReader stderrReader =
      new BufferedReader(new InputStreamReader(p.getErrorStream()));
    String line;

    while ((line = stdoutReader.readLine()) != null)
      stdout.add(line);
    while ((line = stderrReader.readLine()) != null)
      stderr.add(line);
  }

  static File makeTempDirectory() {
    File tmpDirectory;
    do {
```

Listing 12–22 (Continued) `SMCRemoteService.java`

```
      long millis = System.currentTimeMillis();
      tmpDirectory = new File("smcTempDirectory" + millis);
    } while (tmpDirectory.exists());
    tmpDirectory.mkdir();
    return tmpDirectory;
  }

  private static void verboseHeader() {
    verboseMessage("SMCRemoteService--------------------------------");
    verboseMessage(VERSION);
    verboseMessage("port = " + servicePort);
    if (isEmailQuiet) verboseMessage("email is disabled");
    verboseMessage("-----------------------------------------------");
  }

  static void verboseMessage(String msg) {
    if (isVerbose) {
      Date logTime = new Date();
      SimpleDateFormat fmt = new SimpleDateFormat("yyyy.MM.dd hh:mm:ss");
      String logTimeString = fmt.format(logTime);

      System.out.println(logTimeString + " | " + msg);
    }
  }
}
```

Listing 12–23 `UserDirectory.java`

```
package com.objectmentor.SMCRemote.server;

public interface UserDirectory {
  public boolean isValid(String username, String password);
  public boolean add(String username, String password) throws Exception;
  public String getPassword(String username);
  public int incrementLoginCount(String username) throws Exception;
}
```

Listing 12–24 `EmailSender.java`

```
package com.objectmentor.SMCRemote.server;

public interface EmailSender {
  public boolean send(String emailAddress, String subject, String text);
}
```

SMCRemoteServer

SMCRemoteServer is a simple class. It hangs in a loop reading `SocketTransaction` objects from the socket. It uses the VISITOR[8] pattern to decode the transactions it reads. Once the transaction is decoded, SMCRemoteServer sends the appropriate event to the ServerSession instance. See Figures 12–13 and 12–14.

---

8. The VISITOR pattern is described in [Gamma1995], p. 331, and there are significant examples in [Martin2002] p. 388.

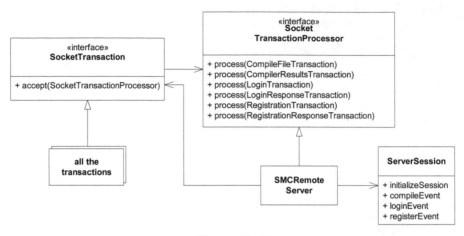

Figure 12–13

`SMCRemoteServer` structure: The transaction Visitor pattern.

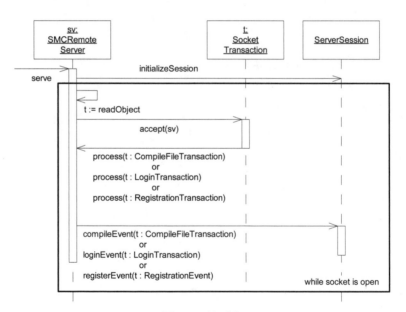

Figure 12–14

`SMCRemoteServer` transaction decoding.

Each time the SMCRemoteServer reads a SocketTransaction from the socket, it passes itself to the accept function of that transaction. This works because SMCRemote-Server implements the SocketTransactionProcessor interface. The transaction calls back through this interface to the appropriate process function. That function, in turn, sends the appropriate event to the ServerSession object. Listings 12–25 and 12–26 show the SMCRemoteServer and SocketTransactionProcessor classes.

Listing 12–25 SMCRemoteServer.java

```java
package com.objectmentor.SMCRemote.server;

import com.objectmentor.SMCRemote.transactions.*;
import com.objectmentor.SocketService.SocketServer;

import java.io.ObjectInputStream;
import java.net.Socket;

class SMCRemoteServer extends SocketTransactionProcessor {
  private ObjectInputStream serverInput;
  private boolean isOpen = false;
  private ServerSession session;

  public void serve(Socket socket) {
    isOpen = true;

    try {
      session = new ServerSession(this, socket);
      session.verboseMessage("Connected");
      serverInput = session.initializeSession(socket);
      while (isOpen) {
        SocketTransaction st = (SocketTransaction) serverInput.readObject();
        st.accept(this);
      }
    } catch (Exception e) {
      SMCRemoteService.verboseMessage("Connection torn down:" + e);
      return;
    }
    SMCRemoteService.verboseMessage("Connection closed normally.");
  }

  public void process(CompileFileTransaction t) throws Exception {
    session.compileEvent(t);
  }

  public void process(LoginTransaction t) throws Exception {
    session.loginEvent(t);
  }

  public void process(RegistrationTransaction t) throws Exception {
    session.registerEvent(t);
  }

  public void close() {
    isOpen = false;
  }
}
```

Listing 12–26 `SocketTransactionProcessor.java`

```
package com.objectmentor.SMCRemote.transactions;

public class SocketTransactionProcessor {
  public void process(CompileFileTransaction t) throws Exception {
    throw new NoProcessorException("CompileFileTransaction");
  }

  public void process(CompilerResultsTransaction t) throws Exception {
    throw new NoProcessorException("CompilerResultsTransaction");
  }

  public void process(LoginTransaction t) throws Exception {
    throw new NoProcessorException("LoginTransaction");
  }

  public void process(LoginResponseTransaction t) throws Exception {
    throw new NoProcessorException("LoginResponseTransaction");
  }

  public void process(RegistrationTransaction t) throws Exception {
    throw new NoProcessorException("RegistrationTransaction");
  }

  public void process(RegistrationResponseTransaction t) throws Exception {
    throw new NoProcessorException("RegistrationResponseTransaction");
  }

}
```

ServerSession

The `ServerSession` class is a finite state machine that controls the communication protocols between the client and the server. The state transition diagram that shows this logic is in Figure 12–15. Note that registrations can take place right from the `Idle` state, but in order to do a compile you must login first.

This finite state machine was translated into SMC code and compiled into Java. The SMC input is shown in Listing 12–27. If you are interested, the generated output is shown in Listing 12–46 at the end of the chapter.

THREE-LEVEL FSM

The `ServerSession` class is part of a design pattern called THREE-LEVEL FSM.[9] Using this pattern we split the finite state machine into three levels, as shown in Figure 12–16. The first level is `ServerControllerContext`. This class contains one degenerate method for every action of the finite state machine. If you examine the code in Listing 12–28, you'll see all the empty methods. They are empty, instead of abstract, because SMC presumes that the context class is not abstract. In this class you'll also see the `FSMError`

---

9. [Coplien1995], p. 383.

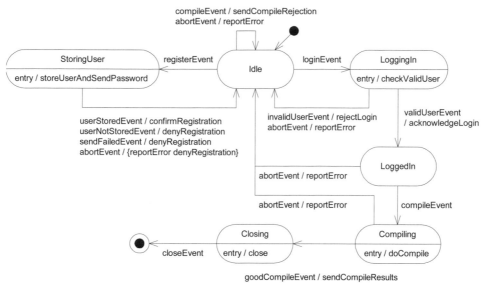

Figure 12–15
`ServerSession` finite state machine.

Listing 12–27 `server.sm`

```
Context ServerControllerContext
FSMName ServerController
Pragma Package com.objectmentor.SMCRemote.server
Initial Idle
{
  Idle {
    loginEvent      LoggingIn    {}
    compileEvent    Idle         sendCompileRejection
    registerEvent   StoringUser  {}
    abortEvent      *            reportError
  }

  StoringUser <storeUserAndSendPassword {
    userStoredEvent    Idle       confirmRegistration
    userNotStoredEvent Idle       denyRegistration
    sendFailedEvent    Idle       denyRegistration
    abortEvent         Idle       {reportError denyRegistration}
  }

  LoggingIn <checkValidUser {
    validUserEvent     LoggedIn   acknowledgeLogin
    invalidUserEvent   Idle       rejectLogin
    abortEvent         Idle       reportError
  }

  LoggedIn {
```

Listing 12–27 (Continued) `server.sm`

```
    compileEvent    Compiling  {}
    abortEvent      Idle       reportError
  }

  Compiling <doCompile {
    goodCompileEvent Closing      sendCompileResults
    badCompileEvent  Closing      sendCompileError
    abortEvent       Idle         reportError
  }

  Closing < close{
    closeEvent        Closed  {}
  }

  Closed  {}
}
```

method. This method is called by the generated code whenever an event occurs in a state
that did not expect it.

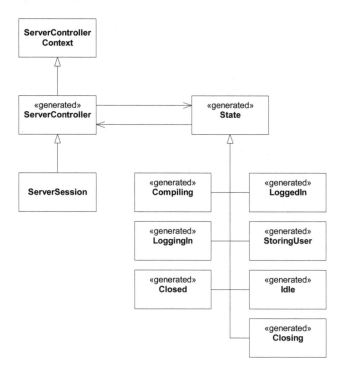

Figure 12–16
THREE-LEVEL FSM.

Listing 12–28 `ServerControllerContext.java`

```
package com.objectmentor.SMCRemote.server;

public class ServerControllerContext {
  public void FSMError(String event, String state) {
    SMCRemoteService.verboseMessage(
      "Transition Error.  Event:" + event + " in state:" + state);
  }

  public void checkValidUser() {
  }

  public void close() {
  }

  public void acknowledgeLogin() {
  }

  public void rejectLogin() {
  }

  public void doCompile() {
  }

  public void sendCompileResults() {
  }

  public void sendCompileRejection() {
  }

  public void sendCompileError() {
  }

  public void reportError() {
  }

  public void confirmRegistration() {
  }

  public void denyRegistration() {
  }

  public void storeUserAndSendPassword() {
  }
}
```

The generated code (Listing 12–46) creates the `ServerController` that derives from `SeverControllerContext`. It also creates `State` and all its derivatives. Finally, I wrote `ServerSession` to derive from `ServerController`. `ServerSession` implements all the degenerate methods of `ServerControllerContext`. As such it contains all of the detailed code that implements the behavior of the server. The code for this class is a bit long, but it's also quite simple. You'll find it in Listing 12–29.

Listing 12–29 `ServerSession.java`

```java
package com.objectmentor.SMCRemote.server;

import com.objectmentor.SMCRemote.transactions.*;

import java.io.*;
import java.net.*;

class ServerSession extends ServerController {
  private ObjectOutputStream serverOutput;
  private ObjectInputStream serverInput;
  private String itsSessionID;
  private Socket itsSocket;
  private Exception itsException;
  private SMCRemoteServer itsParent;

  private String registrationFailureReason = null;

  private CompileFileTransaction cft;
  private File tempDirectory;
  private CompilerResultsTransaction crt;
  private LoginTransaction lt;
  private RegistrationTransaction rt;

  public ServerSession(SMCRemoteServer parent, Socket socket) throws IOException {
    itsParent = parent;
    itsSocket = socket;
    buildSessionID();
    serverOutput = new ObjectOutputStream(itsSocket.getOutputStream());
    serverInput = new ObjectInputStream(itsSocket.getInputStream());
  }

  public ObjectInputStream initializeSession(Socket socket) throws IOException {
    serverOutput.writeObject("SMCR Server. " + SMCRemoteService.VERSION);
    writeMessageFile();
    serverOutput.flush();
    return serverInput;
  }

  private void writeMessageFile() throws IOException {
    if (SMCRemoteService.messageFile == null) {
      serverOutput.writeObject(null);
    } else {
      StringBuffer b = new StringBuffer();
      BufferedReader br = new BufferedReader(new FileReader(SMCRemoteService.messageFile));
      String line;
      while ((line = br.readLine()) != null)
        b.append(line + "\n");
      serverOutput.writeObject(b.toString());
    }
  }

  public void compileEvent(CompileFileTransaction cft) {
    this.cft = cft;
    compileEvent();
  }
```

Listing 12–29 (Continued) `ServerSession.java`

```java
public void loginEvent(LoginTransaction lt) {
  this.lt = lt;
  loginEvent();
}

public void registerEvent(RegistrationTransaction rt) {
  this.rt = rt;
  verboseMessage(rt.getUsername() + " requests registration.");
  registerEvent();
}

public String generatePassword() {
  verboseMessage("Generating password.");
  return PasswordGenerator.generatePassword();
}

public void storeUserAndSendPassword() {
  String password = generatePassword();
  String username = rt.getUsername();
  try {
    boolean stored = SMCRemoteService.addUser(username, password);
    if (stored) {
      verboseMessage("User stored.  Sending password email.");
      boolean emailSent = sendPasswordEmail(username, password);
      if (emailSent)
        userStoredEvent();
      else {
        verboseMessage("could not send email.");
        registrationFailureReason = "could not send email.";
        sendFailedEvent();
      }
    } else {
      verboseMessage("Duplicate Registration");
      password = SMCRemoteService.getPassword(username);
      resendPasswordEmail(username, password);
      registrationFailureReason = "already a member. Email resent.";
      userNotStoredEvent();
    }
  } catch (Exception e) {
    abort(e);
  }
}

private boolean resendPasswordEmail(String username, String password) {
  return SMCRemoteService.sendEmail(username,
                                    "SMCRemote Resending password",
                                    "Your SMCRemote password is: " + password);
}

private boolean sendPasswordEmail(String username, String password) {
  return SMCRemoteService.sendEmail(username,
                                    "SMCRemote Registration Confirmation",
                                    "Your password is: " + password);
}

public void confirmRegistration() {
```

Listing 12–29 (Continued) `ServerSession.java`

```
    verboseMessage("Confirming registration.");
    try {
      RegistrationResponseTransaction rrt = new RegistrationResponseTransaction(true);
      sendToClient(rrt);
    } catch (Exception e) {
      abort(e);
    }
  }

  public void denyRegistration() {
    verboseMessage("Registration Denied: " + registrationFailureReason);
    try {
      RegistrationResponseTransaction rrt = new RegistrationResponseTransaction(false);
      rrt.setFailureReason(registrationFailureReason);
      sendToClient(rrt);
    } catch (IOException e) {
      abort(e);
    }
  }

  public void checkValidUser() {
    String userName = lt.getUserName();
    String password = lt.getPassword();
    if (SMCRemoteService.validate(userName, password))
      validUserEvent();
    else
      invalidUserEvent();
  }

  public void close() {
    itsParent.close();
    closeEvent();
  }

  public void acknowledgeLogin() {
    try {
      int logins = SMCRemoteService.incrementLoginCount(lt.getUserName());
      verboseMessage("Login(" + logins + "): " + lt.getUserName() + " accepted.");
      LoginResponseTransaction lrt = new LoginResponseTransaction(true, logins);
      sendToClient(lrt);
    } catch (Exception e) {
      abort(e);
    }
  }

  public void rejectLogin() {
    verboseMessage("Login: " + lt.getUserName() + " rejected.");
    try {
      LoginResponseTransaction lrt = new LoginResponseTransaction(false, 0);
      sendToClient(lrt);
    } catch (IOException e) {
      abort(e);
    }
  }

  public void doCompile() {
```

Listing 12–29 (Continued) `ServerSession.java`

```java
    verboseMessage("Compiling: " + cft.getFilename() + " using " +
                                  cft.getGenerator() + " generator.");

    try {
      tempDirectory = SMCRemoteService.makeTempDirectory();
      cft.write(tempDirectory);

      compile();
      goodCompileEvent();
    } catch (Exception e) {
      abort(e);
    }
  }

  public void sendCompileResults() {
    try {
      sendCompilerResultsToClient();
      tempDirectory.delete();
    } catch (IOException e) {
      abort(e);
    }
  }

  public void sendCompileRejection() {
    verboseMessage("Not logged in, can't compile.");
    CompilerResultsTransaction crt = new CompilerResultsTransaction();
    crt.setStatus(CompilerResultsTransaction.NOT_LOGGED_IN);
    try {
      sendToClient(crt);
    } catch (IOException e) {
      abort(e);
    }
  }

  public void sendCompileError() {

  }

  public void reportError() {
    System.out.println("Aborting: " + itsException);
  }

  private void abort(Exception e) {
    itsException = e;
    abortEvent();
  }

  private void buildSessionID() {
    InetAddress addr = itsSocket.getInetAddress();
    String connectedHostName = addr.getHostName();
    String connectedIP = addr.getHostAddress();
    if (connectedHostName.equals(connectedIP)) {
      itsSessionID = connectedHostName + ":" + itsSocket.getPort();
    } else {
      itsSessionID =
        connectedHostName + ":" + itsSocket.getPort() + "(" + connectedIP + ")";
```

Listing 12–29 (Continued) `ServerSession.java`

```java
      }
    }

    private void compile() throws Exception {
      String filename = cft.getFilename();
      crt = new CompilerResultsTransaction();
      File batFile = writeCompileScript();

      SMCRemoteService.executeCommand(tempDirectory + "\\smc.bat", crt.getStdoutLines(),
                                crt.getStderrLines());
      batFile.delete();
      File sourceFile = new File(tempDirectory, filename);
      sourceFile.delete();
    }

    private File writeCompileScript() throws IOException {
      File batFile = new File(tempDirectory, "smc.bat");
      PrintWriter bat = new PrintWriter(new FileWriter(batFile));
      bat.println("cd " + tempDirectory);
      bat.println(SMCRemoteService.buildCommand(cft.getFilename(), cft.getGenerator()));
      bat.close();
      return batFile;
    }

    private void sendCompilerResultsToClient() throws IOException {
      String[] filenames = tempDirectory.list();
      crt.loadFiles(tempDirectory, filenames);
      crt.setStatus(CompilerResultsTransaction.OK);
      verboseSendFileReport(filenames);
      sendToClient(crt);
      deleteCompiledFiles(filenames);
    }

    private void sendToClient(SocketTransaction t) throws IOException {
      serverOutput.writeObject(t);
      serverOutput.flush();
    }

    private void deleteCompiledFiles(String[] filenames) {
      for (int i = 0; i < filenames.length; i++) {
        File f = new File(tempDirectory, filenames[i]);
        f.delete();
      }
    }

    private void verboseSendFileReport(String[] filenames) {
      for (int i = 0; i < filenames.length; i++) {
        String filename = filenames[i];
        verboseMessage("Sending: " + filename);
      }
    }

    public void verboseMessage(String msg) {
      SMCRemoteService.verboseMessage("<" + itsSessionID + "> " + msg);
    }
}
```

UserRepository

I chose a very simple implementation for the UserRepository (See Listing 12–30). This class implements the UserDirectory interface and provides the means whereby the registration data is stored. I could have used a database for this, but the need was so simple that it didn't seem to make sense. So, instead, I create a directory named users. Inside this directory I create a file for each user. The name of the file is the email address of the user. The contents of the file are a simple XML record that contains the user's email address, password, and a count of the number of times the user has logged in. This file is created upon registration, and is referenced every time the user logs in.

You might wonder why I didn't use a database, or some other more traditional scheme. The answer is simply that a database wasn't necessary. The kind of data I am storing is very simple, and does not require SQL or any of the other features of a database.

You might also ask why I chose to use XML. It turns out that JDOM is very simple to use, and it allowed me to create user records that were flexible. I could add new fields or change existing fields without a lot of fuss.

Listing 12–30 UserRepository.java

```
package com.objectmentor.SMCRemote.server;

import org.jdom.*;
import org.jdom.input.SAXBuilder;
import org.jdom.output.XMLOutputter;

import java.io.*;

public class UserRepository implements UserDirectory {

  class User {
    public User() {
    }

    public User(String username, String password, int loginCount) {
      this.username = username;
      this.password = password;
      this.loginCount = loginCount;
    }

    String username;
    String password;
    int loginCount;
  }

  private File userDirectory;

  public UserRepository(String userDirectoryName) {
    userDirectory = makeUserDirectory(userDirectoryName);
  }

  private File makeUserDirectory(String userDirectoryName) {
    File directory = new File(userDirectoryName);
```

Listing 12–30 (Continued) `UserRepository.java`

```
    if (!directory.exists())
      directory.mkdir();
    return directory;
  }

  public boolean isValid(String username, String password) {
    return password.equals(getPassword(username));
  }

  public String getPassword(String username) {
    User user = readUser(username);
    return user.password;
  }

  private User readUser(String username) {
    User user = new User();
    try {
      File userFile = new File(userDirectory, username);
      if (userFile.canRead()) {
        SAXBuilder builder = new SAXBuilder("org.apache.xerces.parsers.SAXParser");
        Document userDoc = builder.build(userFile);
        Element userElement = userDoc.getRootElement();
        user.username = userElement.getChild("name").getTextTrim();
        user.password = userElement.getChild("password").getTextTrim();
        user.loginCount =
          Integer.parseInt(userElement.getChild("loginCount").getTextTrim());
      }
    } catch (JDOMException e) {
      System.out.println("e = " + e);
      return null;
    }
    return user;
  }

  public boolean add(String username, String password) throws Exception {
    File userFile = new File(userDirectory, username);
    if (userFile.exists() == false) {
      User user = new User(username, password, 0);
      writeUser(user);
      return true;
    } else {
      return false;
    }
  }

  private void writeUser(User user) throws IOException {
    File userFile = new File(userDirectory, user.username);
    FileOutputStream os = new FileOutputStream(userFile);
    Document userDoc = createUserDocument(user);
    XMLOutputter xmlOut = new XMLOutputter();
    xmlOut.output(userDoc, os);
    os.close();
  }

  private Document createUserDocument(User user) {
    Element userElement = new Element("user");
```

Listing 12–30 (Continued) `UserRepository.java`

```java
    userElement.addContent(new Element("name").setText(user.username));
    userElement.addContent(new Element("password").setText(user.password));
    userElement.addContent(
      new Element("loginCount").setText(Integer.toString(user.loginCount)));
    Document userDoc = new Document(userElement);
    return userDoc;
  }

  public boolean clearUserRepository() {
    boolean cleared = true;
    File files[] = userDirectory.listFiles();
    for (int i = 0; i < files.length; i++) {
      File file = files[i];
      if (file.delete() == false)
        cleared = false;
    }
    if (userDirectory.delete() == false)
      cleared = false;
    return cleared;
  }

  public int incrementLoginCount(String username) throws Exception {
    User user = readUser(username);
    user.loginCount++;
    writeUser(user);
    return user.loginCount;
  }
}
}
```

OReillyEmailSender

The `OReillyEmailSender` is a very simple FACADE[10] that gives the server access to email facilities. I chose to use the O'Reilly engine simply because I've used it before, and it seems to work just fine. See Listing 12–31.

Listing 12–31 `OReillyEmailSender.java`

```java
package com.objectmentor.SMCRemote.server;

import com.oreilly.servlet.MailMessage;

import java.io.*;

public class OReillyEmailSender implements EmailSender {
  public boolean send(String emailAddress, String subject, String text) {
    try {
      MailMessage msg = new MailMessage("cvs.objectmentor.com");
      msg.from("info@objectmentor.com");
      msg.to(emailAddress);
      msg.setSubject(subject);
      PrintStream body = msg.getPrintStream();
```

---

10. The Facade design pattern is explained in [Gamma1995] p. 185. There is a nice example and explanation of Facade in [Martin2002] p. 173

```
Listing 12–31 (Continued) OReillyEmailSender.java
        body.println(text);
        msg.sendAndClose();
        return true;
    } catch (IOException e) {
        System.err.println("Couldn't send email: " + e.getMessage());
        return false;
    }
  }
 }
}
```

PasswordGenerator

The PasswordGenerator class is also very simple and straightforward. This class is used to generate a password for a newly registered user. See Listing 12–32.

```
Listing 12–32  PasswordGenerator.java
package com.objectmentor.SMCRemote.server;

public class PasswordGenerator {
  public static String generatePassword() {
    StringBuffer password = new StringBuffer();
    for (int i = 0; i < 8; i++) {
      password.append(generateRandomCharacter());
    }
    return password.toString();
  }

  private static char generateRandomCharacter() {
    double x = Math.random();
    x *= 26;
    return (char) ('a' + x);
  }
}
```

Conclusion

Apart from the test code, which follows these paragraphs, that's all there is to the SMCRemote system. All in all, including tests, the system is around 3,000 lines of code, with an average cyclomatic complexity of 1.48.

The UML diagrams in this chapter are examples of the kinds of diagrams one might draw in order to explain an existing system to someone else. I kept my diagrams terse, and I tried not to inundate you with them. Mostly they are just there to help you read the code.

Tests for SMCRemoteClient

Listing 12–33 `TestClientBase.java`

```java
package com.objectmentor.SMCRemote.client;

import junit.framework.TestCase;

import com.objectmentor.SMCRemote.transactions.*;
import com.objectmentor.SocketService.SocketServer;

import java.io.*;
import java.net.Socket;

abstract class MockServerBase implements SocketServer {
  private ObjectOutputStream os;
  private ObjectInputStream is;

  public abstract SocketTransactionProcessor getProcessor();

  public void sendTransaction(SocketTransaction t) throws Exception {
    os.writeObject(t);
    os.flush();
  }

  public void serve(Socket socket) {
    try {
      os = new ObjectOutputStream(socket.getOutputStream());
      is = new ObjectInputStream(socket.getInputStream());
      os.writeObject("SMCR Test Server");
      os.writeObject(null);
      os.flush();
      while (true) {
        SocketTransaction t = (SocketTransaction) is.readObject();
        t.accept(getProcessor());
      }
    } catch (Exception e) {
    }
  }
}


public class TestClientBase extends TestCase {
  public static final int SMCPORT = 9000;

  private ByteArrayOutputStream stdoutBuffer;
  private ByteArrayOutputStream stderrBuffer;

  public TestClientBase(String s) {
    super(s);
  }

  protected void setUp() throws Exception {
    stdoutBuffer = new ByteArrayOutputStream();
    stderrBuffer = new ByteArrayOutputStream();
  }
```

Listing 12–33 (Continued) `TestClientBase.java`

```java
  protected String getStderr() {
    return stderrBuffer.toString();
  }

  protected String getStdout() {
    return stdoutBuffer.toString();
  }

  protected void runMain(String[] args) throws IOException {
    PrintStream sysout = System.out;
    PrintStream syserr = System.err;

    System.setOut(new PrintStream(stdoutBuffer));
    System.setErr(new PrintStream(stderrBuffer));

    SMCRemoteClient.main(args);
    System.setOut(sysout);
    System.setErr(syserr);

    stdoutBuffer.close();
    stderrBuffer.close();

    Thread.yield();
  }
}
```

Listing 12–34 `TestClientCommandLine.java`

```java
package com.objectmentor.SMCRemote.client;

import junit.framework.TestCase;
import junit.swingui.TestRunner;

public class TestClientCommandLine extends TestCase {
  public static void main(String[] args) {
    TestRunner.main(new String[]{"TestClientCommandLine"});
  }

  public TestClientCommandLine(String name) {
    super(name);
  }

  public void setUp() throws Exception {
  }

  public void tearDown() throws Exception {
  }

  public void testParseSimpleCompileCommandLine() throws Exception {
    ClientCommandLine c =
      new ClientCommandLine(new String[]{"-u", "user", "-w", "password", "filename"});
    assertEquals("filename", c.getFilename());
    assertEquals(ClientCommandLine.DEFAULT_HOST, c.getHost());
    assertEquals(Integer.parseInt(ClientCommandLine.DEFAULT_PORT), c.getPort());
    assertEquals(ClientCommandLine.DEFAULT_GENERATOR, c.getGenerator());
    assert(!c.isVerbose());
```

Listing 12–34 (Continued) `TestClientCommandLine.java`

```
    assert("simple compile", c.isValid());
  }

  public void testParseComplexCompileCommandLine() throws Exception {
    ClientCommandLine c = new ClientCommandLine(new String[]{
      "-p", "999", "-h", "objectmentor.com", "-v", "-u", "user", "-w", "password",
      "-g", "C++", "f.sm"});
    assert(c.isValid());
    assertEquals("f.sm", c.getFilename());
    assertEquals("bad host", "objectmentor.com", c.getHost());
    assertEquals("bad port", 999, c.getPort());
    assertEquals("bad generator", "C++", c.getGenerator());
    assert("verbose", c.isVerbose());
  }

  public void testRegistrationCommandLine() throws Exception {
    ClientCommandLine c = new ClientCommandLine(new String[]{"-r", "user"});
    assert("registration commandline", c.isValid());
  }

  public void testParseInvalidCommandLine() {
    assert("no arguments", !checkCommandLine(new String[0]));
    assert("no filename", !checkCommandLine(new String[]{"-h", "dodah.com"}));
    assert("too many files", !checkCommandLine(new String[]{"file1", "file2"}));
    assert("Bad Argument", !checkCommandLine(new String[]{"-x", "file1"}));
    assert("Bad Port", !checkCommandLine(new String[]{"-p", "bad port"}));
    assert("generator but no file name", !checkCommandLine(new String[]{"-g", "C++"}));
    assert("filename but no user or password", !checkCommandLine(new String[]{"myFile"}));
    assert("filename but no user",
           !checkCommandLine(new String[]{"-w", "password", "myFile"}));
    assert("filename but no password",
           !checkCommandLine(new String[]{"-u", "user", "myFile"}));
    assert("registration with user",
           !checkCommandLine(new String[]{"-r", "user", "-u", "user"}));
    assert("registration with password",
           !checkCommandLine(new String[]{"-r", "user", "-p", "password"}));
    assert("registration with generator",
           !checkCommandLine(new String[]{"-r", "user", "-g", "gen"}));
    assert("registration with file",
           !checkCommandLine(new String[]{"-r", "user", "myFile"}));
  }

  private boolean checkCommandLine(String[] args) {
    ClientCommandLine c = new ClientCommandLine(args);
    return c.isValid();
  }
}
```

Listing 12–35 `TestRemoteCompiler.java`

```
package com.objectmentor.SMCRemote.client;

import junit.swingui.TestRunner;

import com.objectmentor.SMCRemote.transactions.*;
import com.objectmentor.SocketService.SocketService;
```

Listing 12–35 (Continued) `TestRemoteCompiler.java`

```java
import java.io.*;

class MockRemoteCompilerServer extends MockServerBase {
  public String filename = "noFileName";
  public boolean fileReceived = false;
  public String generator;
  public boolean isLoggedIn = false;

  class RemoteCompilerTransactionProcessor extends SocketTransactionProcessor {
    public void process(CompileFileTransaction t) throws Exception {
      try {
        File f1 = TestRemoteCompiler.createTestFile("myFile.java", "wow");
        File f2 = TestRemoteCompiler.createTestFile("file2.java", "ick");
        filename = t.getFilename();
        generator = t.getGenerator();

        CompilerResultsTransaction crt = new CompilerResultsTransaction();
        crt.loadFiles(null, new String[]{"myFile.java", "file2.java"});

        f1.delete();
        f2.delete();
        crt.getStdoutLines().add("compile diagnostics");
        crt.getStderrLines().add("stderr message");
        sendTransaction(crt);

        fileReceived = true;
      } catch (IOException e) {
      }
    }

    public void process(LoginTransaction t) throws Exception {
      LoginResponseTransaction lrt = new LoginResponseTransaction(true, 0);
      sendTransaction(lrt);
      isLoggedIn = true;
    }
  }

  public SocketTransactionProcessor getProcessor() {
    return new RemoteCompilerTransactionProcessor();
  }
}

public class TestRemoteCompiler extends TestClientBase {
  public static void main(String[] args) {
    TestRunner.main(new String[]{"com.objectmentor.SMCRemote.client.TestRemoteCompiler"});
  }

  public TestRemoteCompiler(String name) {
    super(name);
  }

  private RemoteCompiler c;
  private MockRemoteCompilerServer server;
  private SocketService smc;

  public void setUp() throws Exception {
```

Listing 12–35 (Continued) `TestRemoteCompiler.java`

```
    super.setUp();
    c = new RemoteCompiler("localhost", SMCPORT, new NullMessageLogger());
    server = new MockRemoteCompilerServer();
    smc = new SocketService(SMCPORT, server);
  }

  public void tearDown() throws Exception {
    c.close();
    smc.close();
  }

  static File createTestFile(String name, String content) throws IOException {
    File f = new File(name);
    FileOutputStream stream = new FileOutputStream(f);
    stream.write(content.getBytes());
    stream.close();
    return f;
  }

  public void testFileDoesNotExist() throws Exception {
    c.setFilename("thisFileDoesNotExist");
    boolean prepared = c.prepareFile();
    assertEquals(false, prepared);
  }

  public void testConnectToSMCRemoteServer() throws Exception {
    boolean connection = c.connect();
    assert(connection);
  }

  public void testCompileFile() throws Exception {
    String filename = "testSendFile";
    File f = createTestFile(filename, "I am sending this file.");
    c.setFilename(filename);
    assert(c.connect());
    assert(c.prepareFile());
    assert(c.compileFile() != null);
    Thread.sleep(50);
    assert(server.fileReceived);
    assertEquals(filename, server.filename);
    assertEquals("Bad Generator", "java", server.generator);
    f.delete();
  }

  public void testMainCompileFile() throws Exception {
    File f = createTestFile("myFile.sm", "the content");
    runMain(new String[]{"-u", "user", "-w", "pw", "-g", "C++", "myFile.sm"});

    f.delete();
    File file1 = new File("myFile.java");
    File file2 = new File("file2.java");
    boolean file1Exists = file1.exists();
    boolean file2Exists = file2.exists();
    boolean exists = file1Exists && file2Exists;

    int file1Len = (int) file1.length();
```

Listing 12–35 (Continued) `TestRemoteCompiler.java`

```java
      int file2Len = (int) file2.length();

      if (file1Exists) file1.delete();
      if (file2Exists) file2.delete();

      assert("Not logged in", server.isLoggedIn);
      assert("not received", server.fileReceived);
      assertEquals("bad generator", "C++", server.generator);
      assert("One or more files doesn't exist", exists);
      assert("f1 zero", file1Len > 0);
      assert("f2 zero", file2Len > 0);

      assert("consoleMessage", getStdout().startsWith("compile diagnostics"));
      assert("Stderr Message", getStderr().startsWith("stderr message"));
    }
  }
```

Listing 12–36 `TestRemoteRegistration.java`

```java
package com.objectmentor.SMCRemote.client;

import junit.swingui.TestRunner;

import com.objectmentor.SMCRemote.transactions.*;
import com.objectmentor.SocketService.SocketService;


class MockRemoteRegistrationServer extends MockServerBase {
  public String user;

  class RemoteRegistrationServerTransactionProcessor extends SocketTransactionProcessor {
    public void process(RegistrationTransaction t) throws Exception {
      user = t.getUsername();
      RegistrationResponseTransaction rrt;
      if (user.equals("goodUser")) {
        rrt = new RegistrationResponseTransaction(true);
      } else {
        rrt = new RegistrationResponseTransaction(false);
      }
      sendTransaction(rrt);
    }
  }

  public SocketTransactionProcessor getProcessor() {
    return new RemoteRegistrationServerTransactionProcessor();
  }
}

public class TestRemoteRegistration extends TestClientBase {
  public TestRemoteRegistration(String s) {
    super(s);
  }

  public static void main(String[] args) {
    TestRunner.main(
      new String[]{"com.objectmentor.SMCRemote.client.TestRemoteRegistration"});
```

Listing 12–36 (Continued) `TestRemoteRegistration.java`

```java
  }

  private RemoteRegistrar r;
  private MockRemoteRegistrationServer server;
  private SocketService smc;

  public void setUp() throws Exception {
    super.setUp();
    r = new RemoteRegistrar("localhost", SMCPORT, new NullMessageLogger());
    server = new MockRemoteRegistrationServer();
    smc = new SocketService(SMCPORT, server);
  }

  public void tearDown() throws Exception {
    r.close();
    smc.close();
  }

  public void testRegistration() throws Exception {
    RegistrationResponseTransaction rrt;
    assert(r.connect());
    rrt = r.register("goodUser");
    assert("rrt not null", rrt != null);
    assert("registration passed", rrt.isConfirmed());
    Thread.sleep(50);
    assertEquals("Registration", "goodUser", server.user);
  }

  public void testRegistrationMain() throws Exception {
    runMain(new String[]{"-r", "goodUser"});
    assert("Registration message",
           getStdout().startsWith("User: goodUser registered.  Email sent."));
  }
}
```

Tests for SocketService

Listing 12–37 `TestSocketService.java`

```java
package com.objectmentor.SocketService;

import junit.framework.TestCase;
import junit.swingui.TestRunner;

import java.io.*;
import java.net.Socket;

public class TestSocketService extends TestCase {
  private int connections = 0;
  private SocketServer connectionCounter;
  private SocketService ss;

  public static void main(String[] args) {
    TestRunner.main(new String[] {
        "com.objectmentor.SocketService.TestSocketService"
      });
  }

  public TestSocketService(String name) {
    super(name);
    connectionCounter = new SocketServer() {
      public void serve(Socket s) {
        connections++;
      }
    };
  }

  public void setUp() throws Exception {
    connections = 0;
  }

  public void tearDown() throws Exception {
  }

  public void testNoConnections() throws Exception {
    ss = new SocketService(999, connectionCounter);
    ss.close();
    assertEquals(0, connections);
  }

  public void testOneConnection() throws Exception {
    ss = new SocketService(999, connectionCounter);
    connect(999);
    ss.close();
    assertEquals(1, connections);
  }

  public void testManyConnections() throws Exception {
    ss = new SocketService(999, connectionCounter);
    for (int i = 0; i < 10; i++)
      connect(999);
    ss.close();
```

Listing 12–37 `TestSocketService.java`

```
    assertEquals(10, connections);
  }

  public void testSendMessage() throws Exception {
    ss = new SocketService(999, new HelloService());
    Socket s = new Socket("localhost", 999);
    BufferedReader br = TestUtility.GetBufferedReader(s);
    String answer = br.readLine();
    s.close();
    ss.close();
    assertEquals("Hello", answer);
  }

  public void testReceiveMessage() throws Exception {
    ss = new SocketService(999, new EchoService());
    Socket s = new Socket("localhost", 999);
    BufferedReader br = TestUtility.GetBufferedReader(s);
    PrintStream ps = TestUtility.GetPrintStream(s);
    ps.println("MyMessage");
    String answer = br.readLine();
    s.close();
    ss.close();
    assertEquals("MyMessage", answer);
  }

  public void testMultiThreaded() throws Exception {
    ss = new SocketService(999, new EchoService());
    Socket s = new Socket("localhost", 999);
    BufferedReader br = TestUtility.GetBufferedReader(s);
    PrintStream ps = TestUtility.GetPrintStream(s);

    Socket s2 = new Socket("localhost", 999);
    BufferedReader br2 = TestUtility.GetBufferedReader(s2);
    PrintStream ps2 = TestUtility.GetPrintStream(s2);

    ps2.println("MyMessage");
    String answer2 = br2.readLine();
    s2.close();

    ps.println("MyMessage");
    String answer = br.readLine();
    s.close();

    ss.close();
    assertEquals("MyMessage", answer2);
    assertEquals("MyMessage", answer);
  }

  private void connect(int port) {
    try {
      Socket s = new Socket("localhost", port);
      try {
        Thread.sleep(10);
      } catch (InterruptedException e) {
      }
      s.close();
```

Listing 12–37 `TestSocketService.java`

```java
      } catch (IOException e) {
        fail("could not connect");
      }
    }
  }
}

class TestUtility {
  public static PrintStream GetPrintStream(Socket s)
  throws IOException {
    OutputStream os = s.getOutputStream();
    PrintStream ps = new PrintStream(os);
    return ps;
  }

  public static BufferedReader GetBufferedReader(Socket s)
  throws IOException {
    InputStream is = s.getInputStream();
    InputStreamReader isr = new InputStreamReader(is);
    BufferedReader br = new BufferedReader(isr);
    return br;
  }
}

class HelloService implements SocketServer {
  public void serve(Socket s) {
    try {
      PrintStream ps = TestUtility.GetPrintStream(s);
      ps.println("Hello");
    } catch (IOException e) {
    }
  }
}

class EchoService implements SocketServer {
  public void serve(Socket s) {
    try {
      PrintStream ps = TestUtility.GetPrintStream(s);
      BufferedReader br = TestUtility.GetBufferedReader(s);
      String token = br.readLine();
      ps.println(token);
    } catch (IOException e) {
    }
  }
}
```

Tests for SMCRemoteServer

Listing 12–38 `TestBase.java`

```java
package com.objectmentor.SMCRemote.server;

import junit.framework.TestCase;

import com.objectmentor.SMCRemote.transactions.*;

import java.io.*;
import java.net.Socket;

class MockUserDirectory implements UserDirectory {
  public int incrementLoginCount(String username) {
    return 0;
  }

  public boolean isValid(String username, String password) {
    return true;
  }

  public String getPassword(String username) {
    return null;
  }

  public boolean add(String username, String password) {
    return true;
  }
}

public class TestBase extends TestCase {
  protected ObjectInputStream is;
  protected ObjectOutputStream os;
  protected SMCRemoteService service;
  protected Socket client;

  protected UserDirectory mockUserDirectory = new MockUserDirectory();

  protected UserDirectory mockUserInvalidator = new MockUserDirectory() {
    public boolean isValid(String username, String password) {
      return false;
    }
  };

  public TestBase(String name) {
    super(name);
  }

  public void setUp() throws Exception {
    SMCRemoteService.isVerbose = false;
  }

  public void tearDown() throws Exception {
  }

  protected boolean login() throws IOException, ClassNotFoundException {
```

Listing 12–38 (Continued) `TestBase.java`

```java
      LoginTransaction lt = new LoginTransaction("name", "password");
      sendToServer(lt);
      LoginResponseTransaction ltr = (LoginResponseTransaction) is.readObject();
      return ltr.isAccepted();
    }

    protected void sendToServer(SocketTransaction t) throws IOException {
      os.writeObject(t);
      os.flush();
    }

    protected void disconnectClientFromServer() throws Exception {
      Thread.sleep(500);
      client.close();
      service.close();
    }

    protected void connectClientToServer() throws Exception {
      service = new SMCRemoteService(999);
      client = new Socket("localhost", 999);
      is = new ObjectInputStream(client.getInputStream());
      os = new ObjectOutputStream(client.getOutputStream());

      String headerLine = (String) is.readObject();
      assert("headerline", headerLine.startsWith("SMCR Server"));
      assertEquals("discard message", null, is.readObject()); // discard message
    }
  }
```

Listing 12–39 `TestCommandLine.java`

```java
package com.objectmentor.SMCRemote.server;

public class TestCommandLine extends TestBase {
  public TestCommandLine(String name) {
    super(name);
  }

  public void tearDown() throws Exception {
    super.tearDown();
    SMCRemoteService.messageFile = null;
    SMCRemoteService.isVerbose = false;
    SMCRemoteService.servicePort = Integer.parseInt(SMCRemoteService.DEFAULT_PORT);
  }

  public void setUp() throws Exception {
    super.setUp();
  }

  public void testValidCommandLine() throws Exception {
    assert("Null Command Line", SMCRemoteService.parseCommandLine(new String[0]));
    assertEquals("default port",
                 Integer.parseInt(SMCRemoteService.DEFAULT_PORT),
                 SMCRemoteService.servicePort);
    assert("default verbose", SMCRemoteService.isVerbose == false);

    assert("Parametric Command Line",
```

```
Listing 12–39 (Continued) TestCommandLine.java
        SMCRemoteService.parseCommandLine(
            new String[]{"-p", "999", "-v", "-m", "message.txt", "-e"}));
    assertEquals("port", 999, SMCRemoteService.servicePort);
    assert("verbose", SMCRemoteService.isVerbose == true);
    assertEquals("message", "message.txt", SMCRemoteService.messageFile);
    assertEquals("email", true, SMCRemoteService.isEmailQuiet);
  }

  public void testInvalidCommandLine() throws Exception {
    assertEquals("Invalid Command Line",
                 false, SMCRemoteService.parseCommandLine(new String[]{"-x"}));
    assertEquals("Bad Port",
                 false, SMCRemoteService.parseCommandLine(new String[]{"-p", "badport"}));
  }
}
```

```
Listing 12–40 TestCompilation.java
package com.objectmentor.SMCRemote.server;

import junit.swingui.TestRunner;

import com.objectmentor.SMCRemote.transactions.*;

import java.io.*;
import java.net.Socket;
import java.util.*;

public class TestCompilation extends TestBase {

  public static void main(String[] args) {
    TestRunner.main(new String[]{"TestCompilation"});
  }

  public TestCompilation(String name) {
    super(name);
  }

  public void setUp() throws Exception {
  }

  public void tearDown() throws Exception {
  }

  public void testBuildCommand() throws Exception {
    assertEquals("Build Java Command",
                 SMCRemoteService.COMPILE_COMMAND +
                   " -g smc.generator.java.SMJavaGenerator myFile",
                 SMCRemoteService.buildCommand("myFile", "java"));

    assertEquals("Build C++ Command",
                 SMCRemoteService.COMPILE_COMMAND +
                   " -g smc.generator.cpp.SMCppGenerator myFile",
                 SMCRemoteService.buildCommand("myFile", "C++"));
  }

  public void testExecuteCommand() throws Exception {
```

Listing 12–40 (Continued) `TestCompilation.java`

```java
    File smFile = new File("myFile.sm");
    File javaFile = new File("F.java");

    writeSourceFile(smFile);
    Vector stdout = new Vector();
    Vector stderr = new Vector();
    String command = SMCRemoteService.COMPILE_COMMAND + " myFile.sm";
    assertEquals("exitValue", 0, SMCRemoteService.executeCommand(command, stdout, stderr));
    assertEquals("fileExists", true, javaFile.exists());
    assert("javaFile", javaFile.delete());
    assert("smFile", smFile.delete());
    checkCompilerOutputStreams(stdout, stderr);
  }

  public void testMakeTempDirectory() throws Exception {
    File f1 = SMCRemoteService.makeTempDirectory();
    File f2 = SMCRemoteService.makeTempDirectory();
    assertEquals("MakeTempDirectory", false, f1.getName().equals(f2.getName()));
    assert("f1", f1.delete());
    assert("f2", f2.delete());
  }

  public void testCompileJava() throws Exception {
    connectClientToServer();
    service.setUserDirectory(mockUserDirectory);
    login();
    CompilerResultsTransaction crt = invokeRemoteCompiler("java");
    assertEquals("Compiler Status", CompilerResultsTransaction.OK, crt.getStatus());
    checkCompiledJavaFile(crt);
    checkCompilerOutputStreams(crt.getStdoutLines(), crt.getStderrLines());
    disconnectClientFromServer();
  }

  public void testCompileCPP() throws Exception {
    connectClientToServer();
    service.setUserDirectory(mockUserDirectory);
    login();
    CompilerResultsTransaction crt = invokeRemoteCompiler("C++");
    assertEquals("Compiler Status", CompilerResultsTransaction.OK, crt.getStatus());
    checkCompiledCPPFile(crt);
    checkCompilerOutputStreams(crt.getStdoutLines(), crt.getStderrLines());
    disconnectClientFromServer();
  }

  public void testCompileNoLogin() throws Exception {
    connectClientToServer();
    service.setUserDirectory(mockUserDirectory);
    CompilerResultsTransaction crt = invokeRemoteCompiler("java");
    disconnectClientFromServer();
    assertEquals("Compiler Status", CompilerResultsTransaction.NOT_LOGGED_IN,
                                    crt.getStatus());
  }

  public void testTwoCompilesInARowNotAllowed() throws Exception {
    connectClientToServer();
    service.setUserDirectory(mockUserDirectory);
```

Listing 12–40 (Continued) `TestCompilation.java`

```
    login();
    CompilerResultsTransaction crt = invokeRemoteCompiler("java");
    try {
      crt = invokeRemoteCompiler("java");
      fail("Two Compiles in a row");
    } catch (Exception e) {
    } finally {
      disconnectClientFromServer();
    }
  }

  public void testCloseServer() throws Exception {
    try {
      service = new SMCRemoteService(999);
      client = new Socket("localhost", 999);
      client.close();
      service.close();
    } catch (Exception e) {
      fail("couldn't connect" + e.getMessage());
    }
    try {
      client = new Socket("localhost", 999);
      fail("connected to closed server");
    } catch (Exception e) {
    }
  }

  protected CompilerResultsTransaction
  invokeRemoteCompiler(String generator) throws Exception {
    CompileFileTransaction cft = buildCompileFileTransaction(generator);
    sendToServer(cft);
    CompilerResultsTransaction crt = (CompilerResultsTransaction) is.readObject();
    return crt;
  }

  protected CompileFileTransaction
  buildCompileFileTransaction(String generator) throws IOException {
    File sourceFile = new File("myFile.sm");
    writeSourceFile(sourceFile);
    CompileFileTransaction cft = new CompileFileTransaction("myFile.sm", generator);
    sourceFile.delete();
    return cft;
  }

  protected void writeSourceFile(File smFile) throws IOException {
    PrintWriter w = new PrintWriter(new FileWriter(smFile));
    w.println("Context C");
    w.println("FSMName F");
    w.println("Initial I");
    w.println("{I{E I A}}");
    w.close();
  }

  protected void checkCompilerOutputStreams(Vector stdout, Vector stderr) {
    assert("stdout empty", stdout.size() > 0);
    assert("stderr not empty", stderr.size() == 0);
```

Listing 12–40 (Continued) `TestCompilation.java`

```java
  }

  protected void checkCompiledJavaFile(CompilerResultsTransaction crt) {
    String filenames[] = crt.getFilenames();
    assertEquals("filenames", 1, filenames.length);
    assertEquals("F.java", "F.java", filenames[0]);

    crt.write();

    File javaFile = new File("F.java");
    assertEquals("Compile", true, javaFile.exists());
    javaFile.delete();
  }

  protected void checkCompiledCPPFile(CompilerResultsTransaction crt) {
    String filenames[] = crt.getFilenames();
    Arrays.sort(filenames);
    assertEquals("filenames", 2, filenames.length);
    assertEquals("myFile.cpp", "myFile.cpp", filenames[0]);
    assertEquals("myFile.h", "myFile.h", filenames[1]);

    crt.write();

    File cppHFile = new File("myFile.h");
    File cppCFile = new File("myFile.cpp");
    assertEquals("Compile", true, cppHFile.exists() && cppCFile.exists());
    cppHFile.delete();
    cppCFile.delete();
  }
}
```

Listing 12–41 `TestOReillyEmail.java`

```java
package com.objectmentor.SMCRemote.server;

import junit.framework.TestCase;
import junit.swingui.TestRunner;

public class TestOReillyEmail extends TestCase {
  public static void main(String[] args) {
    TestRunner.main(new String[]{"TestOReillyEmail"});
  }

  public TestOReillyEmail(String name) {
    super(name);
  }

  public void setUp() throws Exception {
  }

  public void tearDown() throws Exception {
  }

  public void testSendEmail() throws Exception {
    boolean emailStatus = false;
    OReillyEmailSender sender = new OReillyEmailSender();
```

Listing 12–41 (Continued) `TestOReillyEmail.java`

```
    emailStatus = sender.send("unclebob@objectmentor.com", "hi bob", "oh boy, email!");
    assertEquals("SendEmail", true, emailStatus);
  }
}
```

Listing 12–42 `TestRegistration.java`

```java
package com.objectmentor.SMCRemote.server;

import com.objectmentor.SMCRemote.transactions.*;

public class TestRegistration extends TestBase {
  private String emailAddress;
  private String mailSubject;
  private String mailText;
  private int emailMessagesSent = 0;

  private EmailSender mockEmailSender = new EmailSender() {
    public boolean send(String emailAddress, String subject, String text) {
      TestRegistration.this.emailAddress = emailAddress;
      TestRegistration.this.mailSubject = subject;
      TestRegistration.this.mailText = text;
      emailMessagesSent++;
      return true;
    }
  };

  private EmailSender mockBadEmailSender = new EmailSender() {
    public boolean send(String emailAddress, String subject, String text) {
      return false;
    }
  };
  private RegistrationResponseTransaction rrt;
  private UserRepository userRepository;
  private String userRepositoryName = "testUsers";

  public TestRegistration(String name) {
    super(name);
  }

  public void tearDown() throws Exception {
    super.tearDown();
    userRepository.clearUserRepository();
  }

  public void setUp() throws Exception {
    super.setUp();
    userRepository = new UserRepository(userRepositoryName);
  }

  public void testRegistration() throws Exception {
    sendRegistration(mockEmailSender);
    assertEquals("emailAddress", "rmartin@oma.com", emailAddress);
    assertEquals("mailSubject", "SMCRemote Registration Confirmation", mailSubject);
    assert("Mail Text", mailText.startsWith("Your password is: "));
    assertEquals("Mail Text Length", 26, mailText.length());
```

Listing 12–42 (Continued) `TestRegistration.java`

```
    assertEquals("Registration", true, rrt.isConfirmed());
    String password = mailText.substring(18);
    assertEquals("User Registered",
                  true, SMCRemoteService.validate("rmartin@oma.com", password));
    assertEquals("email count", 1, emailMessagesSent);
  }

  public void testBadEmail() throws Exception {
    sendRegistration(mockBadEmailSender);
    assertEquals("Registration", false, rrt.isConfirmed());
    assertEquals("Reason", "could not send email.", rrt.getFailureReason());
  }

  public void testDoubleRegistration() throws Exception {
    sendRegistration(mockEmailSender);
    sendRegistration(mockEmailSender);
    assertEquals("second registration", false, rrt.isConfirmed());
    assertEquals("second registration reason",
                  "already a member. Email resent.", rrt.getFailureReason());
    assertEquals("emailAddress", "rmartin@oma.com", emailAddress);
    assertEquals("emailSubject", "SMCRemote Resending password", mailSubject);
    assert("emailText", mailText.startsWith("Your SMCRemote password is: "));
    assertEquals("emailTextLength", 36, mailText.length());
    assertEquals("emailCount", 2, emailMessagesSent);
  }

  private void sendRegistration(EmailSender emailSender) throws Exception {
    connectClientToServer();
    service.setEmailSender(emailSender);
    service.setUserDirectory(userRepository);
    try {
      RegistrationTransaction rt = new RegistrationTransaction("rmartin@oma.com");
      sendToServer(rt);
      rrt = (RegistrationResponseTransaction) is.readObject();
    } finally {
      disconnectClientFromServer();
    }
  }
}
```

Listing 12–43 `TestServerLogin.java`

```
package com.objectmentor.SMCRemote.server;


public class TestServerLogin extends TestBase {
  public TestServerLogin(String name) {
    super(name);
  }

  public void setUp() throws Exception {
    super.setUp();
  }

  public void tearDown() throws Exception {
    super.tearDown();
  }
```

Listing 12–43 (Continued) `TestServerLogin.java`

```java
  public void testAcceptedLoginTransaction() throws Exception {
    boolean loggedIn = false;
    try {
      connectClientToServer();
      service.setUserDirectory(mockUserDirectory);
      loggedIn = login();
      disconnectClientFromServer();
    } catch (Exception e) {
    }

    assertEquals("LoginTransaction", true, loggedIn);
  }

  public void testRejectedLoginTransaction() throws Exception {
    boolean loggedIn = false;
    try {
      connectClientToServer();
      service.setUserDirectory(mockUserInvalidator);
      loggedIn = login();
      disconnectClientFromServer();
    } catch (Exception e) {
    }

    assertEquals("LoginTransaction", false, loggedIn);
  }
}
```

Listing 12–44 `TestUserRepository.java`

```java
package com.objectmentor.SMCRemote.server;

import junit.framework.TestCase;
import junit.swingui.TestRunner;

public class TestUserRepository extends TestCase {
  private UserRepository repository;

  public static void main(String[] args) {
    TestRunner.main(new String[]{"TestUserRepository"});
  }

  public TestUserRepository(String name) {
    super(name);
  }

  public void setUp() throws Exception {
    repository = new UserRepository("testUsers");
  }

  public void tearDown() throws Exception {
    assert("Repository not cleared", repository.clearUserRepository());
  }

  public void testEmptyRepository() throws Exception {
```

Listing 12–44 (Continued) `TestUserRepository.java`

```java
    assertEquals("EmptyRepository", false,
                 repository.isValid("rmartin@oma.com", "password"));
  }

  public void testAdd() throws Exception {
    repository.add("rmartin@oma.com", "password");
    assertEquals("Add", true, repository.isValid("rmartin@oma.com", "password"));
  }

  public void testwrongPassword() throws Exception {
    assertEquals("addFailed", true, repository.add("rmartin@oma.com", "password"));
    assertEquals("wrongPassword", false, repository.isValid("rmartin@oma.com", "xyzzy"));
  }

  public void testDuplicateAdd() throws Exception {
    assertEquals("FirstAdd", true, repository.add("rmartin@oma.com", "password"));
    assertEquals("DuplicateAdd", false, repository.add("rmartin@oma.com", "password"));
  }

  public void testIncrement() throws Exception {
    int logins = 0;
    repository.add("rmartin@oma.com", "password");
    logins = repository.incrementLoginCount("rmartin@oma.com");
    assertEquals("Increment", 1, logins);
    logins = repository.incrementLoginCount("rmartin@oma.com");
    assertEquals("Increment2", 2, logins);
  }
}
```

Other Tests

Listing 12–45 `TestFileCarrier.java`

```java
package com.objectmentor.SocketUtilities;

import junit.framework.TestCase;
import junit.swingui.TestRunner;

import java.io.*;

public class TestFileCarrier extends TestCase {
  public static void main(String[] args) {
    TestRunner.main(new String[]{"TestFileCarrier"});
  }

  public TestFileCarrier(String name) {
    super(name);
  }

  public void setUp() throws Exception {
  }

  public void tearDown() throws Exception {
  }

  private abstract class FileComparator {
    File f1;
    File f2;

    abstract void writeFirstFile(PrintWriter w);

    abstract void writeSecondFile(PrintWriter w);

    void compare(boolean expected) throws Exception {
      f1 = new File("f1");
      f2 = new File("f2");
      PrintWriter w1 = new PrintWriter(new FileWriter(f1));
      PrintWriter w2 = new PrintWriter(new FileWriter(f2));
      writeFirstFile(w1);
      writeSecondFile(w2);
      w1.close();
      w2.close();
      assertEquals("(f1,f2)", expected, filesAreTheSame(f1, f2));
      assertEquals("(f2,f1)", expected, filesAreTheSame(f2, f1));
      f1.delete();
      f2.delete();
    }
  }

  public void testOneFileLongerThanTheOther() throws Exception {
    FileComparator c = new FileComparator() {
      void writeFirstFile(PrintWriter w) {
        w.println("hi there");
      }

      void writeSecondFile(PrintWriter w) {
```

Listing 12–45 (Continued) `TestFileCarrier.java`

```java
        w.println("hi there you");
      }
    };
    c.compare(false);
  }

  public void testFilesAreDifferentInTheMiddle() throws Exception {
    FileComparator c = new FileComparator() {
      void writeFirstFile(PrintWriter w) {
        w.println("hi there");
      }

      void writeSecondFile(PrintWriter w) {
        w.println("hi their");
      }
    };
    c.compare(false);
  }

  public void testSecondLineDifferent() throws Exception {
    FileComparator c = new FileComparator() {
      void writeFirstFile(PrintWriter w) {
        w.println("hi there");
        w.println("This is fun");
      }

      void writeSecondFile(PrintWriter w) {
        w.println("hi there");
        w.println("This isn't fun");
      }
    };
    c.compare(false);
  }

  public void testFilesSame() throws Exception {
    FileComparator c = new FileComparator() {
      void writeFirstFile(PrintWriter w) {
        w.println("hi there");
      }

      void writeSecondFile(PrintWriter w) {
        w.println("hi there");
      }
    };
    c.compare(true);
  }

  public void testMultipleLinesSame() throws Exception {
    FileComparator c = new FileComparator() {
      void writeFirstFile(PrintWriter w) {
        w.println("hi there");
        w.println("this is fun");
        w.println("Lots of fun");
      }

      void writeSecondFile(PrintWriter w) {
```

Listing 12–45 (Continued) `TestFileCarrier.java`

```java
          w.println("hi there");
          w.println("this is fun");
          w.println("Lots of fun");
        }
      };
    c.compare(true);
  }

  public void testFileCarrier() throws Exception {
    File sourceFile = new File("testFileCarrier.txt");
    PrintWriter w = new PrintWriter(new FileWriter(sourceFile));
    w.println("line one");
    w.println("line two");
    w.println("line three");
    w.close();

    FileCarrier fc = new FileCarrier(null, "testFileCarrier.txt");
    assert(fc.isError() == false);
    assert(fc.isLoaded() == true);

    File tmpDirectory = new File("tmpDirectory");
    tmpDirectory.mkdir();

    File newFile = new File("tmpDirectory/testFileCarrier.txt");

    fc.write(tmpDirectory);

    assert("file wasn't written", newFile.exists());
    assert("files aren't the same.", filesAreTheSame(newFile, sourceFile));

    assert("newfile", newFile.delete());
    assert("oldFile", sourceFile.delete());
    assert("directory", tmpDirectory.delete());
  }

  boolean filesAreTheSame(File f1, File f2) throws Exception {
    FileInputStream r1 = new FileInputStream(f1);
    FileInputStream r2 = new FileInputStream(f2);
    try {
      int c;
      while ((c = r1.read()) != -1) {
        if (r2.read() != c) {
          return false;
        }
      }
      if (r2.read() != -1)
        return false;
      else
        return true;
    } finally {
      r1.close();
      r2.close();
    }
  }
}
```

ServerController (SMC Generated)

Listing 12–46 `ServerController.java`

```
//-----------------------------------------------
//
// FSM:      ServerController
// Context:  ServerControllerContext
// Err Func: FSMError
// Version:
// Generated: Wednesday 11/13/2002 at 20:32:13 CST
//
//-----------------------------------------------


package com.objectmentor.SMCRemote.server;

//-----------------------------------------------
//
// class ServerController
//    This is the Finite State Machine class
//
public class ServerController extends ServerControllerContext {
  private State itsState;
  private static String itsVersion = "";

  // instance variables for each state
  private LoggedIn itsLoggedInState;
  private StoringUser itsStoringUserState;
  private Idle itsIdleState;
  private Closing itsClosingState;
  private Compiling itsCompilingState;
  private LoggingIn itsLoggingInState;
  private Closed itsClosedState;

  // constructor
  public ServerController() {
    itsLoggedInState = new LoggedIn();
    itsStoringUserState = new StoringUser();
    itsIdleState = new Idle();
    itsClosingState = new Closing();
    itsCompilingState = new Compiling();
    itsLoggingInState = new LoggingIn();
    itsClosedState = new Closed();

    itsState = itsIdleState;

    // Entry functions for: Idle
  }

  // accessor functions

  public String getVersion() {
    return itsVersion;
  }
```

Listing 12–46 (Continued) `ServerController.java`

```java
public String getCurrentStateName() {
  return itsState.stateName();
}

// event functions - forward to the current State

public void userStoredEvent() {
  itsState.userStoredEvent();
}

public void badCompileEvent() {
  itsState.badCompileEvent();
}

public void invalidUserEvent() {
  itsState.invalidUserEvent();
}

public void compileEvent() {
  itsState.compileEvent();
}

public void loginEvent() {
  itsState.loginEvent();
}

public void abortEvent() {
  itsState.abortEvent();
}

public void registerEvent() {
  itsState.registerEvent();
}

public void closeEvent() {
  itsState.closeEvent();
}

public void userNotStoredEvent() {
  itsState.userNotStoredEvent();
}

public void sendFailedEvent() {
  itsState.sendFailedEvent();
}

public void goodCompileEvent() {
  itsState.goodCompileEvent();
}

public void validUserEvent() {
  itsState.validUserEvent();
}

//-------------------------------------------
//
```

Listing 12–46 (Continued) `ServerController.java`

```java
// private class State
//    This is the base State class
//
private abstract class State {
  public abstract String stateName();

  // default event functions

  public void userStoredEvent() {
    FSMError("userStoredEvent", itsState.stateName());
  }

  public void badCompileEvent() {
    FSMError("badCompileEvent", itsState.stateName());
  }

  public void invalidUserEvent() {
    FSMError("invalidUserEvent", itsState.stateName());
  }

  public void compileEvent() {
    FSMError("compileEvent", itsState.stateName());
  }

  public void loginEvent() {
    FSMError("loginEvent", itsState.stateName());
  }

  public void abortEvent() {
    FSMError("abortEvent", itsState.stateName());
  }

  public void registerEvent() {
    FSMError("registerEvent", itsState.stateName());
  }

  public void closeEvent() {
    FSMError("closeEvent", itsState.stateName());
  }

  public void userNotStoredEvent() {
    FSMError("userNotStoredEvent", itsState.stateName());
  }

  public void sendFailedEvent() {
    FSMError("sendFailedEvent", itsState.stateName());
  }

  public void goodCompileEvent() {
    FSMError("goodCompileEvent", itsState.stateName());
  }

  public void validUserEvent() {
    FSMError("validUserEvent", itsState.stateName());
  }
```

Listing 12–46 (Continued) `ServerController.java`

```java
    }

  //-------------------------------------------
  //
  // class LoggedIn
  //    handles the LoggedIn State and its events
  //
  private class LoggedIn extends State {
    public String stateName() {
      return "LoggedIn";
    }

    //
    // responds to abortEvent event
    //
    public void abortEvent() {
      reportError();

      // change the state
      itsState = itsIdleState;
    }

    //
    // responds to compileEvent event
    //
    public void compileEvent() {
      // change the state
      itsState = itsCompilingState;

      // Entry functions for: Compiling
      doCompile();
    }
  }

  //-------------------------------------------
  //
  // class StoringUser
  //    handles the StoringUser State and its events
  //
  private class StoringUser extends State {
    public String stateName() {
      return "StoringUser";
    }

    //
    // responds to userNotStoredEvent event
    //
    public void userNotStoredEvent() {
      denyRegistration();

      // change the state
      itsState = itsIdleState;
    }

    //
    // responds to userStoredEvent event
```

Listing 12–46 (Continued) `ServerController.java`

```java
  //
  public void userStoredEvent() {
    confirmRegistration();

    // change the state
    itsState = itsIdleState;
  }

  //
  // responds to abortEvent event
  //
  public void abortEvent() {
    reportError();
    denyRegistration();

    // change the state
    itsState = itsIdleState;
  }

  //
  // responds to sendFailedEvent event
  //
  public void sendFailedEvent() {
    denyRegistration();

    // change the state
    itsState = itsIdleState;
  }
}

//------------------------------------------
//
// class Idle
//     handles the Idle State and its events
//
private class Idle extends State {
  public String stateName() {
    return "Idle";
  }

  //
  // responds to abortEvent event
  //
  public void abortEvent() {
    reportError();
  }

  //
  // responds to registerEvent event
  //
  public void registerEvent() {
    // change the state
    itsState = itsStoringUserState;

    // Entry functions for: StoringUser
    storeUserAndSendPassword();
```

Listing 12–46 (Continued) `ServerController.java`

```java
    }

    //
    // responds to compileEvent event
    //
    public void compileEvent() {
      sendCompileRejection();

      // change the state
      itsState = itsIdleState;
    }

    //
    // responds to loginEvent event
    //
    public void loginEvent() {
      // change the state
      itsState = itsLoggingInState;

      // Entry functions for: LoggingIn
      checkValidUser();
    }
  }

  //-------------------------------------------
  //
  // class Closing
  //     handles the Closing State and its events
  //
  private class Closing extends State {
    public String stateName() {
      return "Closing";
    }

    //
    // responds to closeEvent event
    //
    public void closeEvent() {
      // change the state
      itsState = itsClosedState;
    }
  }

  //-------------------------------------------
  //
  // class Compiling
  //     handles the Compiling State and its events
  //
  private class Compiling extends State {
    public String stateName() {
      return "Compiling";
    }

    //
    // responds to abortEvent event
    //
```

Listing 12–46 (Continued) `ServerController.java`

```java
  public void abortEvent() {
    reportError();

    // change the state
    itsState = itsIdleState;
  }

  //
  // responds to goodCompileEvent event
  //
  public void goodCompileEvent() {
    sendCompileResults();

    // change the state
    itsState = itsClosingState;

    // Entry functions for: Closing
    close();
  }

  //
  // responds to badCompileEvent event
  //
  public void badCompileEvent() {
    sendCompileError();

    // change the state
    itsState = itsClosingState;

    // Entry functions for: Closing
    close();
  }
}

//-------------------------------------------
//
// class LoggingIn
//    handles the LoggingIn State and its events
//
private class LoggingIn extends State {
  public String stateName() {
    return "LoggingIn";
  }

  //
  // responds to abortEvent event
  //
  public void abortEvent() {
    reportError();

    // change the state
    itsState = itsIdleState;
  }

  //
  // responds to validUserEvent event
```

Listing 12–46 (Continued) `ServerController.java`

```
    //
    public void validUserEvent() {
      acknowledgeLogin();

      // change the state
      itsState = itsLoggedInState;
    }

    //
    // responds to invalidUserEvent event
    //
    public void invalidUserEvent() {
      rejectLogin();

      // change the state
      itsState = itsIdleState;
    }
  }

  //------------------------------------------
  //
  // class Closed
  //    handles the Closed State and its events
  //
  private class Closed extends State {
    public String stateName() {
      return "Closed";
    }
  }
}
```

Notes

[Beck2002]: Kent Beck, *Test-Driven Development*. Reading, Mass.: Addison-Wesley, 2002.

[Coplien1995]: James O. Coplien and Douglas C. Schmidt, eds., *Pattern Languages of Program Design,* vol. 1. Reading, Mass.: Addison-Wesley, 1995.

[Fowler2002]: Martin Fowler, David Rice, Matthew Foemmel, Edward Hieatt, Robert Mee, Randy Stafford, *Patterns of Enterprise Application Architecture*. Reading, Mass.: Addison-Wesley, 2002.

[Gamma1995]: Erich Gamma, Richard Helm, Ralph Johnson, and John Vlissides. *Design Patterns*. Reading, Mass.: Addison-Wesley, 1995.

[Martin2002]: Robert C. Martin, *Agile Software Development—Principles, Patterns, and Practices*. Upper Saddle River, N.J.: Prentice Hall, 2002.

Index

Symbols

\# protected 28
* 39
– private 28
+ public 28
{abstract} 34
«anonymous» 40
«C-API» 34
«create» 39
«delegate» 40
«extends» 67
«function» 34
«generalization» 67
«interface» 5, 33
«local» 40
«parameter» 40
«persistent» 34
«struct» 34
«utility» 33, 34
«weak» 41

Numerics

0..* 39
0..1 39
1..* 39
3.14159265358979323846264338327950 2
 (I know PI to 110 decimal
 places!) 34

A

abstract
 method 34
abstract class 27, 34
 shorthand 35

abstraction
 imaginary 134
 separation from details 147
acceptance tests 96
action 8, 116
activation 7, 46, 53
active object 59, 111
actor 46, 63, 65, 66
 secondary 63, 65
 tertiary 63
Acyclic Dependencies Principle 105
ADAPTER 19
adornments 21, 28, 33
ADP 105
aerospace 9
aggregation 18, 36, 37
 dropped from UML 2.0 36
algorithm depiction 53
analysis 91
angled lines 53
Ann Marie Martin (my lovely wife) xxiv
anonymous inner class 40, 189
architecture 96
 high-level 104
arrow 4
 dashed 30
 direction of 29
 message 7
 name 29
 number 29
 return 46
 star 29
 with circle 7, 46
association 4, 18, 29, 36, 137
 classes 41
 horizontal 32
 name 4
 qualifier 42

asynchronous message 55, 145
        possible implementation 56
AsynchronousLogger 60
ATM 31

B

Beck, Kent 99, 159, 240
        Good object words. xxiv
behavior 64
        first 16
        hidden 64
        partitioning 133
big picture 113
blank paper 63
blueprints 10
bold lines 113
bold rectangle 113
Booch, Grady ....xxiii, 34, 43
Brooks, Alexis Josephine
        (My granddaughter.) v
Brooks, Angela. (My daughter.) v
Brooks, Matt. (My son-in-law.) v
bubble sort 12
bull pen 98
business analyst 92
business value 93, 94, 96
button 16

C

calling hierarchy 7
card 92
        index 63
        use case 65
CASE ....xxi, 22
castles in the air 20
CCP 104
cellular phone 16
chocolate candy 69

class 28, 46
    abstract 34
    compartments 5
    concrete 27
    fat 87
    god 135
    helper 183
    in sequence diagram 47
class diagram 4, 18, 27, 31
clean code 96
clunky 53
Cockburn, Alistair 66
code
    clean 96
    expressive and readable 49
    generation 23, 199
    improving 98
    never let the sun set on bad 98
    seeing the. 20, 32
coffee maker 129, 130
collaboration 17, 18, 46
    diagrams 7, 16
colon 5, 28, 59
COM 30
Common Closure Principle 104
Common Reuse Principle 105
Comparable 5
compartments 28
component 103
    icon 103
COMPOSITE 40
composition 18, 36, 37
conceptual diagrams 1
concrete class 27
conditions in sequence diagram 53
construction 7
    arguments 7
Construction phase 95
contains relationship 102
continual integration 98
Coplien, James O. (Cope) 240
coupling 72
courage 98

cover page 67
Craftsman 185
creation 47
crossed circle 40
crossed wires 136
CRP 105
customer 92, 93, 95, 96, 98
customer tests 96
CVS 98
cycles of dependencies 105
cyclomatic complexity 208

D

dashed line 46
data token 7, 46
DATA TRANSFER OBJECT 172
database 73
    facade 73
DECORATOR 40
deep copy 37
defect rate 96
degenerate method 86, 196
dependency
    cycles 27
    management 70, 158
    relationship 40, 103
    structure 27
Dependency Inversion Principle 86, 106, 141
depiction of algorithms 53
design 91
    heuristics 129
    mistakes 129
    phase 22
    principles 69
        when to apply them. 89
    quality 69
    smells 70
destruction 37, 47

diagram
    class 4, 18, 27, 31
    conceptual 1
    implementation 1
    object 5, 109
    package 107
    physical 3
    specification 1
    state 7, 115
    static 3
    use case 66
diagrams
    discarding 22
    dynamic 3, 18, 20
    incomprehensible 45
    redundant and wasteful 49
    simple and clean 21
    useful 14
    when not to draw. 22
    when to draw. 22
Dialer 16
DIP 86, 106, 141
disciplines 91
documentation 22, 23, 45, 91, 97, 99
    back-end 13
    design 13
    Martin's first law of 99
    the value of. 24
dog 2
Don't Panic v
dot structure 7
downcasts 84
duct tape 70
dX 91, 99
dynamic diagram 3, 18, 20
dynamic model 45

E

Elaboration phase 95
embedded real-time system 132
engineers
    aerospace 9

structural 9
essence of OOD 148
estimation
    calibration 95
    use cases 65
    user stories 92
event 7, 116
    custom 117
    entry 117
    exit 117
    use case 64
event-based system 115
evolution 20
evolving diagrams 20
exploration 91
Extreme Programming 91, 99

F

FACADE 73, 207
Feathers, Michael 89
feedback 95
FileCarrier 183
finite state machine 7, 115
fitnesse, see also: *http://fitnesse.org* 97
FLIP-FLOP 83
folder 102
the force 67
Fowler, Martin 1, 8, 99, 240
    Who has a music note on his head xxiv
Fragility 70, 71
Francis, Alan
    (LSF) xxiv
function
    argument 28
    declaration 28
functional decomposition 104

G

Gamma, Erich 43, 240
garbage collector 37, 47

generalization relationship 2
generation, code 23
glitzy UI 94
god classes 135
goodies 45
grandchildren v
Grenning, James. (A good friend.) 45
guard 7, 51, 53
GUI 71, 73
    isolation 74
guillemet 33
guilty 22

H

half-arrowheads 55
has 29
HASA 29
Helm, Richard 43
heuristics
    design 129
    package 104
hidden behavior 64
hideous 18, 132
HTTPRequest 11
HTTPResponse 11

I

ICE 123
icon
    state 115
if statement 53
Illustrator. See Brooks, Angela v
imaginary abstraction 134
Immobility 70
implementation 91
implementation diagrams 1
import 103
impossible task 63
impunity 98
Inception phase 95

incomprehensible diagram 45
index card 63
inheritance 30
    relationship 2
    vertical 32
initial pseudo state 116
inner classes 40
    anonymous 40
instance variables 29
`instanceof` 84, 86
integration
    continual 98
interface 5, 30, 33
    in sequence diagram 60
    shorthand 34
Interface Segregation Principle 87, 105
ISA 29
ISP 87, 105
italics 34
iteration midpoint 94
iteration planning 93
iterative 20
Iterative Development 91
iterator 51

J

jar 101, 103
Javadocs 24
JDepend. See also: *www.clarkware.com* ....
    105
JDOM 71, 205
Johnson, Ralph 43
just in time requirements 63
Justin Michael Martin
    (will invent cold-fusion) xxiv

K

key 42
kitchen garbage 70
Koss, Bob *(Young Bob)* xxiv

L

laboratory 98
library paste 70
lifeline 46, 47
lifetime responsibility 37
`LinearObject` 13
link 5, 7, 18
Liskov Substitution Principle 84
`List` 29
local variable 40
`Logger` 60
`LoginServlet` 11
lollipop 30
    on lifeline 61
loop condition 48
loops in sequence diagrams 48
LSP 84

M

Martin, Angelique Thouvenin
    (My daughter-in-law.) v
Martin, Gina
    (My Daughter) xxiv
    (Singer Extraordinaire) 15
Martin, Luka Jean. (My grandson.) v
Martin, Micah. (My son.) .... v, 185
Martin's First Law of Documentation 99
`Math` 34
McBreen, Pete xxii
meat 69
    rotting 69
member functions 27
member variables 27
message 7, 46
    arguments 46
    arrow 7
    asynchronous 55
    label 7, 46
    synchronous 55
    that take time 53
    to interfaces 60

method 28
    abstract 34
    degenerate 86, 196
midpoint of iteration 94
minimalism 21
modeling 9
MODEL-VIEW-CONTROLLER 73
multiple threads 59
multiplicity 38
multithreaded systems 55, 111, 145
music note on Martin Fowler's head. ...xxiv
MVC 73
    variation 75

N

names, underlined 46
namespace 101
Needless Complexity 70
Needless Repetition 70
nitty gritty details 49
NULLOBJECT 189

O

object 46
    creation 47
    destruction 47
    diagram 5, 109
    name 5, 46
OCP 73, 84, 106
office
    open 98
OOD
    the essence of 148
    training 129
OOPL 70
OOverkill 158
Opacity 70
open office 98
Open–Closed Principle 73, 84, 106
organic chemistry 187

oval 67
overdocumenting 161

P

package 101
    abstractness 106
    dependencies 103
    dependency diagrams 107
    design principles 104
    icon 102
    nesting 102
pair programming 96
perfect programming days 92
Persistable 72
phone call 54
physical diagrams 3
PI 34
plan 91
    iteration 93
    release 93
Point 13
Pollable 145
polling 145
PolyLine 13
polymorphism 70
postconditions 63, 65
practices 91
preconditions 63, 65
primary course 64
principles 20
    design 69
    OOD 69
    package 104
priorities 92
private 28
process 22, 91, 99
productivity 96
properties 35
protected 28
PROXY 40
pseudo code 51
public 28

Q

QA 96
    manager 97
qualifier 42
quality assurance 96

R

race condition 54
Rational xxiii
RDD 136
realizes relationship 31
real-time system 132
rectangle 4, 28, 102
    bold 59
    skinny. See activation.
recurrence expression 51
refactoring 98, 144
relationship
    aggregation 18, 36, 37
        dropped from UML 2.0 36
    association 4, 18, 29, 36, 137
    composition 18, 36, 37
    contains 102
    dependency 40, 103
    generalization 2
    inheritance 2
    realizes 31
    use case 67
release
    granule 104
    planning 93
Release/Reuse Equivalency Principle ... 104
REP 104
requirements 91, 92, 96
    analysis 63
    document 97
    just in time 63
responsibility 71
    driven design 136
return value 28

reuse 70, 104
    granule 104
rework 96
Rigidity 70
RMI 83
road maps 13
rocket science 184
ROPE 185
Ruby 185
Runnable 113
RUP 95

S

SAP 106
SAX 71
SCCS 98
scenarios
    failure 65
SDP 105
SELF SHUNT 79
separation of concerns 71, 147
sequence diagram 6, 7, 16, 45
    angled lines 53
    condition 53
    crossed lines 54
    high-level vs. low-level 49
    interfaces 60
    lollipop 61
    loops 48
        advanced 51
    scenarios 49
    the kind to avoid 49
    thread identifier 59
sequence number 7
    becoming unworkable 187
    dot structure 7
Servlet 11
short cycles 20
Single Responsibility Principle 71, 104
SMC 121, 161
socket 111
SocketService 111, 186

software architects 22
Software Craftsmanship xxii
source code control system 98
source code dependencies 27, 30
Space 13
spaghetti code 70
Sparky 2
specification diagrams 1
spike 93
SQL 205
SRP 71, 104
Stable Abstractions Principle 106
Stable Dependencies Principle 105
star 16, 51
STATE 122
state
    final pseudo 119
    icon 115
    initial pseudo 116, 119
    super 116
state diagram 7, 115
State Machine Compiler 121, 161
state transition diagram 115
state transition table 120
static diagrams 3
static variables 33
stereotypes 33
    custom 34
    listed in first page of index
stick figure 6, 46
stimulus 64
story points 92, 94
subway turnstile 7, 120
superstate 116, 118
synchronous message 55
system behavior 64
system boundary diagram 66

T

tab 102
tangle 13
task 94

team 98
    sitting and spinning 63
test 91
    acceptance (See acceptances tests)
    unit (See unit tests)
test-first 83, 97
Thread 113
thread 55, 56
    identifier in sequence diagram 59
    internal 59
THREE-LEVEL FSM 196
thrill xxiii
transition 8, 116
    reflexive 117
Transition phase 95
tricky things 134
turnstile 7

U

UI
    glitzy 94
UML .... xxiii, 1
    language lawyer 42
    method, not 99
    misuse of 9
    not using it. 161
    overuse of 9
    perversity 55
UML Distilled .... xxi, 8
Uncle Bob xxiii
underline 5, 46
underlying problem, the 136
Unified Process 95
unit tests 73, 78, 83, 89, 97, 162
use case 63, 92, 96, 137
    alternate course 65
    capturing them all 63
    card 63, 65
    details 63
    diagrams 64, 66
    estimation 65
    failure scenarios 65

name 65
postconditions 65
preconditions 65
primary course 64
relationships 67
simplicity 63
tomorrow they change 63
vastly overcomplicated 63
writing 64
user story 92, 96
estimating 92
merging 93
points 92
splitting 93
utility 34

Mitchell, William H.
(Formerly known as "Red".) xxiv
wind tunnels 9
wires
crossed 136
wisdom 49
www.objectmentor.com 71

X

X on lifeline 47
XML 71, 205
XP 91, 99

V

vapor classes 134
variable 28
declaration 28
static 33
VECTOR 29
velocity 93, 95
Viscosity 70
VISITOR 176, 193
Vlissides, John 43
Vogel, Billy xxiii

Z

zone 32

W

war room 98
waste of time 45
expensive 61
huge 49
weak reference 41
Welter, Lance *(sales creature)* xxiv
whatchamajiggers 42
white board 13, 14, 20, 62, 94, 99, 129
whole/part 36
wiki 24

1) Abstract class
2) Interface
3) Isa
   Hasa } relationships
4) Mike Sharp's notes
5) UML Books in the library —
   find out + borrow
   • p.8 [Fowler 1999a]
   • p.43 [Booch 1994]

6) association
   generalization
   :

7) Christina e-mail lecture
   notes
8) Lecture Notes you have
   saved in
   • PE2 Folder
   • PE1 Folder

9) The Lecture on UML in
   the UML folder

10) consider using class diagrams
only and not sequence diagrams

11) Swing (before OOP or
MVC
rather design principles